BABY GIRL:

BETTER KNOWN AS

Aaliyah

ALSO BY KATHY IANDOLI

God Save the Queens:
The Essential History of Women in Hip-Hop

BABY GIRL:
BETTER KNOWN AS

Aaliyah

KATHY IANDOLI

ATRIA BOOKS

New York   London   Toronto   Sydney   New Delhi

ATRIA
BOOKS

An Imprint of Simon & Schuster, Inc.
1230 Avenue of the Americas
New York, NY 10020

First Atria Books hardcover edition August 2021

ATRIA BOOKS and colophon are trademarks of
Simon & Schuster, Inc.

For information about special discounts for bulk purchases,
please contact Simon & Schuster Special Sales at 1-866-506-1949
or business@simonandschuster.com.

The Simon & Schuster Speakers Bureau can bring authors to
your live event. For more information or to book an event, contact
the Simon & Schuster Speakers Bureau at 1-866-248-3049
or visit our website at www.simonspeakers.com.

Interior design by Alexis Minieri

Manufactured in the United States of America

1   3   5   7   9   10   8   6   4   2

Library of Congress Cataloging-in-Publication Data has been applied for.

ISBN 978-1-9821-5684-8
ISBN 978-1-9821-5686-2 (ebook)

For Aaliyah, who changed music as we know it.
Tell my mother I love her.

TABLE OF CONTENTS

AUTHOR'S NOTE

When I first began working on *Baby Girl*, I decided not to write about the circumstances surrounding Aaliyah's involvement with R. Kelly and how it unfolded over time. Considering word had finally gotten out about his predatory and criminal behavior with minors, mentioning him within Aaliyah's life story cheapened the narrative, in my opinion. As someone who loved Aaliyah dearly from afar, I felt I was disrespecting her legacy by spreading this part of her life on Front Street when her family never had. I also didn't want to dignify R. Kelly with any credit for her career, despite him being one of the main reasons we learned about Aaliyah in the first place. His crimes have left most with a pit in their stomachs, anguished at the thought of once supporting him and his music.

I will never forget the day I interviewed a then-teenage Ciara for her 2004 debut album, *Goodies*. On the album is a cut called "Next to You," featuring R. Kelly, which he also wrote and produced. The lyrics place Ciara in the position of coaxing R. Kelly into letting her stay the night, with R. Kelly being blissfully down for whatever. I noted in my feature how R. Kelly's lyrics written for a teenager were inappropriate, as two years prior his child pornography tape had surfaced. It boggled my mind how he could continue writing songs like this for young women and be so well compensated to do so.

Members of Ciara's team contacted both my editor and me. They threatened me with slander (in reality they meant "libel").

"She's not Aaliyah," was their pointed, succinct rebuttal. But Ciara could have been. My remarks weren't even against Ciara; she is incredibly talented and one of the torchbearers of Aaliyah's legacy. But the mention of Aaliyah by her team, as if it were a mark of shame, felt so wrong since the blame was again placed upon the teenage girl and not the predator. Again, this was 2004, and while no one really understood what had happened between him and Aaliyah back then, I still felt it was an unfair burden to place on someone who was no longer alive to defend herself. Ciara never knew this exchange existed, I'm sure. She has always held Aaliyah's name in the highest regard, considering Ciara and many artists who followed were undoubtedly inspired by Aaliyah's work. This wasn't the first time that Ciara would be compared to Aaliyah in some way, and years after that magazine article (in 2019) Ciara pulled her R. Kelly collaborations from streaming services. I call that a tiny (albeit delayed) victory.

I watched Lifetime's *Surviving R. Kelly* (parts one and two) series with unease, a decade and a half following my article, wondering how his predilection for young girls had fallen under the radar for so long. I grimaced as young girls were held hostage, their families telling horror stories of their daughters still being in his clutches, while others who managed to escape revealed what they endured, with disturbing detail.

You could see the torture on many of the girls' faces, and in others' you could see blankness and reprogramming. As a viewer, there's an inherent fear for what their post-traumatic futures will look like once they've inevitably realized they're in an abusive holding pattern. Like everyone else, however, I too was separating Aaliyah from R. Kelly's victims. I was categorizing her the way the media (and the music industry) had done so often in the past, by viewing their relationship as a mutually loving one, not one rooted in grooming and latent sexual violence. Abusive patterns don't discriminate. Prey is prey, and Aaliyah had fallen prey to R. Kelly. He was just as damaging a force in Aaliyah's life as he was to the other very young women he violated. Theirs wasn't a love story that defied age; it was a tragedy that Aaliyah endured and somehow moved past to become an icon in her own right without him. That is the only reason why R. Kelly is discussed in this book. It was only in watching this docuseries and dissecting newfound evidence did I realize that disregarding R. Kelly's chapter in Aaliyah's life would be denying Aaliyah another title she so greatly deserved: "survivor."

INTRODUCTION: GOOD-BYE, SUMMER

August 25, 2001

Where were you when you heard that Aaliyah died?

Generational celebrity deaths are such an interesting part of popular culture, aren't they?

You remember every detail: where you were, what you were doing, who you were with. You might even hold on to these fragments of memories tighter than you would over the passing of your own distant relatives. That's because those who touch the world on a grander scale—for better or worse—have the potential to reach more people, and yet affect every single one of them individually and uniquely. JFK, MLK, Kurt Cobain, Tupac Shakur, The Notorious B.I.G., Michael Jackson, Whitney Houston, Prince, Kobe Bryant—the list goes on and on. Through the duration of their lives—no matter how long or short they may be—these humans become our superheroes. Their mortality, however, is our brutal reminder of the former. Their deaths become historical events in and of themselves, usually involving some anniversary people grimly commemorate. Since the advent of social media, that now includes a picture posted with some warm words, a vague memory associated with the dearly departed person, and a quote honoring their lives. Certain calendars even regard these deaths as international holidays, again showing the correlation between a celebrity's death and their impact on the world. Many, many people have only a rudimentary understanding of world history and key dates, yet they can tell you the exact date that their favorite singer died.

With the passing of Aaliyah, it was a double whammy of devastation, where there was little time to process her death before a global crisis hit.

Just two and a half weeks following Aaliyah Haughton's death, on September 11, 2001, the United States was thrust into a world-changing tragedy.

The news of the destruction of the Twin Towers overshadowed her passing, with fans left wondering what even happened, considering the details of her plane crash appeared so vague and before we even knew it two more plane crashes arguably eclipsed hers. Once award show season rolled around, Aaliyah was honored during artist memorial segments and through posthumous accolades. Still, her death left fans bewildered with little time to manage their grief; so even now when you scan the comments of her videos on YouTube, the responses almost always include a dismal "I still can't believe that she's gone."

Before I continue, let me answer my own question: *Where was I when I heard that Aaliyah died?*

I was four months out of college and still hanging out at the local diner. It was around 11:30 PM when New York City's HOT 97 was reporting the news. I was standing in the diner's parking lot with my friend exchanging our good-byes after a late dinner. He had an Acura Integra with a custom-designed sound system, so every time he turned on his car the radio would shake the pavement beneath the vehicle, as if it were directed to on command. This time, when he turned on his car the first thing blaring out of the radio speakers and shaking the pavement was famed radio personality and the Voice of New York Angie Martinez saying Aaliyah's name on New York's HOT 97. Her wildly bold voice was breaking as she spoke in her thick, immediately recognizable Brooklyn accent. That should have been my first clue, but I continued walking to my car. After all, it was not unusual to hear Aaliyah's name all over the radio airwaves, with her songs following in tandem. It was 2001, and Aaliyah had the world in her palm. Her eponymous album had been released a month prior and *Queen of the Damned* was being filmed, so Aaliyah was everywhere. Still, Angie's voice aroused my suspicions, especially since this wasn't her usual time slot, so my brisk pace downgraded itself to a tiptoe, as my body involuntarily timed its own movements to the stillness of her tone.

"Hey, I think Aaliyah was killed in a plane crash," my friend called to me. I came to a full stop. You know that feeling like the sound is sucked out of a room and you suddenly can't hear a thing but the warbles of airflow? Well, imagine it being sucked out of the planet, because I was standing outside.

I ran back over to his car, listening in disbelief. The news was being reported as information filtered through the pipeline in real time from the Bahamas, where she was killed. The crash happened hours before, though by midnight it was confirmed that she was gone, which explains why most online news articles show a published date of August 26, 2001, at the tops of their reported stories. (This predates the TMZ era, where it now literally takes five minutes to confirm or deny any piece of information.) Back then, there was an unspoken respect for families' finding out first, albeit their window was small. But as the evening came to a close, it was confirmed that so had Aaliyah's life.

I drove home crying that night. And not like a single glistening tear in memoriam, but full-on weeping as Aaliyah's songs filled my car from various radio stations blaring her hit after hit. It was like a continuous bout of punches to the gut, every time another song played. I had experienced the losses of the aforementioned Tupac, Biggie, and Kurt Cobain, but this one felt so different. It was *Aaliyah. Baby Girl.* She wasn't supposed to die yet. How could this have happened? These were all of the thoughts swirling in my mind as I drove home in a fog.

When I walked into my house, my eyes were so swollen that my mother thought I had gotten into an argument with my friend. This may sound dramatic to some, but to others it makes perfect sense. I felt this stranger's death on a deeply personal level. Aaliyah was born just a month before me, so she was almost exactly my age. I was a newly minted college graduate and my life was just beginning, while hers had just ended. I didn't just look up to her; I stood beside her. She felt like my very best friend, the cooler one of the duo where you oftentimes wonder why she chose you to be her partner in crime. That's how close my imaginary friendship was with Aaliyah, much like so many other people I know. I mean, she died on my friend Christina's birthday, and the next day she cut off all of her hair because she grew it long to be like Aaliyah's signature long tresses, even covering her one eye with half of her hair like Aaliyah had. For many Halloweens thereafter, friends wore Aaliyah "costumes" before it became a vintage homage to her on prime-time TV series like *Grown-ish* or Halloween pics by celebrities like Kim Kardashian and Kash Doll posted across Instagram. When I interviewed Quincy Jones in 2007, he asked me if I was Aaliyah's friend since we shared a similar "vibe," as he punned (he founded *Vibe* magazine in 1993). I still haven't completely recovered from that compliment and I still wear it like a badge of honor.

It became clear to me just how powerful Aaliyah truly was when I covered the two-year anniversary of her passing at Ferncliff Cemetery in Hartsdale, New York, on August 25, 2003. To say there was a crowd gathered would be an understatement. Aaliyah had been put to rest in the cemetery's marbled mausoleum, and fans congregated, leaving balloons and flowers, cards, poems, photos with her, and her albums at the foot of the wall bearing her name. (Her father now rests right above her, as he died on November 8, 2012.) My best friend, Maryum, and I stood there in awe at the number of kids around our age (some younger, some older) who stood at that mausoleum wall and publicly mourned Aaliyah. TV camera crews were present, documenting the phenomenon. I remember I scribbled in my little reporter notebook: "Girls dressed just like Aaliyah are sobbing, boys crying because their crush is gone" (gender normativity notwithstanding; it was a different time, and now I've seen such an even split between men and women being inspired by Aaliyah and applying her tenets to their own lives). Regardless of their reasons for attending, it was all so intense, and when you bring Aaliyah's death up even two decades later the reaction is still intense. Whenever I watch her "Rock the Boat" video, I feel that intensity knowing it was that very music video shoot that ultimately took her life—a life that ended abruptly at the age of twenty-two.

Aaliyah was described by music industry people as "cool," with a subtle air of mystery, yet she lit up any room when she entered. She was known as LiLi by her team and those closest to her, the goal was to protect her and shield her from the chaos in which she entered into the business. Her final year of life was an important one, where Aaliyah inadvertently made every moment count. She was coming off five years of redevelopment. Like her mentor Missy Elliott's 2002 album title, Aaliyah was *under construction*. She sacrificed a fraction of her teenage self to the abusive hands of R. Kelly, where she was sketched like a neophyte with raging hormones and a taste for older men on her debut album, 1994's *Age Ain't Nothing but a Number*. Her recovery time in the media post-controversy was impressively swift, though the healing of her internal trauma seemingly wasn't. She found ways to piece her old self together with her new self on 1996's *One in a Million*, as Timbaland and Missy allowed Aaliyah's airy vocals to be a musicology experiment in their tempering of time-honored R&B music with fragments of electronic music, which in turn elevated the entire genre. Her 1996 Tommy Hilfiger campaign proved she could model, and 2000's *Romeo Must Die* proved she could act. She even dominated soundtracks thanks to songs like "Are You That Somebody?" and "Try Again." So in the last year of her life, she had finally found herself. Her final album was aptly titled by her mononym, *Aaliyah*, and she was more hands-on than ever, working with the late producer and songwriter Static

Major. Her lyrics were more personal, displaying a maturity into young adulthood while still remaining young, wild, and free. Her starring role in *Queen of the Damned* was setting the stage for her *Matrix Reloaded* role, which would later lead to *The Matrix Revolutions*. Aaliyah was the Phoenix, who rose from the ashes, yet returned to them just as she reached full form.

It felt so unfair.

Regardless of what you believe or who you believe in, seeing someone die so young makes you question everything. There was so much more to be done, and now we were left with unfinished business in this story we watched unfold right before our eyes. Would Aaliyah have married Damon Dash and started a family? How many films could she have starred in? What about all of the albums left to record? Would so many of the R&B and hip-hop artists who followed ever have gotten their shot had Aaliyah remained here? There were so many possibilities for what could have become her life, but none of that happened. Aaliyah was just getting warmed up and it felt like she was taken away. Yet through the duration of her physical absence, she's evolved into this mythical creature. A goddess, whose art transformed into this fantastical silhouette that hangs over music. You feel Aaliyah in the songs of today; you see her spirit in the artists who arrived after her. The "Princess of R&B" is an understatement; Aaliyah is at the crown of music royalty.

While she wasn't particularly known as some resounding balladeer, Aaliyah musically possessed a skill set that dubbed her a chameleon. Her voice was a flexible instrument; it could recline on any sound bed and elicit a dreaminess that most couldn't touch and still can't. And, of course, her style—where baggy pants and midriffs were the uniform—is still omnipresent. No comeback needed; the Aaliyah swag is always here in full effect. Designers still replicate the looks she pioneered, through working with either them or her fashion choices outside of them.

Hearing Aaliyah speak about her passion for music in interviews or watching her move fluidly through her music videos, it's apparent she was otherworldly, even when she walked this earth. She possessed a different kind of aura, where her magnetic personality came through in her music. She was something special, very special, and fans still mourn the loss of their hero and that intangible something she emitted. Those who knew her even expressed to me through conversations that in her presence they felt like she was nothing short of angelic. In fact, the word "angel" was used to describe her by so many people throughout my writing of this book.

And perhaps that's the most magical part of Aaliyah: she felt abstract and yet tangible at the same time. Her story is one of the last of its kind, where when she walked into a room she exuded stardom, and her charisma disarmed anyone who encountered her. While she had family in the music industry, she wasn't an industry plant. She really wanted to be a star. She loved every moment on that stage and loved every fan and every chapter of her story—both good and bad.

While her impact is palpable and her influence is so easy to spot, we have ultimately forgotten that she was a human being who once walked this earth. She was someone's daughter, sister, girlfriend, best friend. Sometimes it's as if Aaliyah were conjured up within our own imaginations, where we can pull from very little to create a real-life picture. Unlike other tragic deaths of young stars, like Selena, we haven't been given a clear, linear story about who Aaliyah was, what she endured, and why she was so special. That is what I have attempted to do with *Baby Girl: Better Known as Aaliyah*: provide those who loved her from afar some semblance of what her real life was like, while providing a small amount of closure in knowing that she made the most out of her twenty-two short years. We can always honor her as an angel, but it's time to pay homage to the beautiful Black woman who kept her inner strength tucked away and persevered through an unforgiving music industry in the name of her love of her craft.

Over the course of twenty years, the life of Aaliyah Haughton has transformed from fact to fan fiction. We have pieced together this super-icon of sorts, based upon the parts of what we knew about her during her short time here, mixed with what we hoped she'd become had she not died at the age of twenty-two. Since Aaliyah was always wrapped in this air of mystery, it's easy now to idealize every aspect of her. She didn't provide ample information about herself while on earth, so we know about as much in the afterlife as we did back then. It's only now that we are starting to learn more about her, both good and bad. And there's nothing to balance these revelations, especially without her music, since at the time this book was written Aaliyah's catalog still sat in streaming platform purgatory, despite the teasing of talks with record labels about finally distributing her music to a whole new audience. That lever is waiting to be pulled by her uncle, Barry Hankerson, who has been holding these songs for what feels like an eternity. It was rumored that the music would be released on what would have been her forty-first birthday, January 16, 2020, but that day came and went, and by August 25, 2020, there was the promise that talks had finally begun. By January 16, 2021, we were still left waiting. So what we're left with now is just a trickle of new information about Aaliyah's life, without music readily available to temper it.

Aaliyah changed the world, both on earth and beyond. What you're about to experience is how she did it and how she still does it posthumously. Most of all, this is a book by an Aaliyah fan, for the Aaliyah fans, both new and old. The ones who cried the day she died and the ones who discovered her after decades past. The dedicated day ones and the newcomers, along with those who don't even know they're fans yet.

After all, Aaliyah was more than a woman. She was one in a million.

CHAPTER ONE: GET YOUR MOTOR RUNNING

Detroit turned out to be heaven, but it also turned
out to be hell.

—Marvin Gaye

Detroit, Michigan, was once a city decorated with industrial domination and strong music-industry roots. Eventually dubbed the Motor City, Detroit would emerge as the epicenter for the automotive industry. Henry Ford drove the first car down a Detroit street in 1896. Three years later, he formed the Detroit Automobile Company. Almost every automotive company followed, forming their home bases in or around Detroit. It was like an industrial mecca, and one by one it was dismantled. Historians mark the year of 1958 as the beginning of the end for Detroit, once the Packard Motor Car Company closed shop after fifty-five years. What was once fueled with promise was now exhausting itself, as the city was losing its industrial steam.

However, as the automotive industry had begun its downward spiral there, music brought new life. In 1959, a Detroit native by the name of Berry Gordy started a musical empire that would change history when he borrowed $800 from his folks and formed Tamla Records. The following year, it was officially incorporated and renamed as Motown Records Corporation. Motown, a portmanteau of Detroit's Motor City roots and the word "town," was quite frankly the heart of what has now become American popular music, thanks to the Black musicians who encompassed it. Berry Gordy psychically named the headquarters of Motown Hitsville USA, the physical address being 2648 West Grand Boulevard. Artists like Diana Ross (and the Supremes), the Temptations, Smokey Robinson (and the Miracles), the Jackson 5, Marvin Gaye, Gladys Knight (and the Pips), and Stevie Wonder were all residents of Motown at one point or another. Detroit would later become the hub of techno music thanks to a DJ named Juan Atkins and the center point for popularized battle rap, once Eminem became the pale face of Detroit's hip-hop scene.

Detroit had grit and glamour. It was perhaps the perfect place to grow a complicated superstar, who ironically never owned a car.

Aaliyah Dana Haughton wasn't actually born in Detroit but in New York, in Brooklyn's Bedford-Stuyvesant neighborhood, on January 16, 1979. Her family had roots in the New York Transit Authority, along with operating several small businesses, including a laundromat and a tailor shop. Her father, Michael "Miguel" Haughton, worked several jobs before later becoming his daughter's personal manager. Her mother, Diane Haughton, was also a singer, traveling early on with a touring theater company, though eventually she became a teacher. She left teaching to be a stay-at-home mom once her kids were born, later co-managing Aaliyah with her father. First came Aaliyah's brother, Rashad, on August 6, 1977, and then Aaliyah arrived less than two years later. Her name is a spelling variation of "Aliya," the feminine version of the name "Ali," which in Arabic means "the highest, most exalted one." It can also mean "the best" and "the champion," like Muhammad *Ali*. When Aaliyah was five and Rashad was seven, the Haughton family moved to Detroit, Michigan.

There's something very telling about Aaliyah being born in Brooklyn and raised in Detroit. For almost the entire duration of her musical career, she would self-identify as "street but sweet." It was a cute little rhyme that truncated her style into two words, ones oftentimes diametrically opposed in society, though paired side by side to describe Aaliyah they were quite fitting. By the 1990s, Brooklyn supplanted the Bronx to become the heartbeat of hip-hop music alongside Queens, as artists like The Notorious B.I.G., Lil' Kim, Nas, Foxy Brown, Mobb Deep, and Jay-Z ran the city. Those Brooklyn roots gave Aaliyah her edge—and she later returned to New York City during this heyday once she became a star. Meanwhile, Detroit's smooth soul of Motown still gave Aaliyah this indescribable delicacy amid an inner city on the verge of decline. Street but sweet.

By the time the Haughtons relocated to Detroit in 1984, America—already deep into a recession on President Reagan's watch—was just beginning to rebound. Despite the economy firing back up, work opportunities were still scarce. Diane's brother, Barry Hankerson, had a few businesses in the Midwest, including a food distribution company and some warehouses, so Michael was bringing the family to Detroit so he could work with his brother-in-law.

Barry Hankerson was a former football player turned businessman and politician, who eventually worked his way into the music industry through the back door of local TV production. He married Motown's own Gladys Knight in 1974 at the height of her career with the Pips, after helping her to produce a TV special. After five years, the two divorced and became entangled in a dramatic custody battle over their son, Shanga Hankerson. At one point, when Shanga was just two and a half years old, Barry was accused of attempting to kidnap his son. An article printed in the March 10, 1979, edition of the *Indianapolis Recorder* stated: "Sources said the couple has a temporary custody order which allows the child to spend one day with his mother and the following day with the father. It was after the day with the father that Hankerson did not return the child. According to news reports, Hankerson then called Knight and told her he would defy the court ruling, and would keep the child." Shanga was finally returned back home to his mom. While Gladys Knight was already estranged from her ex-husband by the time Aaliyah was born, she still looked at Aaliyah and Rashad like her niece and nephew.

❧

When Aaliyah was around four years old, her mother realized she had the talent growing within her. It started with a young Aaliyah humming back to music playing in the house. Her tone, even at that age, showed that not only could Aaliyah recognize notes as they were being sung; she could also repeat them herself. Aaliyah then started inching her way into the business. Her family enrolled her in Gesu Catholic Church and School, located on the West Side of Detroit. While Gesu was called "one of the most influential Catholic parishes in the city of Detroit" by former *Detroit Free Press* writer Patricia

Montemurri (who wrote an entire book on the church and school's history), it was also known for its robust theater program. Students of all-spanning grades would perform in theater-company-quality musicals, oftentimes held in larger auditoriums like the 375-person theater at Marygrove College.

It was here that Aaliyah got her first break. At six years old, she was cast in the school musical of *Annie*. She had a supporting role as an orphan, with one line, as she told the *New York Post* in July 2001: "You're gonna get the paddle." Three years later, she starred in *42nd Street*, only this time, through old, grainy video footage of Aaliyah at her rehearsals, she's seen dancing and singing front and center as the director Suzanne McGill-Anderson's voice is heard saying, "It's wonderful because these kids have no inhibitions." The local news interviewed Aaliyah, then nine, about her role, which also included leading the song "We're in the Money." Aaliyah made a joke about her director yelling a lot, though the reporter regarded her as a seasoned little veteran in the local theater circuit. After the show's run, Aaliyah became a local singing fixture, from talent shows and more school productions such as *Hello, Dolly!* and *42nd Street* to small events like weddings and other parties. Aaliyah took part in New Detroit, a racial-justice organization that would throw annual events around Dr. Martin Luther King Jr.'s birthday, where Aaliyah would perform mostly covers of Whitney Houston songs. She was also enrolled in vocal training with Detroit vocal-music teacher Wendelin Peddy, who later taught at the Detroit Academy of Arts and Sciences.

Aaliyah attempted to build upon her acting career when she auditioned in 1989 for the role of kid sister Judy Winslow on ABC's prime-time comedy *Family Matters* about a Black middle-working-class family. She didn't land the role, though Aaliyah's first real taste of stardom wasn't far away.

CBS's *Star Search* was one of the earliest examples of what would become the reality competition series of later years. *Star Search*, a precursor to *America's Got Talent*, was where acts of all ages competed against one another. It was similar to an "amateur hour" style show, though ramped up to make the payoff far greater than a pat on the back and fifteen minutes of fame. As contestants continued to compete weekly, they would eventually reach a championship show, where the grand prize was $100,000 and an air-quoted possibility of a future recording contract, putting the "star" in *Star Search*. Many legends have lost on that show to opponents whose careers never saw the light of day. A prime example of that is Beyoncé's 1993 loss with her group Girls Tyme (later morphing into Destiny's Child) to a five-person band called Skeleton Crew. The wounds of that loss run deeply to this day, as Bey used footage of her losing performance for her 2014 single "***Flawless" off her surprise self-titled album in 2013. Justin Timberlake and Christina Aguilera both also lost on *Star Search*.

It was a show that Aaliyah not only was a fan of, but also saw as a game-changing opportunity to enter American households with one short performance. "My mother and I watched faithfully," Aaliyah remarked about *Star Search* in her interview with *Teen People* in 1999. "And I always wanted to be on it." Aaliyah competed against one of the returning *Star Search* champions, Katrina Abrams, in round one of the 1990 competition. Host Ed McMahon described Aaliyah as a "little person with a big voice" before announcing her to the stage. At ten years old, Aaliyah didn't look like her future would be spent in loose jeans and tight tank tops. Her grandmother had sewn her a pretty dress, a black form-fitted top with a white ruffled bottom and a white half blazer. She had on white tights and black shoes, with her makeup and hair done elegantly. She sang the *Babes in Arms* show tune "My Funny Valentine" in a vocal combination of the theatrical version mixed with the Ella Fitzgerald cover. She chose that song because it was one that her mother had sung in the past during her time in theater, and Aaliyah wanted to be just like her. Her performance was dramatic, staged even, where her raw talent is cloaked beneath the obvious preliminary instructions to remain poised and demure while trying to steady her nervously shaking voice. Even when she's interviewed by McMahon, Aaliyah's expressions are very theatrical. Perhaps that was from her previous training, or it's the result of child stars misinterpreting fame as maturity and their familial network cosigning it.

Aaliyah lost on *Star Search*, like most superstars do. Katrina received four stars; Aaliyah 3.25. She shook her winning opponent's hand and left the stage. Aaliyah broke down in tears once she was off-camera. You can mask a child with layers of adult-leaning decorations, but at the end of the day, they're just a kid. She didn't head home right after her loss; on the contrary, she stayed and watched the show as a spectator and not the winner.

Still, Ed McMahon saw something in Aaliyah.

In *Vibe*'s August 2001 cover story on Aaliyah (circulated during the time of her death), Ed McMahon spoke on remembering her drive in that moment eleven years prior. "There's a thing that you see when somebody walks out on the stage," he told writer Hyun Kim. "I call it the fire. They got that inner fire, which has nothing to do with the schooling, nothing to do with the teacher, nothing to do with the parents. There is a desire in that person to please the audience. You see enough of it to recognize it. And that's what I saw with Aaliyah." While the loss was upsetting, Aaliyah pushed on. She would ask her mother every day if record labels saw her on television and called the family to sign her. It's an endearing inquiry but really just showed how, even at ten years old, she knew what she wanted and was figuring out ways to get it. Having some famous family members didn't hurt, either.

Despite Gladys Knight's parting with the Hankerson family, she still stayed close to her niece. She arguably saw herself in the young star, considering Knight got her big break at seven years old competing on and winning the *Original Amateur Hour* TV program in 1952. In fact, when "Auntie Gladys" had her sold-out five-night residency at Las Vegas's Bally's Casino, she had an eleven-year-old Aaliyah accompany her for each of the five performances. The two would sing a duet of "Believe in Yourself" and Aaliyah had a solo moment performing "Home," both from *The Wiz*. The first night, Aaliyah was so nervous that she stood in one spot on the stage, sang, and got right off. Knight pulled her aside afterwards to offer some encouragement. "[Knight] told me, 'You've gotta learn how to move and work an audience,'" Aaliyah told MTV years later. "It was a great learning experience for me." Aaliyah would later credit that string of performances as her greatest training for singing and performing live.

"From an early age, I knew she had enormous talents, an intrinsic gift," Knight spoke of Aaliyah to BBC News following her passing. "When she first performed with me in Las Vegas, she was still quite young, but she already had it—that spark the world would later see and fall in love with."

Aaliyah was groomed to be a superstar, in the most organic way possible. In the late eighties and early nineties, artists didn't have YouTube to film song covers or post, nor did they have Instagram and TikTok (or any social media for that matter) to develop fan followings based upon fifteen-second clips. Aaliyah was too young for open-mic nights, like most rising stars back then who showed up with an acoustic guitar and gumption. Even in those instances, how many *really* make it into the business? What Aaliyah did have were two dedicated parents who wanted her to achieve her dreams, as they too recognized the intangible something that she had, even at such a young age. They also noticed an overgrown maturity.

"I was *hot* at ten. I had the little sex appeal working back then," she told the *Late Late Show* with Craig Kilborn in 2000. "When I was younger, we were getting me ready to come out in the business—I was looking for agents, so [my mother] was taking pictures of me, and she said, 'Yo, she's got this kind of sex appeal working. It comes through in the pictures and on the camera.'"

She also had her grandmother Mintis Hicks Hankerson, who supported her vision for stardom as a kid. "If there's anything that inspired me, it's my grandmother," she told *Black Beat* magazine in 2001. "She always wanted to hear me sing. She would say, 'Come here and sing "Get Here" for me!' It made her so happy to hear me sing, so whenever I am down on myself and feeling down, I think of her." Aaliyah later had a dove tattooed on her lower back in honor of her late grandmother, who passed in 1998. She also dedicated her final album, *Aaliyah*, to her grandmother.

Another person who saw that spark in a young Aaliyah was her uncle Barry, who by that point was no stranger to the biz. Hankerson was already cutting his teeth in theater, producing Ron Milner's gospel musical *Don't Get God Started* from 1987 to 1988 and *One Monkey Don't Stop No Show* in 1991. He was managing The Winans, also acting as percussionist while coproducing 1985's *Let My People Go* and 1987's *Decisions* with Quincy Jones. While Hankerson was in Chicago holding auditions for *Don't Get God Started* at the New Regal Theater, a young man was attempting to audition, but the auditions were closed per the security guard at the theater door. The young man desperately sang "Amazing Grace" for the guard, and one of the actors in the musical overheard. It was Chip Fields, known for her part on the seventies sitcom *Good Times*, and mother to Kim Fields from *The Facts of Life* and *Living Single*. Fields paid the young man $5 to return the next day and sing for Hankerson, along with reading a part of the script. There was one glitch: he didn't know how to read, so the next day when he returned he played his demo tapes for Hankerson. What Hankerson witnessed was something far greater than a small supporting actor role in an Off-Broadway musical. This was a superstar in the making, and Hankerson wanted in on his inevitable success story.

The artist was Robert Sylvester Kelly, a twenty-two-year-old Chicago native who started as a street performer after dropping out of high school. He would sing with his keyboard under

Chicago's "L" Metro transit as morning commuters would drop donations into his hat. It became his full-time job, where in an average "workday" he would take home $400. He later formed the group MGM (which stood for Musically Gifted Men) with a few friends; Robert was the front man. The group competed on the *Star Search*–esque show *Big Break,* hosted by Natalie Cole, and took home the $100,000 grand prize and released the single "Why You Wanna Play Me?" Their union was ill-fated, since the group couldn't agree on money matters, yet their contract was binding. By the time Robert met Barry, he was attempting to untangle himself from MGM. After hearing him sing, Barry slid Robert out of one contract (with MGM) and into an exclusive management agreement with him. This was in 1990, and that summer, while Robert was at his friend's barbecue, he returned to busker mode and performed for the guests. One of whom was an A&R executive at Jive Records named Wayne Williams. Williams approached him after the performance, and Robert was later signed to Jive Records as the artist R. Kelly. Barry Hankerson negotiated the deal.

A year later, in 1991, while R. Kelly was working on his debut album, *Born into the 90's* with Public Announcement, Barry brought his twelve-year-old niece to the studio to meet him. "I sang for him," Aaliyah told *Vibe* in 1994, "and he liked my sound."

Barry Hankerson was hoping to use R. Kelly as leverage to secure a record deal for Aaliyah, since R. Kelly was not only growing in popularity as a star but also a hit-making song-writer/producer for other artists. Labels weren't quite ready for Aaliyah, but Aaliyah was ready to be a star. While Barry's son Jomo was in his last year at Pepperdine University, he and his father decided to start a record company once Barry's attempts to lock a record deal for Aaliyah failed.

In 1991 Blackground Entertainment was formed, and two years later its flagship artist started working on her debut album.

CHAPTER TWO: AGE AIN'T NOTHING BUT A NUMBER

It was basically like listening to an R. Kelly album,
but with a little girl singing.

—Jeff Sledge, *Vibe* magazine, 2016

"May 5, 1993. Aaliyah's Diary. Got it," Aaliyah says with a coy giggle on the intro to the title track off her 1994 debut album, *Age Ain't Nothing but a Number,* as pen scribbles accent dramatic, rolling piano keys like she's about to tell her whole life story. It's a subtle nod to the simplicity of being a teen, documenting life between the pages of some glittery Lisa Frank journal with a unicorn jumping over a rainbow on the cover and a padlock on the side, while simultaneously alluding to the idea that her project was semi-autobiographical.

Age Ain't Nothing but a Number was a complex work, for a number of different reasons. Adhering to the date that Aaliyah herself set on that song, she was fourteen years old when the process had begun for piecing together her big debut. While her uncle Barry Hankerson previously couldn't secure an exclusive major-label deal for her, his newly minted Blackground Entertainment was able to score her a deal with Kelly's label, Jive Records.

R. Kelly released his solo debut album, *12 Play*, on November 9, 1993. His first Jive release, *Born into the 90's* with his group, Public Announcement, was met with mild critical acclaim. Hankerson was executive producer on both projects. Kelly's pre-solo work with Public Announcement made him a prominent fixture in music's teetering New Jack Swing Era. Groups like Jodeci were becoming the face of that movement, making sure a de facto figurehead (in Jodeci's case, it was singer K-Ci Hailey) could always saunter to the front of the stage during choreographed performances to woo the ladies with his abs exposed. Kelly was primed to stand out among his group members, but he needed to do more. It was his solo album that marked him as a sexual dynamo.

12 Play's cover shows R. Kelly gripping a black cane that extends outward across his baggy black denim, a position proudly extending his cane as a phallic symbol, since it's sprouting directly from below his belt. At the end of the cane is a tiny mirror, which used to be a device for young boys to mischievously look up girls' skirts. Kelly is inconspicuously staring off into the distance in blacked-out shades concealing his eyes, wearing a vest with no shirt on underneath. In the nineties this was popular for both R&B singers and college men. In fact, historically Black fraternity members would carry canes as accessories to twirl and make thuds to the floor with the tips, adding bass lines to their step show routines. Series like *A Different World* popularized this Black college lifestyle and brought it to television. However, R. Kelly was nearing twenty-seven when this project was released, despite presenting far younger during the album promo with this collegiate flair.

12 Play was brilliantly executed, by erotic R&B standards.

Songs like "Bump n' Grind" and "Sex Me (Part I) / Sex Me (Part II)" cast sexual innuendos to the side and cut straight to the chase, while "Your Body's Callin'" and "It Seems Like You're Ready" were more suggestive, leading women to believe he understood their bodies perhaps better than they did. It was a power play that worked incredibly well for him, especially when he learned to translate it live. While his early performances opening for R&B acts such as Gerald Levert and Glenn Jones during their tours bruised his ego due to low attendance, Kelly started infusing his live sets with more sexuality. The world caught on, and in 1993 *12 Play* hit Number One on *Billboard*'s Top R&B/Hip-Hop Albums chart and Number Two on the *Billboard* 200.

12 Play's success was enough to prove R. Kelly could craft hits, so Hankerson knew what he was doing when he introduced the star to his niece. Theoretically, the creative pairing of R. Kelly and Aaliyah seemed perfect, considering both had strong classic soul foundations and Aaliyah's goal was to mix that old-school sound with the new school, much like what R. Kelly had already done with his career thus far. It was a win-win situation, and when Aaliyah first met R. Kelly at twelve and sang for him, Barry knew that Kelly could mold her into something more successful than anyone had ever imagined.

By the time they began working together, Aaliyah was a freshman attending Detroit High School for the Fine and Performing Arts, majoring in dance. The school was on par with Fiorello H. LaGuardia High School of Music & Art and Performing Arts in New York City, also known as the school from the movie *Fame*. Using her first name as a mononym, Aaliyah took part in school talent shows. She quickly built a buzz within her high school. Barry had Aaliyah cutting demos well before that, at Detroit's Vanguard Studios, bringing her to record-label meetings everywhere from Warner to MCA to take meetings. Aaliyah was also no stranger to Jive, as Barry was shopping her to the label at eleven years old, though they were reluctant to sign her so young and wanted to wait a bit longer. Once Aaliyah was a teenager, signed to her uncle's company and working with R. Kelly—who was already considered a talent and a genius under their own roof—Jive was all in. R. Kelly was brought on board to both write and produce the entire project, a dream for any label since there were no publishing complications and, again, it would be in the hands of a certified hit maker.

So at fourteen years old Aaliyah entered the studio with R. Kelly to create her debut album.

It took about nine months to record *Age Ain't Nothing but a Number*. Aaliyah recorded some at the top of 1993 but picked it back up around May of that same year. During her summer break from school, Aaliyah flew to Chicago from Detroit, where she spent two months on and off with R. Kelly to create the project at the nation's largest independent studio, the Chicago Recording Company. It's the same studio where R. Kelly would later record his massive commercial hit "I Believe I Can Fly." They hung out together in Chicago, outside of the studio, going bowling, playing video games at arcades, going out to dinner, and watching movies—all of the cutesy activities high school sweethearts do on their date nights. Throughout their time together, R. Kelly would observe Aaliyah and her behaviors, even her interactions with her peers, listening in on their girl talk. He and Aaliyah continued to work on the project until around February of the following year. All of this time together was credited as his technique for gaining inspiration and fodder to write her album material. The product proved he had done his homework, in the most unconventional sense.

"Working with him, he's unpredictable," Aaliyah said of Kelly in an audio interview circulated by Jive to press in 1994. "It's not like when we go in the studio we have the song written out and we just go in and we just sing it through. Really, this whole album came off the top of his head. We'll just go in, go to the mic, and he'll tell me to say something and sing it and I'll sing it. If we like it, we keep it; if we don't, we don't. It's really a special kind of way we do that. It's something that's not written out and planned; it's something that really happens."

When the promotional copies of the album circulated to press and music critics, the back cover showed a picture of Aaliyah with R. Kelly. Aaliyah is grinning in red lipstick and a white bandana, cupping her hands across R. Kelly's bald head. He's smirking and wearing his usual vest with no shirt on underneath. They both have on matching sunglasses. The back cover reads: *"AGE AIN'T NOTHING BUT A NUMBER* was written and produced by R. Kelly. specially for Aaliyah." (Yes, they included those typographical errors.) It also reveals a release date of June 14, but since the music video for "Back & Forth" became an MTV rotation darling, Jive opted to push the album up three weeks early.

On May 24, 1994, *Age Ain't Nothing but a Number* was released. On the cover, Aaliyah is up close within focus, leaned up against a white wall with her face turned toward the camera. She's dressed in all black, with a beanie, blacked-out shades, a black hoodie from nineties fashion staple Karl Kani, and a leather vest. Out of focus in the background stands R. Kelly, wearing the same leather vest with nothing on underneath, staring longingly at Aaliyah and leaning his head on the top of his omnipresent black cane. He too is wearing blacked-out shades. What was once regarded as symbolic imagery of a mentor watching his protégé flourish has taken on new meaning over the years. In the upper right-hand corner of the album cover is Aaliyah's name written phonetically ("ah-lee-yah") since she was still a newbie and people struggled with pronouncing her name correctly.

The project was expertly sequenced by former Jive A&R executive Jeff Sledge to allow for a non-stop playing experience, where the goal was to start at the intro and end at the final track, "I'm Down." With twelve songs, the album cuts straight to the point. R. Kelly's fingerprints are all over the project, with the exception of Aaliyah's cover of the Isley Brothers' "At Your Best (You Are Love)," but even there, when the song was released as a single with a video, R. Kelly produced it, touted as "the remix." His influence was apparent throughout. "It was basically like listening to an R. Kelly album, but with a little girl singing," Sledge told *Vibe* in 2016.

From the top to the bottom, *Age Ain't Nothing but a Number* is the perfect mid-nineties R&B album. It adheres to everything that made that era great—part soul, part hip-hop, with flecks of New Jack Swing. It is, in fact, an R. Kelly album . . . sung by a little girl.

That little girl, however, was portrayed as far older, and we're only reminded of her age in small doses on the project. Spending enough time with such a young girl could have theoretically given R. Kelly an advantage to write breezy tracks about young love and growing up. He instead took it in another direction in moments, where the project was more seeped in Aaliyah rebelling against her age rather than embracing it. There were only flecks of innocence sprinkled throughout an adult-leaning project, when in reality it should have been the other way around.

Tracks like "Throw Your Hands Up" have lighter messages woven into the lyrics like, "If you're not down with the crack, throw your hands up!" While lines like those err on the side of cheesy, it's really the only reminder of Aaliyah's age, since she was still an early teen on the project, and the "Just Say No" initiative and the D.A.R.E. campaign were still popular in middle schools and high schools during that time period. Another young artist, Tia Hawkins, provides guest vocals and ad-libs on this track and a few others. Hawkins was around sixteen when the songs were recorded.

The album feels light and airy, filled with young love. It's no wonder why both R. Kelly and Aaliyah spent so much time together in Chicago that prior summer, hanging out and having fun. The album perfectly captures that spirit of a summertime love story. It speaks of uncertainty, flirtation, gaining confidence, moving forward with cautious optimism, and eagerly solidifying love. Only this story is about a fourteen-year-old girl and a twenty-six-year-old man.

In the liner notes, Aaliyah thanks R. Kelly as her "mentor, best friend, and producer." The ranking bookended by "mentor and producer" is only a tiny red flag, though peeling back the layers of the album reveals something far more sinister than what the radio allowed. "Back & Forth" is a clear hit, bouncing through synths and heavy drums, as Aaliyah is talking about going to the club, while R. Kelly commands in the background, "Let me see you go back; now let me see you come forth." These instructions on *12 Play* would theoretically be perceived as sexual directions, and here he is inserting them into Aaliyah's first single about dancing at a party with her friends. The album track "No One Knows How to Love Me Quite Like You Do" opens with Aaliyah and Tia at the studio talking about a boy named Chris when R. Kelly bursts into the room to get Aaliyah back in the booth to work on music. His ad-libs on that song are repeated over and over: "Liyah, you're the only one for me."

Other songs have little innuendos and overgrown flirtatious subtleties, indicative of the fact that these were not lyrics for Aaliyah to be singing at her young age. The person wielding the pen made millions off songs about straight-up sex, so while R. Kelly could create purely sanitized songs on the album (check the song "Young Nation," where Aaliyah really just carries on about being young), the moment there's any reference to love he forcibly inserts a reference to sex. It's almost as if it's beyond his control and there's just involuntary blurting in song. Take the track "I'm So into You," where in the midst of cheeky banter about checking out a guy, Aaliyah sings the line "Take control of me; fulfill my fantasies."

The most glaring example by far is "Age Ain't Nothing but a Number." On the album's title track, Aaliyah is portrayed as the instigator, luring an older man as she sings about him knocking and her letting him in. Throughout the song, she's asserting that her age means very little in the way of experience. A part of the song where Aaliyah sings, "'Cause tonight we're gonna go all the way," was later changed during some live performances to "'Cause tonight we're gonna chill 'round the way," perhaps due to the obviously suspicious lyrics, again penned by R. Kelly. Three years later, a lawsuit was filed against Aaliyah specifically by music publisher Windswept Pacific. The agency alleged that Aaliyah copied the 1978 track "What You Won't Do for Love," by Bobby Caldwell. Ironically, the suit was filed against Aaliyah only, and years after she stopped working with Kelly, who both wrote and produced the song. Caldwell was ultimately given credit for the interpolation of his song.

❀

The album version of "At Your Best (You Are Love)" encapsulates the remnants of Aaliyah's innocence through her delicate vocals. Her candy-coated falsetto shows that there's more to her range than she was offered to express on the rest of the project. It's here that you remember the young girl from Motor City, raised on Motown. Her soulful roots were strong. She wanted to be a singer, perhaps even more than she wanted to be a star. This song, this version, is the heart of who Aaliyah was at the time, and it was the only part that R. Kelly didn't have complete control over, as it was originally an Isley Brothers song. In interviews, Aaliyah herself says it's her favorite track on the album.

R. Kelly appears on five of the fourteen songs on the album (including the bonus Mr. Lee and R. Kelly Remix to "Back & Forth"). On one of the first songs recorded for the album, "Old School," R. Kelly dedicates the entire third verse to telling *his* career story, from listening to old records to waiting tables and hoping for his big break. He even sends a nod to Barry Hankerson on the verse: "'Til I met the B.H. and bust down A Capella to him / He said you got talent and you're going places." It was a poorly placed homage, though only further proved how so little of the project's direction was within Aaliyah's grasp. The only thing she could preserve was her undeniable ability to take someone else's musical vision, interpret it, and somehow make it her own. That would prove to be her superpower throughout her entire career.

In the midst of Aaliyah's own release, R. Kelly had her slide in two remixes for his projects: "Summer Bunnies" and a "His & Hers Extended Remix" for his hit single "Your Body's Callin'." These came within months of Aaliyah's album release—and again, while she was only fifteen on a grown man's love songs, she continued to show her versatility.

❁

Age Ain't Nothing but a Number arrived at an ideal time during music. The year 1994 had a mixed bag of R&B hits, leaving room for some innovation, since so much of what was being pushed through the music industry pipeline was beginning to sound formulaic, despite the slew of career artists searching for reinvention. While groups like Boyz II Men topped the charts with their fan favorite hits like "I'll Make Love to You" and Jodeci with "Cry for You," TLC was swapping condoms on their clothing for silk pajamas with *CrazySexyCool*. Janet Jackson's *janet.* arrived the year before, so Ms. Jackson was still riding high off her latest reinvention as a soulful sexy bohemian. The same successful stability can be said for Mariah Carey, since *Music Box* dropped in 1993 and she was still surfing that wave a year later. Newcomers were being added to the fold too. Brandy, Xscape, Brownstone, Changing Faces, and BLACKstreet were all introduced in 1994. Aaliyah not only fit into that roster, but she also stood out. While she fell in line at times with the New Jack Swing Era sound, there was still something forward thinking about her vocals. She wasn't belting, but her coos were so unique and smooth; this offered her the balance of being very in the now, but not completely written off as a trend. Many artists of that era leaned too heavily upon what was current, and within a few short years their careers were over.

Not Aaliyah. She was soulful, but not too intimidating. Pop, yet not too mainstream. R&B without being too niche. A flair for hip-hop gave her an edge, which again set her apart from some of her peers, like the aforementioned Brandy, whose big hats and childish suspenders as she sang saccharine love songs created a "do no wrong" air to her. That might work for a younger audience, but certainly not for the adults. Brandy, however, was also creating age-appropriate music, which can inevitably narrow her lane. Aaliyah could serve any listener, and she did so very well. Like the born actor that she was, she knew just when to turn one side of herself on and the other side of herself off. It was felt in both the music and her interviews.

Critics liked the project enough, mainly for where they felt Aaliyah existed within the Black female R&B artist paradigm of the nineties. *Billboard* described it as "Essential for those fiending for Mary J. Blige–style Hip-Hop/R&B," while Dimitri Ehrlich of *Entertainment Weekly* remarked: "Imagine En Vogue packed into one teenage body and backed by hip-hop Svengali R. Kelly, and you have Aaliyah." Dimitri also ran a comparison to Blige, though he argued that Aaliyah's vocals were more "agile" than Mary's. However, once later lined up against her work with Timbaland, Missy Elliott, and Static

Major, Aaliyah's first album loses its luster after witnessing her potential once she's washed from R. Kelly's artfully soiled hands. In *The New Rolling Stone Album Guide*, it's argued that Aaliyah's debut was overshadowed by the later controversy involving its collaborators.

Age Ain't Nothing but a Number reached the Top 20 on the *Billboard* 200 (at Number Eighteen) and Number Three on the *Billboard* Top R&B/Hip-Hop Albums chart, with the two singles "Back & Forth" and "At Your Best (You Are Love)" being Certified Gold. When "Back & Forth" reached Number One on the Hot R&B/Hip-Hop Songs chart, it ironically knocked R. Kelly's single "Your Body's Callin'" from its chart-topping pedestal. To date, the album has gone Double Platinum, moving over 3 million units in the United States, and Gold in the UK, Japan, and Canada.

Beyond sales, the album showed promise in a rising star, whose inherent mystique and vocal capabilities were the real star of the show. Everything else was purely an added bonus. Her promotional photos showed a budding fashion maven, as Aaliyah's dark shades, cutoff tops, and baggy jeans were first introduced during this era.

The album's music videos remained in line with that specific aesthetic, as well. Director Millicent Shelton—whose career started as the wardrobe assistant on Spike Lee's 1989 film *Do the Right Thing*—was the music-video director for all three of the album's singles ("Back & Forth," "At Your Best [You Are Love]," and "Age Ain't Nothing but a Number"). "Back & Forth" has kids and R. Kelly hanging out and dancing, with Aaliyah taking center stage. The camera then switches to scenes of Aaliyah and R. Kelly in matching tracksuits sitting on the bleachers.

The video for "At Your Best (You Are Love)" shows Aaliyah singing into an old-school Kellogg telephone in a booth, while R. Kelly waits for her in the car. The two then start step dancing with each other against a brick overlay before pivoting to the obligatory hip-hop music video parking lot scene. The "Age Ain't Nothing but a Number" video travels along that same vein with the parking lot posse shots. The one thing all of the videos have in common is they all possess a vignette effect, where Aaliyah is almost haloed, as the color schemes change from warm earth tone tints to black and white.

The visuals seemed to reflect Aaliyah's personality. "She was very quiet and she was very shy," Shelton said on BET's TV special *Aaliyah: One in a Million* in 2011. "A lot of people thought she was wearing the sunglasses because there was something wrong with her eyes, but she was wearing the sunglasses because it helped calm her down because she was nervous." Shelton remarked how Aaliyah was kind to everyone on set from director to extras, yet she also made note of how Aaliyah had a distinctive ability to embody her music early on. "A lot of new performers that I work with, you have to really teach them how to sell their own song," she continues. "Aaliyah, you didn't have to teach. I mean, she was a natural, and she just turned it on."

While the music videos took a deeper dive into Aaliyah's musical personality, behind the scenes they reflected something else to some of the people in the room during filming. April Walker, Kimya Warfield-Rainge, and Nicole "Cola" Walker of famed heritage lifestyle clothing line and styling company Walker Wear, styled Aaliyah and R. Kelly for her "Back & Forth" video.

Prior to the video, the Walker Wear team was brought on as image consultants for both the video and also the album's promotional photos. "April and I started with the Aaliyah record," Kimya remembers. "We were given an unofficial copy of the album to be able to hear where she was going with her music." They went back and shared it with Cola and "began building upon where we thought her image should go and how we planned to take it there," Kimya says. "The next week, Cola and I had a meeting with Aaliyah and her management team, and that is when we met R. Kelly."

The meeting included Aaliyah's team/family (mother, father, brother, Barry, Jomo) plus R. Kelly. "At that meeting, he pretty much took over," Kimya says of Kelly. "He was the influencer. They already had an image set for her." The image per R. Kelly was a "girl from around the way in Chicago." When they questioned his vision for the young artist, he snapped, "Well, what do the girls in *your hood* wear?" He then requested that the Walker Wear team purchase an Air Jordan sweat suit that was several sizes too big for Aaliyah. He wanted multiple dark sunglasses and a focus on her bare midsection, with her pants slung low. In essence, he wanted Aaliyah to be dressed just like him, in female form. "We kind of joked that we're just gonna dress her like Jodeci," Kimya says with a laugh, "but we decided that it was best that we mimic *his* look for *her*, but put a little feminine touch to that look."

Kimya and Cola were then scheduled to meet Aaliyah and her team at Los Angeles's Beverly Center shopping mall. The two put some looks together, making sure Kelly's requisite dark sunglasses were paired with each outfit. When Aaliyah, R. Kelly, and the rest of her team arrived, they came with bags of clothing, having already chosen the looks for her. "They took the rest of our budget," Kimya recalls.

During the meeting, R. Kelly pulls out a leather vest from a plastic bag. It's a vest created by the same designer who made his infamous ones that he would wear on his album covers and on tour. Only this vest had a license plate on the back side with his home state of Illinois and "LIYAH1" sprawled across it. "Our jaws dropped," Cola says. "We were at a loss for words." Not only was it peculiar that Aaliyah would be rocking a license plate from R. Kelly's stomping grounds across her backside like you would on a vehicle, but the concept of wearing a license plate at all made no sense to the fashion team. Beyond looking like a symbol of ownership, it really didn't fit Aaliyah's vibe.

"Aaliyah was adamant about wearing that," says April Walker, founder of Walker Wear. "I felt it was very country, so to speak. We always felt like it was important to keep the artist authentic to who they were, but this was such a sticking point. So we were like let's just go with it."

That vest made its grand appearance in the "Back & Forth" video a few days later.

The video had some parts shot in Detroit and was partially filmed on Aaliyah's fifteenth birthday at a gymnasium in Los Angeles. The next day, the infamous Northridge Earthquake hit and production was halted, resuming once the coast was clear. The earthquake reached 6.7 on the Richter scale, sending violent rumbles throughout Southern California and causing multi-billion-dollar damage. The earthquake was so intense that R. Kelly claimed to the ladies of Walker Wear that he slept in his car out of fear once the earthquake struck at 4:30 AM. When the aftershocks of the earthquake shook the trailers on location for the video later that day, everyone was a little triggered.

On set, the chemistry between R. Kelly and Aaliyah was shockingly palpable. Kelly would watch her as her makeup was being applied and hair being done, rubbing her back and telling her how beautiful she looked and how she was going to be the best. Aaliyah would look up at him with doting eyes. "Any time we asked for her opinion, the response we would get was, 'Whatever Robert says,'" Kimya adds. "Her whole family was around, so it was interesting how they can say they didn't know anything." Cola continues, "Everyone was so comfortable with all of the interaction that was going on there." A particular scene in the video shows R. Kelly and Aaliyah wearing matching red, white, and black tracksuits. "That was a very Chicago thing," Cola remarks. "Couples would wear matching outfits. Some of them still do!" When they went home after filming, Kimya and Cola agreed that their instincts told them there was more going on between R. Kelly and Aaliyah than just friendship and mentorship. "It wasn't something we kept thinking about," Kimya explains, "but once the world found out about them, let's just say we weren't surprised."

The Walker Wear team was called right after they wrapped "Back & Forth" to style R. Kelly for his "Your Body's Callin'" video, which Kimya saw as a deliberate attempt to quiet them with more work. "It felt like 'if we keep it going, they won't say anything,'" she expresses. A few years later, when Walker Wear attempted to work again with Aaliyah, they were shut down because they previously worked with R. Kelly. "They said if you worked with R. Kelly, you couldn't work with her," April Walker explains. "We had already worked with both of them, so I didn't even understand that."

All awkward witnessing of an inappropriate dynamic aside, they too saw something in Aaliyah. "She definitely was a star," Kimya says enthusiastically. "When they were shooting that video, you could tell she was a natural. She didn't even need R. Kelly." Contrary to their opinions, R. Kelly was front and center for every part of the process.

Promotion for *Age Ain't Nothing but a Number* was often conducted by Aaliyah and R. Kelly together. The two were often dressed identically, at times in flannels with Disney's Mickey Mouse logo or matching shirts wearing *Looney Tunes* character Pepé Le Pew, the predatory skunk who would attempt to romance a female black cat with a fraudulently painted white stripe. Other times they were both dressed in all black with their eyes concealed by those dark sunglasses. Their jewelry was also strategically matched. Aaliyah was often spotted during album promo wearing a gold chain of a silhouette of R. Kelly on his *12 Play* cover, alternating with a chain of another *Looney Tunes* character, the Tasmanian Devil. In his *Vibe* winter 1994 cover story, R. Kelly is described wearing a Tasmanian Devil chain, which he says is "lucky." Aaliyah later sported a Pepé Le Pew chain well into the recording of her second album.

During their interviews together, R. Kelly would code-switch from grown mentor to boyish sidekick at the drop of a hat, while Aaliyah would hover between doe-eyed ingenue and knowing minx. Their combined wavering maturity allowed them to meet somewhere in the middle, making their disparity in age almost forgettable. Their banter was playful, a little less brother and sister and more like the handsome big brother of your best friend, leaving ample room for the unknown.

That is, until it was made known.

On August 31, 1994, Aaliyah and R. Kelly were married at the Sheraton Suites in Rosemont, Illinois. The marriage certificate shows R. Kelly at his real age of twenty-seven and Aaliyah's age as eighteen, three years older than she actually was. Decades later in 2019, it was reported that R. Kelly allegedly bribed a government employee from his home state of Illinois for a fake ID reflecting Aaliyah at a legal age. The marriage certificate was registered in Illinois as well, so it would all add up. News of their marriage circulated, though they continued to deny it, even when further rumors started about Aaliyah being seen in Chicago, coming in and out of R. Kelly's house and walking his dog named 12 Play. Kelly also bought Aaliyah her own puppy during the album run, which she named Tour.

"I was a writer at MTV News then, and I called the Cook County Clerk's office and got a copy of their marriage certificate—which said that she was 18, even though she was not—so Kurt Loder could break the story," famed journalist Touré wrote in *Rolling Stone* in 2018. Kurt Loder then broke the story in a televised MTV News break: "Hip-hop star R. Kelly did indeed marry his protégé, the fifteen-year-old singer Aaliyah Haughton," Loder reported. "Kelly stated his age as twenty-seven, two years older than he previously claimed to be, and Aaliyah produced two pieces of ID that appeared to show her to be eighteen."

Loder continued to say that Aaliyah's age was already publicly a point of contention, since she was dropped from the

Budweiser Superfest Tour that year due to her being under eighteen, so there's really no way that anyone could allege they weren't aware that she was a minor.

Vibe magazine was the first to publish the story in print, dropping the bomb about the marriage officially in their December 1994/January 1995 issue, where they printed a copy of the false documentation that reflected the two as being married. On the cover of the issue was R. Kelly with the giant words "THE SEX, THE SOUL, THE SALES—AND THE SCANDALOUS MARRIAGE TO TEENAGE SUPERSTAR AALIYAH" beneath his face and his name. In the article, the writer, *Vibe* editor-in-chief Danyel Smith, tells a quick story of how an anonymous caller phoned the *Vibe* offices to say that the relationship between Aaliyah and R. Kelly was "sick" and when she was asked her name her response was "Ms. Snoop with the scoop." The marriage was eventually annulled in February of 1995 by Aaliyah's parents, and Aaliyah later had the marriage record expunged in 1997, when the file was sealed shut. Case closed. In future interviews, she denied that it ever happened.

"I'm not married. That's all I really want to say about it. I like to handle the scandal; I don't let the scandal handle me," she told writer kris ex for *Vibe* in 1996. "I don't like to go into the details on it, because it was a very . . . scandalous thing. I don't like to get into details and add fuel to the fire. I had a lot of drama back then, and I don't really want any more. And out of respect for my family and what I went through, I just answer, I'm not married. At all."

Her father came the closest to even confirming it on her family's side in an interview with *i-D* magazine in their March 1995 issue, where he tells interviewer Frank Broughton: "I'd rather not comment on that. To be honest with you, it was a situation that happened. It's gone now. She's getting on with her life."

There was no real shock at learning that there was a supposed relationship between the two; it was really the marriage that threw everyone off. Earlier, in the summer of 1994, Aaliyah and R. Kelly both appeared on BET's *Video Soul Gold* and the hosts almost immediately inquired about their connection to each other. It was a fair question, one that everyone was wondering during that time. "Everybody seems to think that y'all are either girlfriend and boyfriend, or cousins or friends. Let's get the record straight," the co-host Sherry Carter says, to which Aaliyah responds. "Well, no, we're not related. At all. We're just very close. This is my best friend in the whole wide world." Prior to her responding, R. Kelly mimicked a nervous "hot under the collar" gesture and quipped, "I better go get me a white Jeep. Uh-oh." Kelly was referencing the then-recent event on the evening of June 17, 1994, where O.J. Simpson hopped in his white Ford Bronco and peeled down the freeway in Los Angeles for two hours while the cops chased him in an effort to arrest him for the alleged murder of his ex-wife Nicole Brown Simpson. In essence, Kelly was insinuating that he was fleeing from guilt. That joke would quickly speak volumes following this televised moment.

In the same interview, Aaliyah is asked about her age. "That's a secret," she says coyly, placing her index finger to her lips. "Shhhhhh."

For the first year of her career (and arguably those thereafter), Aaliyah did exist in this world of ambiguity. She defied age, presenting as far older yet still holding on to pieces of girlish giddiness. She defied race, with long straight hair and light skin—a combination of Jamaican roots mixed with Native American blood, and an Arabic name to boot. And she defied the confines of gender, as her baggy clothes were paired with a fully made-up face, making her visually the best of both worlds. Aaliyah was unclassifiable.

While that made her both mysterious and alluring, the lack of disclosure of her age early on served to implicate her once everything involving R. Kelly was made public. The first question isn't whether there's foul play happening; it's "Where are this girl's parents?" The sped-up maturity is presumed to be the product of a young girl's upbringing, not the older man who kicked it into overdrive. There's also this age-old tale of younger girls wishing to "grow up too fast," again placing little blame on the man who helped her get there. During that time, there was a bigger debate of whether or not Aaliyah was concealing an eye deformity beneath her dark glasses than there was over whether it's proper if it's proper to call an unrelated grown man your "best friend in the whole wide world."

Music has a tangled history with older men and younger women finding romance with little consequence. Elvis Presley was twenty-five and Priscilla Beaulieu (later Presley) was fourteen when they first got together. Celine Dion was twelve years old when she had begun being managed by René Angélil, who was thirty-eight. They eventually married, so who really knows when their romantic involvement started? Rolling Stones bassist Bill Wyman was forty-seven years old when he started dating thirteen-year-old Mandy Smith. And of course, who could forget twenty-three-year-old Jerry Lee Lewis marrying his thirteen-year-old cousin Myra Williams? A more recent example is reality TV star and young mogul Kylie Jenner's relationship with rapper Tyga. The two went public when Jenner was seventeen and Tyga was twenty-five, though footage has shown the two being flirtatious when Kylie was as young as fourteen. That's the effect of being followed around by cameras your entire life. These instances are all suspicious, some even downright illegal.

At face value, the relationship between R. Kelly and Aaliyah was just another case of history repeating itself. When two artists work together extensively to create art, feelings sometimes seep into the work. The creative and romantic pairing seems almost idyllic, where in one breath you exchange meaningful glances and the next you're sharing a love for whatever it is you create, be it songs, paintings, whatever. Take John Lennon and Yoko Ono, or even Frida Kahlo and Diego Rivera. Lauryn Hill and Wyclef Jean. The story is retold in so many different versions, all with a similar theme: they came for the art and stayed for each other.

Likewise, the dynamic between a grown male pop star and his teenage core fan base is always tricky. In the 1990s we saw it happen time and time again, where an artist like Kevin Richardson of the Backstreet Boys was twenty-seven during the group's prime, singing love songs to thirteen-year-olds. It creates this veil of illusion, where both the artist and the fan are ageless through the music. That's the relationship the music industry creates for album sales and global popularity. It doesn't matter how disturbing it plays out in real life; this is the business of selling a fantasy. Men with chest hair and possible grays in their goatees are gyrating for girls licking their braces and adjusting their training bras. It's capitalism in theory, criminal in reality.

Aaliyah was the median age of a typical fan who would lust after an older R&B star, and R. Kelly was in fact a bona fide star when they met. So combine the fandom with the creative partnership and sparks were bound to fly. At least that's how it was played out in the media. The idea of getting "too close" through the duration of creating an album became the narrative. Their relationship was almost normalized, with the predator sounding more like Aaliyah than Kelly. It was even right down to her debut album, where the title track incriminates her through the music, despite the pen belonging to R. Kelly. Even Kelly's legal representatives in the past have attempted to allege that R. Kelly didn't know Aaliyah's age, despite footage from an old documentary in 1994 surfacing years later where R. Kelly says, "Right now I'm producing a very talented lady, a young lady. She's fourteen, Aaliyah. She's real street; she just be chillin'."

It was an unfair imbalance where the blame fell more upon Aaliyah. After all, she was the one who had to do serious recon following the news breaking. Their partnership ended, and Aaliyah now had to rebuild her career from the ground up, while R. Kelly exited unscathed—until the truth about him got out.

CHAPTER THREE: R. KELLY'S LOST SURVIVOR

That n***a raped my girl.

—Damon Dash, *Cannon's Class*, 2019

D ash was the first to call it rape—and it took nearly twenty years for him to say it publicly. While the media tossed around phrases like "forbidden love," "secret romance," and "love affair" to describe R. Kelly's relationship with Aaliyah, none of those descriptors were accurate. It wasn't until the true sexually abusive patterns of R. Kelly were brought to light that the question of how Aaliyah fit into that narrative came into play, and even then she was still portrayed more like the blushing young bride than the teenage victim.

R. Kelly's relationship with sex was warped since childhood. In his 2012 autobiography, *Soulacoaster: The Diary of Me*, Kelly details his first sexual experience. He was eight years old. The woman was "at least ten years older than me," he reveals. He was molested by that same woman repeatedly for years.

"No matter how many times it happened, I knew I could never tell anyone," he writes. "I was too afraid and too ashamed." Psychology experts consistently point to repeated patterns following trauma, where the abused evolves into the abuser if they don't seek proper mental health treatment. Even in *Soulacoaster*, while R. Kelly delves shallowly into the damaging effects of that abuse, he places the shame and the blame upon himself, never tackling his need to heal. Instead, he used it as a springboard into his hyper-sexualization that made him millions.

R. Kelly's book arrived a decade following numerous accusations of pedophilia and statutory rape over the years. The first teenager to come forward was Tiffany Hawkins in 1996. Also known as Tia Hawkins, she was the vocal collaborator on Aaliyah's *Age Ain't Nothing but a Number* album. Hawkins, a Chicago native, met Kelly in Chicago's Hyde Park neighborhood at the Kenwood Academy, where she sang in the choir. She was fifteen; Kelly was twenty-four. This was 1991, when R. Kelly's star was just beginning to shine. So when she and her friend spotted him hanging around near her high school, Hawkins—an aspiring singer—had to walk up to Kelly and introduce herself. They formed a rapport rather quickly, which gave Hawkins a false sense of hope that he would help her get her big break. Instead, he made her his teenage madame. Initially, Hawkins served as the wrangler, bringing her young friends over to R. Kelly's home, where he would have sex with them. Eventually, Hawkins was coerced into the sexual encounters herself. That's when her sexual relationship with R. Kelly really took form. She eventually moved in with him and stayed for three years, advised by Kelly to cut off contact with all of the people around her. When she learned she was pregnant, Hawkins alleged that she was urged to "handle" the pregnancy and never again mention the possibility that the child was Kelly's.

About two years into her relationship with R. Kelly, in 1994, Aaliyah came into the picture. Both Hawkins and Aaliyah became good friends, hanging frequently around one of Hawkins's classmates and also with a background singer of R. Kelly's named Jovante Cunningham. Together they called themselves Second Chapter. In that infamous interview on BET's *Video Soul Gold*, Kelly says the concept behind the title of *Age Ain't Nothing but a Number* came from Second Chapter bantering about boys. "She's running around the studio one day with her friends talkin' a lot of smack . . . 'tell her age ain't nothing but a number, girl. . . .' I'm like, 'So whatchu tryin' to say?'" He wrote the title track in fifteen minutes and had Aaliyah sing it shortly thereafter. Hawkins became a part of the project, as mentioned, even sitting beside Aaliyah on top of a Jeep in Aaliyah's "At Your Best (You Are Love)" music video. Essentially, they were friends and collaborators, brought together by what has later become known to be a very typical play in R. Kelly's luring girls together harem-style. Aaliyah was an unfortunate part of this, long before Kelly's diabolical ploys came to light.

In author and journalist Jim DeRogatis's book *Soulless: The Case Against R. Kelly*, he reveals: "All but one of my sources said she and Kelly began having sexual contact during her first recording sessions." Hawkins says in Lifetime's *Surviving R. Kelly Part II: The Reckoning*, "When I found out Robert married Aaliyah, I didn't care because if someone else was sleeping with him that was great because I didn't have to." Her claims in the docuseries were that she was never particularly attracted to R. Kelly, but since he was holding her potential singing career in his hands, she felt as if she had no choice but to obey his wishes. Other girls in the R. Kelly sex circle have stated that eventually Aaliyah and Hawkins fell out, because Hawkins was rumored to be jealous of Aaliyah—maybe due to her sleeping with R. Kelly or because of the fame she had that Hawkins never achieved.

In 1996, the situation came to a head when Hawkins sued R. Kelly for emotional distress, as Hawkins was riddled with trauma and even suicidal. The suit was for $10 million in damages, but by 1998 she settled for $250,000. "I was the first girl, and nobody believed me," she said in *Surviving R. Kelly*, "and after that it continued to happen again and again and again."

Still, the line was hardly drawn to connect R. Kelly's history with younger girls to his relationship with Aaliyah, perhaps again because it was so clandestine.

"I thought that they had fallen in love, that it was wildly inappropriate on R. Kelly's part, but that it was some legitimate mistake that her parents had swooped in to correct," remembers dream hampton. Hampton, executive producer for *Surviving R. Kelly*, was a writer for *Vibe* in the late nineties and early aughts and was assigned a cover story on R. Kelly for *Vibe*'s November 2000 issue. "I wrote the *VIBE* story that ended up being used in the trial because we shot the cover of him inside the sauna where the rape tape was," hampton explains. "I was told by his publicist Regina Daniels that I couldn't ask about Aaliyah when I interviewed him and I was there to basically do an observational kind of 'making of an album' piece which is pretty fluffy." Daniels later had her own issues with R. Kelly, upon learning that he had a secret affair with her young daughter Maxine. During hampton's assignment, she was scheduled for two days of observation for the profile, but it ended up being nearly a week. "He kept putting off the actual interview," she adds. "I remembered asking him about Aaliyah, and he was pissed and he glared at me because I had broken the rule that his publicist laid down. Then when the piece came out he called me and cursed me out. And I was like, 'Did you think we were friends because I'd been there for five days?'"

A month later, Pandora's box was opened.

On December 21, 2000, DeRogatis, then a writer for the *Chicago Sun-Times*, printed the article "R. Kelly Accused of Sex with Teenage Girls" with Abdon Pallasch, which came following an initial piece on R. Kelly. Shortly before the Thanksgiving holiday that year, DeRogatis—the *Sun-Times*'s resident pop critic on and off for nearly a decade—received a mysterious fax addressed to him in response to his album review of R. Kelly's fourth studio album, *TP-2.com*, the sequel to *12 Play*. On his prior album *R.*, Kelly reached new heights with his squeaky-clean mainstream hit "I Believe I Can Fly," and DeRogatis challenged his ability to volley back and forth seamlessly between sanitized pop hits and sexually charged anthems on this next project, citing examples of other artists like Marvin Gaye who code-switched far more fluidly.

Then the fax arrived, one page and single-spaced:

Dear Mr. DeRogatis,

I'm sending this to you because I don't know where else to go. You wrote about R. Kelly a couple of weeks ago and compared him to Marvin Gaye. Well, I guess Marvin Gaye had problems, too, but I don't think they were like Robert's. Robert's problem— and it's a thing that goes back many many years—is young girls.

The letter cited clear examples—one of which named R. Kelly's goddaughter Reshona Landfair as a victim—with the anonymous writer noting: "I'm telling you about it hoping that you or someone at your newspaper will write an article and then Robert will have no choice but to get help and stop hurting the people he's hurting."

It was signed, "A friend," and so began DeRogatis's extensive coverage of R. Kelly's diabolical history, which eventually found Kelly in prison.

Within a month, DeRogatis's article was printed, calling out not only R. Kelly's pathological behavior—complete with nods to court records and interviews—but also the mechanisms with which he encounters his underage prey. "Sources said Kelly continues to seek meetings with underage girls by having an assistant press tiny balled-up notes with his phone number into the palms of their hands backstage at concerts or at video shoots," the article states. DeRogatis later gave R. Kelly's troubled history a panoramic view with *Soulless: The Case Against R. Kelly* in 2019. Two weeks after DeRogatis and Pallasch's article, an anonymous VHS cassette was delivered to their *Sun-Times* office. On it was a light-skinned girl with long dark hair, kneeling on a pillow and performing oral sex on R. Kelly, among other disturbing visuals. Neither DeRogatis nor Pallasch could identify the girl or her age. They turned the footage over to the police. By this point, Barry Hankerson was long out of the picture. In February of 2000, Hankerson resigned from managing R. Kelly, after riding with him for eight long years—six of which were a part of the tangled allegory involving his niece. Hankerson resigned via a letter to Kelly's attorney at the time, Gerald Margolis, where Jive Records founder and head Clive Calder was cc'ed. In DeRogatis's book, he notes that Hankerson's lawyer advised that "he was leaving because he believed Kelly needed psychiatric help for a compulsion to pursue underage girls." Many have villainized Hankerson when it comes to his protection of Aaliyah or lack thereof. Many have surmised that he made this union possible and through it allowed for Aaliyah to be fed to the predatory wolf, only to continue managing the wolf in an effort to double dip and cash out on both Kelly's and Aaliyah's successes.

It wasn't that easy. It never is.

Hankerson rarely speaks about what happened between Aaliyah and R. Kelly, but his retributory presence was and still is felt. It's very possible that he had no idea of how vile R. Kelly was to Aaliyah and that his niece—mature beyond her years—fell for a man who seemed immature beyond his own. If Dash was the first to learn of R. Kelly's abuse toward Aaliyah, then Barry would have equally been in the dark. However, Barry Hankerson is no fool. He's a gangster by design and put two and two together when Tia Hawkins came forward. If it could happen to Tia Hawkins, then it could happen to Aaliyah Haughton.

Things seemed to change after that realization.

Hankerson allegedly contacted Minister Louis Farrakhan. Farrakhan delivered a speech in 2019 where he revealed to his congregation that he met with R. Kelly, amid boos from the crowd. Farrakhan hushes them, before continuing. "He was managed by a friend of mine," Farrakhan says, asking someone side-stage, "What's that brother's name? Barry Hankerson." He continues, "And Barry told me, 'I'm gonna get rid of him.' I said, 'Barry, be patient. That boy is deeply spiritual. A man can't write no songs like that and not have God all up in him, but he's got to be cleansed.'" The phrase "get rid of him" would lead most to believe that Barry meant he was going to have R. Kelly murdered. DeRogatis inquired about that speech over text to Barry Hankerson. This was his reply: "The Minister prays for the worst of the worst; that's why he's the Minister. However, he has guided me well." He closed the text with "ASA," an abbreviation for "Assalamu alaikum" or *Peace be with you*.

"I'm a Muslim. I do my prayers every day," Hankerson told Geoff Edgers in his 2018 interview with the *Washington Post*, after being asked if he had any regrets about R. Kelly. Hankerson revealed he was prohibited by law from speaking about his former artist. "I lost my niece in a plane crash, and please excuse my language, but I don't really give a fuck about none of them people you're talking about." While Hankerson clearly didn't follow through with those plans at the behest of Farrakhan (and Farrakhan warned R. Kelly about the pending threat), he was rumored to have found redemption in other ways.

Information slowly began trickling in about R. Kelly's despicable patterns. Reshona Landfair's aunt was R&B singer and R. Kelly protégé Stephanie Edwards, better known as Sparkle. When DeRogatis previously attempted to speak with her, based on the mystery fax's allegations, she didn't provide much information. She later called DeRogatis and explained to him that she was shown a VHS tape as well, but this one seemed far different and more revealing than the one sent to the *Sun-Times*. It wasn't enough information to implicate R. Kelly without DeRogatis receiving the tape himself.

In February 2002, Jim DeRogatis received a phone call. "Go to your mailbox," the mysteriously deep voice bassed on the other end. In his mailbox was now a second unlabeled VHS cassette in a manila envelope. On the video was what was later discovered to be three-year-old video footage showing R. Kelly having sex for nearly thirty minutes with a girl who could now be identified as his goddaughter. The video closes with him urinating on her.

Chicago police began an investigation of child pornography, following the police's anonymous receipt. The footage was then leaked, packaged, and sold by street vendors as a "sex tape," in response to which R. Kelly denied the claims that it was him on the tape. He later said he had a twin brother, placing the blame on his non-twin brother Carey Kelly and offering him $50,000, a recording contract, and a new car to take the fall.

The accusations piled on, primarily involving underage girls. By August 2001, an Epic Records intern in Chicago, Tracy Sampson, sued R. Kelly for forcing her into oral sex with another woman at seventeen, though years later she told *Dateline* that their sexually abusive relationship started around 1999 when she was just sixteen. They ended their relationship when Sampson turned eighteen, and while the suit was for $50,000, she received a $250,000 settlement in 2002. In addition to the leaked video, that year proved to be monumental in R. Kelly's twisted history of sexual allegations.

It's unclear whether Barry Hankerson orchestrated the leaking of the tape, or was it simply Sparkle who hand delivered the video to DeRogatis's mailbox? DeRogatis to this day doesn't know who brought him that tape, but he has his suspicions. If Barry was the man behind R. Kelly's downfall, it would make perfect sense; he hurt Barry's niece. The abuse didn't start or end there, though.

In April of 2002, Patrice Jones filed a $50,000 lawsuit against R. Kelly, alleging he had sex with her when she was sixteen, impregnated her, and then forced her to have an abortion. Jones settled her case as well. In May of that same year, Isley Brothers backup dancer Montina "Tina" Woods sued R. Kelly for filming them having sex without her consent, the product distributed as a sex tape titled *R. Kelly: Triple-X*. By June, he was indicted on twenty-one counts of child pornography. While he posted his own $750,000 bail, he also pleaded not guilty in court. A six-year span stretched between the accusations and the trial, despite R. Kelly racking up twelve more counts of child pornography between 2002 and 2004. Footage was seized from a Florida home that Kelly was renting, including cameras showing film of minors engaging in sexual activity; R. Kelly is in some of the photos. However, because the footage was illegally obtained, it couldn't be used during his trial. That trial wouldn't happen until May of 2008, and a month later he was acquitted on all counts of child pornography. The reason for the acquittal stemmed from one woman: Reshona Landfair. She denied claims that it was her in the tape, refused to appear in court to testify, and dismissed any allegations that she had a sexual relationship with her godfather. This ultimately forced the court's hand, and so R. Kelly was acquitted.

Eleven years later, in 2019, his goddaughter came forward once Kelly's abusive patterns finally came into focus after two and a half decades of failing to adequately charge him. An article in the *Chicago Tribune* reported that his goddaughter's long-awaited cooperation was an act of "bravery," where she more than likely lied previously for her own self-protection. "It will be harder for Kelly to wriggle out of this one," *Chicago Tribune* reporter Dahleen Glanton writes. "The 52-year-old R&B singer is battling charges of sexual assault, obstruction of justice, child pornography and racketeering. Prosecutors said Kelly sexually assaulted 12 women, at least eight of whom were underage at the time and some as young as seventh and eighth graders." New video also surfaced seventeen years after the first tape, showing R. Kelly urinating in the face of a minor and choking her, saying out loud on the tape that she is only fourteen and having her reiterate her age. Another victim, Joycelyn Savage, came forward later in 2019 and told stories of R. Kelly urinating and defecating in her mouth. This is all on top of further investigations starting in 2017 that R. Kelly was running an underage sex cult.

When DeRogatis moved over to penning pieces for *Buzz-Feed*, he wrote one in July 2017 breaking down how families were torn apart over their daughters being locked in a sex cult with the self-proclaimed Pied Piper of R&B. "Kelly confiscates the women's cell phones," DeRogatis writes in the piece, "so they cannot contact their friends and family; he gives them new phones that they are only allowed to use to contact him or others with his permission." They're also forced to call him Daddy, as he calls them his babies, and they're dressed in baggy jogging suits because he doesn't want their bodies "exposed." If other men are in the room, the girls must face a wall so they can't be looked at or show their eyes to anyone, particularly men. Heartbroken parents detail that they felt their children were brainwashed once in his clutches. However, the ones who have escaped over the years eventually found their voice.

The boost in confidence from the victims happened once an entire series was dedicated to documenting R. Kelly's aggressions. Lifetime, the same network that released the *Aaliyah: The Princess of R&B* biopic—which portrayed Aaliyah's relationship with R. Kelly as true romance in 2014—then released *Surviving R. Kelly* in 2019 and *Surviving R. Kelly Part II: The Reckoning* in 2020, complete with interviews about Kelly's abusive nature toward young girls. "I was invited into the project," dream hampton expresses. "I couldn't say no. He was my generation's problem to solve. I felt that there was some movement happening with #MuteRKelly and another showrunner wouldn't honor the activism."

During the New York City screening of *Surviving R. Kelly*, a threat of violence was called in, after which the NeueHouse Madison Square theater had to evacuate.

❀

Prior to *Surviving R. Kelly*, it felt as though everyone had forgotten about his criminal behavior, especially in the absence of convictions, along with denials on R. Kelly's behalf. Everyone, that is, except for Damon Dash. Once he and Aaliyah started dating in 2000, he "knew everything." In *Surviving R. Kelly Part II: The Reckoning*, Dash refers to Aaliyah as the "sacrificial lamb" of R. Kelly's twisted world. He explained in the docuseries that Aaliyah referred to R. Kelly as a "bad man," though she held no malice against him. Per Dash, Aaliyah's standpoint was, "Let that man live, but just keep him the fuck away from me."

However, Dash's animosity toward R. Kelly eventually trickled into his business. As the co-founder of Roc-A-Fella Records along with Jay-Z, Dash was faced with a dilemma toward the end of 2000 when Jay-Z agreed to appear on the remix to

R. Kelly's *TP-2.com* single "Fiesta." By this point, Dash was almost thirty and had already been dating Aaliyah for several months, aware of what R. Kelly had done to her. In a video interview on Nick Cannon's *Cannon's Class*, Dash broke it down: "If me and you are cool and you know that I got a girl that your man raped and I tell you and you gonna still work with him, whatchu gonna feel?" he hypothetically asks Cannon, referring to Jay-Z's awareness of what R. Kelly had done to Aaliyah and still agreeing to work with him. "That n***a raped my girl, that he liked as well, and went on a tour with him."

Dash also told Page Six in 2019 that Jay-Z had a failed attempt to woo Aaliyah before he did. "He tried very hard," Dash told Page Six. "But you know, we were both going hard . . . . everybody was trying to get to Aaliyah—it was not just Jay. I did not know Jay was trying to holler at her, but then it just happened like that. He was trying; I was trying. Everybody was trying—he was going hard." Many have argued that Jay-Z did date Aaliyah before Dash had, while others claim the two were just hanging out. Hampton remembers first introducing Aaliyah and Jay-Z one night at a club in New York City and then learning they kept in touch after that evening. Jay-Z had already been a fan, having sampled Aaliyah's "One in a Million" for his track "Intro: A Million and One Questions/ Rhyme No More" off *In My Lifetime, Vol. 1*. All of this predates Aaliyah's relationship with Dash.

But that acknowledgment of Jay-Z's feelings for Aaliyah in any capacity left Dash shocked that he would agree to work with someone who violated her. Then again, maybe it was spite? A retaliatory move, where again Aaliyah was the unfortunate pawn. There is no real way to prove the motive behind Jay-Z's decision to work with R. Kelly, though Dash argues it frayed the already-weakening Roc-A-Fella bond.

The final straw snapped in 2002, after Aaliyah had died, when Jay-Z joined forces with R. Kelly for the *Best of Both Worlds* collaborative album. On the title track, Jay-Z even goes as far as mentioning grieving Aaliyah, and then saying, "But I hope my boy Dash gets to see her when he passes." Dash refused to have his name on the project, and whatever proceeds he received from anything involving *Best of Both Worlds* he donated to a breast-cancer charity in honor of Aaliyah's late grandmother. This was also the rumored reason why Roc-A-Fella Records was dismantled a short while later.

All of this begs the question of what exactly happened to Aaliyah during her time with R. Kelly. Damon Dash called it rape, arguably beyond statutory, though he's one of very few people who are vocal about anything criminal regarding Aaliyah and R. Kelly. Prior to their public marriage annulment in 1995, on September 29, 1994 (less than a month after the date on their marriage certificate), a document was signed by R. Kelly, Aaliyah, and both of Aaliyah's parents. The document was anonymously sent to DeRogatis, all of which he reports in *Soulless*. The agreement states that R. Kelly is to pay $100 to Aaliyah in exchange for cutting ties altogether and never mentioning their relationship again, "due to the nature of the music industry and its ability to engender rumors and disseminate personal information, both true and untrue," as per the agreement. That $100 was also rumored to actually be $3 million "off the books," as DeRogatis puts it. Further, R. Kelly was not held accountable for anything that happened, or anything that *may* happen, even "a decline in her ability, reputation, or marketability . . . emotional distress caused by any aspect of her business or personal relationship with Robert . . . [or] physical injury or emotional pain and suffering from any assault or battery perpetrated by Robert against her person." R. Kelly's attorney in the matter, Arnold E. Reed, and Barry Hankerson were the mediators who would police and prevent any further interaction. This prevented Aaliyah from vocalizing her experience publicly. Years later, it may have even prevented her from coming forward as a survivor with the rest of the young women. The situation was written off many times as having never happened, despite so many bearing witness to the traumatizing disaster that continued on for far too long.

During *Surviving R. Kelly*, Jovante Cunningham tells a startling story, where she and Kelly's entourage were all sitting on their tour bus when the back-bedroom door flew open to expose Kelly having sex with Aaliyah in plain view. Per Cunningham, R. Kelly was doing "things that an adult should not be doing with a child." She punctuated that sentiment with expressing "how people are still suffering behind things that went on twenty years ago." Aaliyah's mother, Diane Haughton, released a statement calling Cunningham a liar and saying that both she and Aaliyah's father, Mike, were always on tour with Aaliyah, leaving no room for this behavior to occur. "These lies and fabrications cannot be tolerated and allowed to be spewed from the forked tongues of saboteurs of Aaliyah's legacy," Diane Haughton added in the statement.

Lisa Van Allen—who also appeared in *Surviving R. Kelly* to detail her abusive relationship with Kelly when she was just seventeen—shed further light on Kelly's relationship with Aaliyah in an interview with VladTV in 2019. Van Allen said she first developed a trusting relationship with R. Kelly, who through discussing how he was molested by his sister growing up formed a bond with Van Allen. He then went on to discuss Aaliyah. "They had a pact," she says. "Pins in Eyeballs—no matter what anyone said or if anyone stuck pins in their eyeballs, they would never tell about their relationship." If what Van Allen is saying is true, then Kelly again created this juvenile circle of trust, like two kids spitting in the palms of their hands and shaking on it. Van Allen also made another harrowing claim. "He did get a little more in depth in details when her mother found out. He actually stayed in their home in Detroit, and her mother actually was sexually attracted to him as well," she continues. "He said when Aaliyah would go to sleep that he would—now this is what *he* said—he said that he would go in the living room and him and her would do sexual acts on the couch, while Aaliyah was asleep in the bedroom." Diane Haughton has vehemently denied those claims. Van Allen then continued to explain that Kelly confided that he did marry Aaliyah with a doctored marriage certificate and that she was pregnant at the time. R. Kelly supposedly felt that if he could say he didn't know she wasn't eighteen, then he wouldn't get in trouble if anyone found out about her pregnancy before Aaliyah was able to have an abortion, because she was now his wife.

"And this came out of his mouth," Van Allen adds. "I could take a lie detector test to this. This is what he told me." An extended version of the pregnancy story is also told in the 2011 book *The Man Behind the Man: Looking from the Inside Out*, where a man named Demetrius Smith—who was once employed by

R. Kelly—states that during his Miami tour stop, Aaliyah frantically called Kelly to tell him that she ran away from home and that she thought she was pregnant. The two flew to Chicago for the fake ID and marriage certificate, and once the marriage was secured, R. Kelly jumped right back on his tour. In court documents, Aaliyah admits that she lied about her age on the marriage certificate. Smith appears in *Surviving R. Kelly* to acknowledge his own guilt, as he was there for the wedding. "I was in the room when they got married," Smith said. "I'm not proud of that. I had papers forged for them when Aaliyah was underage. It was just a quick little ceremony; she didn't have on a white dress; he didn't have on a tux. Just everyday wear. She looked worried and scared." Aaliyah ran away from home prior to the wedding and after being left in the hotel room as R. Kelly went back on tour following their marriage she returned home and confessed to her parents and to Barry what had happened.

In 2016, R. Kelly spoke with *GQ* magazine in what was described as a candid interview, with no restrictions and no holds barred. Kelly echoes his childhood trauma, as well as highlighting the cyclical nature of sexual abuse. "R. Kelly, a man who has been accused of multiple sexual offenses against underage girls, has just explained that he believes the sexual abuse he suffered is something that is passed down from generation to generation, so that in each new generation, victim becomes perpetrator," journalist Chris Heath writes. "Once he has said these words, and they are hanging in the air between us, it just seems impossible to imagine that he won't at least address the obvious question—the question, he must surely realize, that anyone reading this would immediately ask: *By that logic, wouldn't that make you the next in the cycle of child molesters?*"

Naturally, R. Kelly's response to his own guilty admission led to a deflection of any further probing, amplifying his denial yet again.

When the subject of Aaliyah arrives, he acknowledges that they loved each other but still remains vague. "Well, because of Aaliyah's passing, as I've always said, out of respect for her mother who's sick and her father who's passed, I will never have that conversation with anyone," he says. "Out of respect for Aaliyah, and her mother and father who has asked me not to personally. But I can tell you I loved her, I can tell you she loved me, we was very close. We were, you know, best best best best friends." He then adds that Aaliyah and her family had an opportunity to talk publicly about this when she was still alive, with no mention of their agreement of silence. His obtainment of false identification to marry Aaliyah in 1994 came back around in 2019, when he was indicted on a new count of bribery for bribing an official for a fake ID. Aaliyah is listed as Jane Doe #1 on the indictment. He pleaded guilty at the brief hearing, which he attended over video from jail.

R. Kelly's unhinging in the media happened right before our eyes. A year earlier, in 2018, a video resurfaced from an interview with Touré for BET, which birthed the quote heard round the world:

Touré: Do you like teenage girls?
R. Kelly: When you say teenage, how old are we talking?

The Q&A went retroactively viral in the wake of social media, especially upon realization that Kelly was in his forties when he supplied that answer. Then, in 2019, *CBS This Morning*'s co-host Gayle King interviewed R. Kelly for a prime-time special, where she sat calmly as he rose from his seat and beat his chest in both a televised and choreographed meltdown. This unraveling only set the stage for what was to come. On July 23, 2018, R. Kelly released a nineteen-minute song called "I Admit," where he goes controversy by controversy, defending his "innocence" in parts, and confessing in others. There's a part in the song where he details an interaction with Wendy Williams, where Williams is asking him a series of questions. "She said, 'What about Aaliyah?'" R. Kelly sings of Williams's inquiry, to which he responds to himself, "I said, 'Love.'" He follows the line with Williams asking about his sex tape, referring to the situation as a setup.

Currently, R. Kelly sits in prison since the summer of 2019, following his arrest for sex trafficking that July. His requests for release have been denied, including one plea in March 2020 from his own concern for his health and safety during the COVID-19 pandemic. That same month, he was charged with nine more counts of sex trafficking, with racketeering, and eight violations of the Mann Act filtered in. The Mann Act, passed in 1910 by President William Howard Taft, prohibited the transporting of women and girls for "immoral purposes," i.e., prostitution. Also called the White-Slave Traffic Act of 1910, it was later considered weaponizing to consensual sex workers, though the stringency of the law has been useful in charging for sex trafficking. In Kelly's case, these charges stem from 2015, when he had sex with more underage girls, allegedly giving one herpes. His plate is now full, with twenty-two federal criminal charges for allegedly sexually abusing eleven girls between the years of 1994 and 2018, along with four other indictments of sexual assault and abuse. He and his team still argue there's a lack of evidence to implicate him.

R. Kelly's Facebook page is flooded with comments from female fans of all ages, not promoting his innocence but rather acknowledging his guilt and expressing their desire to be added to his diabolical harem. Young girls stating their age, asking to meet him along with older women willing to be the exception, are just a few examples of what happens when fame produces nefarious results. His abusive history is less of a timeline and more of a snowball: it started with a ten-to-twelve-year disparity in age, picking specific young girls and so-called dating them, though as he reached his thirties, forties, and fifties it evolved into a sex cult, complete with charges of sex trafficking and sexual abuse that has only escalated in vileness. It's what happens when a court of law witnesses the patterns and still releases the perpetrator. Add to that global recognition and acclaim even during the mayhem: during the twenty-year span of R. Kelly's sexual violence, he released thirteen albums (including a Christmas album in 2016 titled *12 Nights of Christmas*), two collaborative projects with Jay-Z, went on eleven headlining tours and two co-headlining tours, released a memoir, and won nearly one hundred awards that include Grammy Awards, BET Awards, American Music Awards, Billboard Awards, and NAACP Image Awards, among many others. It's impossible to see one's own guilt when the rest of the world has turned a blind eye; only now in a post-#MeToo world are we now seeing some action. However, while his label, RCA Records, "parted ways" with Kelly following the release of *Surviving R. Kelly* and the #MuteRKelly campaign that followed, there is still a growing interest in the singer. Per Nielsen, following the airing of *Surviving R. Kelly*, his streaming data saw a 116 percent surge, jumping from 1.9 million streams on January 2, 2019, to a staggering 4.3 million streams by the following day. The enthusiasm for the music remains; though is this separating the artist from the art, and if so, how far do you separate the two?

❀

Specifically to Aaliyah, it's more a matter of reading between the lines when deciphering their collective narrative, using parts of what was pattern behavior for Kelly. If there are known instances of R. Kelly's sexual abuse in the double digits involving girls who have barely left their single-digit age, then what would lead anyone to believe that he somehow spared Aaliyah? There are a number of known observations between R. Kelly and Aaliyah that fall in line with his treatment of other survivors. It's neither impossible nor inconceivable to put two and two together.

His track record of impregnating young girls and forcing them into abortions would lead to the unfortunate presumption that he probably did get Aaliyah pregnant. And considering she was both underage and high profile, a quick marriage was the Band-Aid before an inevitable abortion. Per Van Allen, following Aaliyah's abortion it was then that the marriage was annulled, though there was a six-month time frame between their marriage date of August 1994 and the rumored annulment date of February 1995.

Further, R. Kelly's desire to keep young girls in baggy clothing in an effort to prevent them from being ogled by other men would explain his desire to have Aaliyah wear that same loose-fitting gear during her first album campaign. Add to that having her eyes concealed by dark shades, where now he simply has his victims face the wall. None of these similarities are coincidental, and there was one person who added it all up in real time: Barry Hankerson.

It's not to say that Aaliyah never believed she was in love with R. Kelly. She probably did at one point. His affirmations, charisma, and guidance built Aaliyah's confidence as she started her road to stardom. We've heard this story countless times, but R. Kelly had a responsibility to Aaliyah as the adult in the room, and he failed her with behavior that is now known to be pathological. This was more than a one-off coincidence of "accidentally" falling in love with a child. This is who R. Kelly is, and considering the new information consistently being made available implicates him even more as an abuser, it's painful to fathom his concealed treatment of Aaliyah. We may never know the depths of the abuse she specifically endured or when she even realized that what was happening was wrong.

Aaliyah didn't just have a crush on an older man; she was violated by her mentor. And while she wasn't able to tell her story of surviving R. Kelly while alive, the hope is that maybe one day her family will do it for her. "I wish that Aaliyah's family would speak, because I think there are so many young Black girls who have been hurt," DeRogatis reflects in *Surviving R. Kelly*. "What it would mean to know that Aaliyah was hurt that way too . . ."

CHAPTER FOUR: TABULA RASA

. . . it was really like Aaliyah kind of got villainized
somehow.

> —Jomo Hankerson, V-103 interview, 2014

The show must go on.

The year 1995 was a transformative one for Aaliyah. On January 14, just a few short days before her sixteenth birthday, she performed at the legendary Apollo Theater. Prior to that performance, she spoke with *Video Music Box*'s DJ Ralph McDaniels and for the first time hinted at her true age. "You know I don't tell you my age; it's a secret," she says with a smile, her eyes no longer concealed by dark shades. "I'll give you a hint . . . it's gonna be a very 'sweet' birthday." She also confirmed in this interview, "I'm Aaliyah, not Aaliyah Kelly," after being asked about the marriage rumors. Aaliyah also went into detail discussing some of the first album's video concepts, including "Age Ain't Nothing but a Number," where she mentions coming up with the treatment with her brother, Rashad. She never mentions R. Kelly. In an interview a month later with Brett Walker of BET's *In Your Ear*, she says that there won't be any more singles off *Age Ain't Nothing but a Number* and that the plan was to jump right into her next album.

Her label did later attempt to squeeze out two more singles that went straight to the European market—"Down with the Clique" in May and "The Thing I Like" in August, the latter bringing her early soundtrack success when it appeared on the soundtrack to the 1994 film *A Low Down Dirty Shame*. Both songs had very little traction Stateside (and weren't officially released as singles there), though Aaliyah was bubbling overseas. She had embarked on a world tour, touching places like Western Europe (England, France, the Netherlands), South Africa, and Japan. Her stage setup included a live band, with some choreo-graphed backup dancers and singers, as Aaliyah alternated between dancing and singing during her performances. She was going global, and fans who didn't even speak English were latching on to her songs. Plus, she was making all of that hap-pen while still a sophomore attempting to continue her high school education. That made her, in many ways, so relatable to her core fan base. In music industry speak that's the perfect time to get to work on your follow-up album, striking while the iron is hot, as they say. However, controversy is a double-edged sword. While Aaliyah and her team managed to keep a tight lip (via NDA or otherwise) about her now-faded connection to R. Kelly, the music industry didn't forget. It remained a mys-tery waiting to be solved, yet in the wake of her making new music it resurfaced in a way that was creatively unimaginable.

It was clear that while Aaliyah's interchangeable family and music team wanted her name removed from sentences including R. Kelly, he was the force behind that debut project that brought her to the public eye and ultimately made her a star. In addition, following their creative and personal split, it was Aaliyah's reputation that was hanging in the balance and not R. Kelly's. In March of 1995, during the airing of the Soul Train Music Awards—when Aaliyah's name was mentioned during her nominations for Best R&B Soul or Rap New Artist and Best R&B/Soul Album, Female (for *Age Ain't Nothing but a Number*)—the audience booed. In those early days following the R. Kelly scandal, Aaliyah suffered through several negative responses from audiences near and far. A teenager, who just endured so much, was being chastised for choosing to leave a volatile situation. Further, all she had was her music to keep her going, and the threat of losing that came with every boo, hiss, and howl. It was psychological warfare, but Aaliyah endured it with grace.

"What was surprising to me was after it all came out, it was really like Aaliyah kind of got villainized somehow," Jomo Hankerson told Atlanta's V-103 radio station in 2014 about the aftermath of her R. Kelly storm. "That's the part that I never understood. And that's what made the transition to the second album very difficult."

Coming off a successful debut album, the move to the sophomore project is supposed to be smooth. Sure, there's the theory of the "sophomore curse," where the success of your start doesn't materialize into an entirely successful career. Oftentimes artists are regarded as a "one-hit wonder" once that first project leaves and little success follows. It's tough for anyone labeled as a "star," especially when you're young and wondering what the future has in store for you and your craft. However, in Aaliyah's case, she had the makings of a hit maker: she had a highly musical pedigree since childhood, she was able to readily adapt to the music she was given and adopt it in a way that felt seamless, she already had a trendsetting style in place, and she had a voice that wasn't like any other artist out there. With all of that talent, she still couldn't find collaborators.

Hankerson stated that while the label had a few key relationships, they struggled with finding more producers who would work with them. Calls weren't returned, especially when the bigger-named producers learned that they'd be producing a song for a fledgling sixteen-year-old singer and no longer the protégé of superstar R. Kelly. It almost felt like Aaliyah was being blacklisted. There was no way that Aaliyah was going to give up, but she had to hit the reset button.

Blackground eventually parted ways with Jive Records, where they let Aaliyah out of her contract through Jive founder Clive Calder in an effort to continue her disassociation from R. Kelly. Geoff Edgers reported on the details of what happened in the *Washington Post.* "In 1994, Hankerson and the Haughtons came to Calder's office," he wrote. "There was no talk of reprimanding Kelly. Instead, the family demanded that Jive let Aaliyah go." The further argument from Aaliyah's family was that she wouldn't be promoted as fairly with R. Kelly as her labelmate. While it was agreed upon that she could cut ties with Jive Records, Aaliyah had to forego a percentage of her future album sales to Jive, despite being with a new label. Aaliyah was then signed by Atlantic Records.

Craig Kallman, who was the vice president of A&R at Atlantic Records at the time (later moving up to chairman and CEO in 2005), signed Aaliyah to Atlantic when she was sixteen.

He told *Vibe* in 2016 that she was a "complete package" and he saw that from the moment he met her. "She immediately had this kind of electrical charm about her," he shared with *Vibe*. "She was incredibly charismatic and just the sweetest, nicest artist, but also carried herself with a real, kind of almost mysterious air about her. She had this way about her that was very intriguing and telling."

The goal for Aaliyah was to rebrand: find a new team, work with new people, and wipe the slate clean. It was the best and only way for her to truly break free from her ties to R. Kelly, while building upon her own identity as she was growing up and going further into her teenage years. The press was still regarding her as a "new" artist—evidenced by a small spot in the February 1995 issue of *Ebony* magazine, where she's flanked by Brandy and Larenz Tate as the "New Teen Sensations." There was still time to fix things, despite the reluctance of new collaborators.

So Aaliyah started spreading her wings.

In April 1995, Aaliyah appeared alongside top female hip-hop and R&B artists like Mary J. Blige, Queen Latifah, TLC, and many others on the soundtrack to the film about the Black Panther Party, aptly titled *Panther*. Aaliyah sang a part on the film's powerful theme "Freedom," a song about resisting the discriminatory practices set in society for generations against Black people. While the project didn't bring mainstream appeal, it did diversify her portfolio a bit. Here was an artist who broke moments before her other female R&B counterparts like Brandy and Monica hit the scene. "She came out before Monica and I did; she was our inspiration," Brandy told

Billboard in 2011. "At the time, record companies did not believe in kid acts and it was just inspiring to see someone that was winning and winning being themselves."

And while Monica is also featured on the "Freedom" song, Aaliyah wasn't always offered the luxury of starting out with a squeaky-clean slate, so every new endeavor beyond her *Age Ain't Nothing but a Number* period was a step in an entirely new direction since she was now doing it alone.

The producers invested in her were scarce, but they were there. Sean "Puffy" Combs showed interest early on in working with Aaliyah and had even thrown his hat into the ring to take the bulk of production duties on her follow-up album. (The stars never completely aligned there, but that didn't stop them from later working together in other capacities.) Two producers stepped up to start working with Aaliyah once her recording budget was sorted. There was Craig King, who produced on R&B duo Zhané's breakout album, *Pronounced Jah-Nay*, in 1994, along with other nineties acts, later working with the likes of Ludacris, Kanye West, and Wiz Khalifa among others. There was also Vincent Herbert, who worked with Dionne Warwick, The Winans, Toni Braxton, Al B. Sure!, Babyface, and many other acts before working with Aaliyah. Later Herbert was credited for his work with Destiny's Child and Lady Gaga. He also assisted with later Blackground artists like JoJo.

King told *Vibe* in 2016 that for three months they were staying in a condo over in Detroit, cranking out songs at Vanguard Studios (the same place where Aaliyah cut her very first demos) that would later appear on Aaliyah's second album. The goal here was to diverge from the sound R. Kelly had created for her; this would be a 2.0 version of Aaliyah. It was time to transform her and make her the star of the show. After all, by the mid-nineties R&B was yet again in need of a reboot as hip-hop stars were growing accustomed to sampling soul, funk, and jazz records, leaving a run-of-the-mill R&B songs in the dust if it didn't have some gusto. "Vincent [Herbert] and I were the first people she called; we were the first group," he told *Vibe*. "That's why we had so much freedom to go in and create a sound because we didn't have to do a song here or there. They wanted us to go in and build a sound. We built a sound and it was a departure from R. Kelly."

When Aaliyah arrived in the studio to work, King had her sing "At Your Best" with him at the piano to test her range. "I turned the lights down, she sat next to me on the stool, and we started to play the song," King continued, "and I got chills all over my body."

Together (with Herbert) they recorded eight songs; three made it to the album with one on a Japanese bonus release. That moment singing "At Your Best" stuck, as the songs they recorded in the studio included another Isley Brothers cover, the smoothly R&B "Choosey Lover (Old School/New School)," which was produced by Vincent Herbert with Rashad Smith, a hip-hop-accented Marvin Gaye cover of "Got to Give It Up" (featuring rap pioneer Slick Rick), and the nineties soulful "Never Givin' Up" (featuring Tavarius Polk), co-written by Monica Payne. The mid-tempo song "No Days Go By" made it as a bonus track on the Japanese release, co-written and coproduced by Rheji Burrell, and co-written by Aaliyah.

Aaliyah was then bound for Atlanta with her mother and brother. The Hankersons reached out to Jermaine Dupri, who was already building a movement with his label So So Def

Recordings, breaking acts like the backwards-clothing-wearing Kris Kross, Da Brat, and even working with Lil' Kim. "I think it was fly that she took chances on her music," Dupri told MTV News in 2001. "Just the softness of how she sang over them hard-ass beats, it was something different." With Dupri (and producer Carl So Lowe) she cut "I Gotcha Back," a rhythmically breezy love song. She enlisted new producer J. Dibbs to write and produce the contemporary R&B cut "Giving You More."

Legendary songwriter Diane Warren also requested to work with Aaliyah. Warren has penned hits for everyone, from Cher to Patti LaBelle, Celine Dion, Whitney Houston, and later Beyoncé, Lady Gaga, and many, many others. "I remember really liking Aaliyah and wanting to work with her," she told *Vibe* in 2016. "I think I reached out to Craig Kallman at Atlantic and said I wanted to work with her. They were down." She wrote the ballad "The One I Gave My Heart To," and while Babyface was the intended producer, he couldn't make it to the session with Aaliyah. He was in Los Angeles, and she was still in Atlanta at the time. Babyface tagged in Atlanta-based co-collaborator Daryl Simmons, who scored a major hit co-writing and coproducing Boyz II Men's "End of the Road" with L.A. Reid and Babyface. When Simmons arrived at the studio, it was with Aaliyah and her father. He had her warm up and was floored. "She started singing and I heard this voice. I looked out in the room, and I was like, 'Is that you?'" he told *Vibe*. "She goes, 'Oh yeah, that's how I warm up.' She was doing all this incredible opera. It was the furthest thing I would have ever thought that she could do. It just blew my mind."

The then-new producer Rodney Jerkins produced and co-wrote the dancy track "Everything's Gonna Be Alright."

Jerkins, going by the stage name Darkchild, moved on to produce for Brandy, Monica, Mary J. Blige, and Destiny's Child among others. He also produced the Gina Thompson single "The Things That You Do"—the song in which Missy Elliott appeared on the remix, which for many was the first time they'd heard Elliott.

New Jersey rap trio Naughty by Nature was already a force, thanks to songs like "O.P.P." and "Hip Hop Hooray." Group member and producer KayGee produced the song "A Girl like You" for Aaliyah and it features Naughty's group leader, Treach. The song is very much in line with a Naughty by Nature–style song, with harmonizing horns and strong bass lines. "She was like my li'l sis," Treach told MTV News in 2001. "She'd come up and put her arm next to me like, 'Listen, we gonna make this song together. I don't want you to do just one verse and it's over. We gonna do the hook together.'" Aaliyah returned the favor in 1999 by appearing in Naughty by Nature's music video for their single "Holiday."

The consensus was that Aaliyah was highly musical but also shy and demure. She had a quiet roar about her, where once she entered the booth it was like she came alive. This idea of hopping around and working with multiple people was something entirely new for her. After all, she came from a setup where it was a one-on-one creative process. As predatory and traumatic as it was, R. Kelly created a world where only the two of them existed. He watched her, observed her, and wrote about her. Sure, the product was a certified hit (while simultaneously incriminating him with a whole album about what he hoped were her thoughts about him), but there can be some comfort in isolation, especially when it's made to feel like it's just the two of you. Now Aaliyah was seeking out new collaborators, hoping she could find a second life for her music. And yes, while some requested to work with her themselves, there was still an overarching hope that this could all work. It wasn't a surefire win, no matter how talented the artist and her assembled team were.

Plus, the nineties were defined by artists and their "crews" and Aaliyah still needed one.

Puffy was perhaps one of the first to invite Aaliyah into a new sense of community. Puffy discovered the late Notorious B.I.G. in 1992, after seeing the Brooklyn-bred phenomenon's spread in *The Source*'s "Unsigned Hype" column. From there, he signed Biggie to his newly minted Bad Boy Records after being fired from Uptown Records, led by the late industry visionary Andre Harrell, and home to future legendary acts like Mary J. Blige. Notorious B.I.G. dropped his magnum opus *Ready to Die* in September 1994, setting a whole new bar for hip-hop music. While Bad Boy was a record label, it was also very much a tight-knit crew. Aaliyah appeared to fit right in.

In June of 1995, Biggie released the single "One More Chance / Stay with Me (Remix)" and Aaliyah appears in the video mouthing the chorus alongside other R&B mavens like Mary J. Blige and the hook's actual singer, Biggie's then-wife, Faith Evans. Biggie's crew (and also baby act) Junior M.A.F.I.A. released their own project *Conspiracy* in August, and while Faith Evans sings on the album version of their song "I Need You Tonight," it's Aaliyah who sang the hook when the track became a single and appeared in the single's music video. Aaliyah maintained her ties to Bad Boy. In February 1996, Puffy orchestrated a trip to Trinidad to work on The

Notorious B.I.G.'s *Life after Death* (a project that would eventually be released posthumously on March 25, 1997, as he died on March 9 before the album arrived). On this trip was production collective the Hitmen, who at the time was comprised of Deric "D-Dot" Angelettie, Steven "Stevie J" Jordan, Nashiem Myrick, Ron "Amen-Ra" Lawrence, and Carlos "Six July" Broady. The team holed up in the Caribbean Sound Basin studio in Port-of-Spain to create Biggie's final project with him (unbeknownst to them). In addition, 112, Faith Evans, and Aaliyah flew out there to help on the album. Ironically, R. Kelly appears on *Life after Death* on the song "#!*@ You Tonight," though he wasn't a part of this now-infamous work trip. This was also going to be the trip where Aaliyah was going to cut a few tracks of her own for *One in a Million,* but time escaped them. "We started working together, but we couldn't finish the songs on time," Aaliyah told journalist Michael Gonzales in the November 1996 issue of *Request* magazine, the publication printed by former music retailer Sam Goody. "I had to leave, because I had to go to Atlanta to record with Jermaine Dupri."

On the evening of March 9, 1997, Aaliyah was out partying with Biggie in Los Angeles, right before he was murdered. Following his passing, Lil' Kim released the music video for her *Hard Core* single "Crush on You" in June 1997. Aaliyah can be seen dancing in the video. On that same album, Aaliyah was featured on the radio edit of Kim's "Queen B@#$H." Prior to that, Kim can be found a year earlier starring in the video for Aaliyah's single "If Your Girl Only Knew" and appearing in 1997 in the "Hot like Fire" video alongside fellow Junior M.A.F.I.A. member Lil' Cease. Since both Junior M.A.F.I.A. and Aaliyah were distributed by Atlantic Records, they were frequently placed together and grew quite close. "I always looked at her like my sister," says Lil' Kim. "Because we were so opposite, we attracted to each other. I was the sexy, hardcore gangstress, and she was the sexy empress with a little edge. We fit together like a hand in a glove."

Another Puffy affiliate made her way into Aaliyah's world and changed the course of Aaliyah's career, with the help of some "super" friends.

❧

In 1989, a local artist in Portsmouth, Virginia, named Melissa Elliott formed a girl group with some friends from her high school. The group was called Fayze, and Melissa also recruited another friend to help with production. His name was Timothy Mosley, a Norfolk, Virginia, native, deejaying under the name DJ Timmy Tim. In 1991, Fayze recorded a track called "First Move," and the group was determined to make it big. They understood that it was all about who you know, so with a song in tow it was time to network. Fayze showed up to a local Jodeci concert that same year, and after making their way backstage they sang an impromptu a capella performance for Jodeci member DeVanté Swing. He, in turn, signed the group to his imprint over at Elektra Records called Swing Mob. He also changed Fayze's group name to Sista. The group moved to New York City, and Melissa brought Timothy with her. DeVanté renamed him Timbaland, like the Timberland boot (a hip-hop fashion staple), and Melissa started going by "Missy." They also brought along their friend Melvin Barcliff, also known as Magoo.

While Sista found some success with their 1993 single,

"Brand New," Missy saw a bigger picture for herself and her friends. Coincidentally, so did DeVanté. His Swing Mob went from imprint to community, as he made a compound out of a two-story building upstate in Rochester, New York, where about twenty creatives all holed up to make music. They started calling themselves Da Bassment Crew. In that crew: Missy, Timbaland, Magoo, singer Tweet (as part of the group Sugah), Ginuwine, veteran recording engineer Jimmy Douglass, and R&B group Playa (which included the late Static Major), among others. It started as something fun and organic, where artists could come together and really become a creative force. For two years, Da Bassment spent hours on end every day writing and producing songs. Their collaborative mission was Jodeci's third album, 1995's *The Show, the After Party, the Hotel*. DeVanté took most of the writing credits on the project, despite it being a team effort, though both Missy and Timbaland received co-writing credits on just a few songs (Missy on "S-More" and Timbaland on "Bring On Da' Funk" and "Time & Place"). The process to even have their uncredited work appear on the album was strict. It was orchestrated like a battle royale, where DeVanté would instruct people to write either alone or in groups, competition-style, and he would select whichever songs he liked best. It was intense, highly competitive, and also traumatic.

Timbaland's 2016 memoir, *The Emperor of Sound*, tells a whole different side of Da Bassment, filled with behavior that was borderline torture, where DeVanté created an aggressively competitive world for all of the artists. "We would go for days without eating," Timbaland says in his memoir. "We would be woken up in the middle of the night to run crazy errands. We were knocked around, kicked around, and beat down." Their access to the outside world was limited, almost like a prison. It was nothing short of abusive, where the end result was not even getting to grow as a credited musician. Artists like Ginuwine and Magoo have spoken differently of the experience over the years. They speak of the hard work and the sport of it all, where writing a song in the fastest time was more of a lesson in speed than inducing anxiety—though Ginuwine has compared it to the boot-camp style of Death Row Records, which operated under the venomous Suge Knight. Still, there was struggle, and if the struggle didn't result in gaining adequate songwriting credits (when DeVanté took the bulk of them, it led to an inevitable lack of publishing royalties for everyone else) then it was done in vain, at least from Timbaland and Missy's standpoint.

Missy Elliott was the first to ultimately leave that camp (followed by Timbaland and later Ginuwine and the rest of the musicians), and with good reason. As a child, she endured her fair share of abuse. VH1's *Behind the Music* highlighted that bumpy early road in 2011, where Missy details being molested for close to a year by her sixteen-year-old cousin when she was just eight years old. Add to that, growing up in poverty with no running water and watching her father pull a gun on her mother. There would be no way that she would allow another abusive pattern to seep into her life any longer.

And so she left the Swing Mob for good, yet used her ties to the treacherous camp as networking leverage once she was back out in the world. She began linking with industry bigwigs, particularly Puffy, who was enjoying the success of The Notorious B.I.G., following the release of his aforementioned

Bad Boy Records debut album, *Ready to Die*. They also shared a mutual friend in Mary J. Blige (Puffy's former artist at Uptown Records), as Missy was present during Mary's studio sessions for her sophomore album, 1994's *My Life* (Mary was in a relationship with K-Ci Hailey, DeVanté's groupmate from Jodeci).

Through her reputation for stellar songwriting and artistry, Missy was able to grab a handful of opportunities—like singing backup and on the hook to MC Lyte's "Cold Rock the Party," off her fifth studio album, 1996's *Bad As I Wanna B*, and grabbing a guest feature on the aforementioned Bad Boy Remix to R&B singer Gina Thompson's single "The Things That You Do." Meanwhile, Da Bassment Crew fell apart shortly after Missy Elliott departed. That wouldn't be the last time the lineup would work together, though. Missy, Timbaland, Magoo, and Playa reassembled as the crew later known as Tha Supafriendz, releasing music for Ginuwine still and even Tweet.

Though once leaving the trauma of Swing Mob, their collective (and individual careers) hung in the balance. They managed to cut some tracks for Ginuwine upstate, using the song "Pony" as the centerpiece for their soon-to-be definitive sound. As he drove away from the Rochester ruins of Swing Mob with Ginuwine's masters in tow and no deal in sight, engineer Jimmy Douglass was struck with hope once he heard Missy on the radio, on that Gina Thompson song. One of their own escaped the madness and still made it. Douglass managed to secure a deal for Ginuwine with Sony, and so the team regrouped in Ithaca, New York, to start creating what would become Ginuwine's 1996 debut album, *Ginuwine . . . the Bachelor*.

In the midst of recording that project, the team caught wind that Aaliyah was searching for new producers to work with. The songs previously recorded for the album were great, but she needed her own sound, one where if you closed your eyes and heard it you'd be able to instantly recognize that it was her. That would be the thing to truly push her into icon territory. Craig Kallman was on the hunt.

"I really just started meeting with tons and tons of new songwriters and producers, just looking for someone creative that had their own spin on things," Kallman recalled to *Vibe*. "And one day, this young kid came in." It was Timbaland. He played beats for Kallman, and he was blown away. He phoned Aaliyah and told her about this new producer on the scene. There was even a songwriter to match: Missy Elliott.

Timbaland and Missy sent over a demo track that she and Timbaland had worked on called "Sugar & Spice," a song written and produced by Missy and Timbaland, with the reference track recorded by Tweet and her group Sugah. The song also appeared on Da Bassment's first mixtape, recorded during their tenure at the Swing Mob compound. When the track landed in Jomo and Barry Hankerson's hands, they weren't too keen on the song for Aaliyah's next project. They felt like the song sounded too "kiddie" and unfit for what was going to be Aaliyah's first post–R. Kelly debut.

"Kiddie" might not have been the best word to describe "Sugar & Spice," though it was a step in reverse for an artist who sang that "age ain't nothing but a number" at the age of fifteen. While the track boasted some innocence in the lyrics, as Sugah cooed that they were sweet like "sugar and spice, and everything nice," one aspect that managed to stick out was the intricate beat. It was an amalgam of what was happening in R&B around 1995: fragments of the soon-to-be bygone

New Jack Swing Era, though it was mixed with soul, a little funk, and then this unorthodox triple-beat pattern. It was the beginning of Timbaland's soon-to-be notorious style of beat making, though in its rough early stages. When Jomo passed the track off to Aaliyah, he had no real thought of where that track would go or any real intentions of using it. Again, it was too "kiddie" for his liking.

Aaliyah, however, loved it.

Up until this point, she lacked any real control over her own musical destiny. She started under the tutelage of her uncle and then quickly moved over to R. Kelly. Decisions were made for her, and while she showed no reluctance in acquiescing, this sophomore album was going to be the proof that she was fine without the watchful eye of her former mentor. Yes, *Age Ain't Nothing but a Number* gave Aaliyah her start, but this time around had to be different. She had nothing to lose and everything to gain by turning her situation around and showing who she was as a solo star. So Aaliyah made her first real artistic call and advised her uncle and cousin that she wanted to work with Timbaland and Missy. They listened to her.

Everyone got on a phone call, where Aaliyah told Missy and Tim her artistic vision: she was known for this "street" appeal, but she wanted to add a sexier vibe to her art now. She was no longer fourteen years old, having songs written for her about overly mature indiscretions. There was ample room where she could spread her wings a bit and tread into grown territory, now that she was nearing a more appropriate age for it. She requested that Timbaland and Missy travel to Detroit to meet with her. Craig Kallman also urged that the two head out to Detroit for this fateful meeting. So Missy and

Timbaland agreed and were on their way but kept it all under wraps until they actually landed the gig. They were knee-deep in recording the debut project for Ginuwine, but they hit the pause button once the Aaliyah opportunity arose.

"Here we all are in this isolated studio up in Ithaca, and then Missy is out doing whatever, and then Tim had to go away to do something that Missy had for him," Jimmy Douglass recalls, "and apparently they went to Detroit and cut a record."

He was correct, but there was a bigger goal at the heart of that trip: to head out to Detroit and figure out if they were going to be the production team that Aaliyah needed in her corner for her next album.

"They was testing us out to see if we could make a hit record for Aaliyah," Missy told *The FADER* in 2011, "because she was coming off the project with R. Kelly and I guess they wanted to try some new producers." For all intents and purposes, Aaliyah was a big star and Missy and Tim were still so new. "We was kinda nervous because we hadn't done records for any artists of that caliber," Missy continued, "but when we first met her, she treated us like she knew us for years, like we grew up with her. She was always very sweet, always smiling, and she made us feel like we was big producers when we didn't have no record out. Even coming off a big album, she never once treated us like we were beneath her."

The reality was that Aaliyah, Timbaland, and Missy were all expats from their previous worlds. Those worlds were very similar: they worked under superstars who later turned out to be abusers, and when they disengaged there was a question of whether or not they could ever get their careers to continue without those very people who originally helped guide them.

It was a fair enough question, though the mutual bravery of escaping their pasts and still taking that risk to leap into the unknown future made this new union a community of commonality, but also one where Aaliyah was finally in the driver's seat. She had been down this road before, knew the ropes already, and could navigate from a position of confidence and experience over her previous constant journey of learning. She was also growing up, now sixteen, and learning the value of her own choices. And so she chose this team to guide her into the next iteration of her career.

Everyone knew that there was a lot riding on this partnership. Whatever Aaliyah did next had to be *big* and whatever Timbaland and Missy created, following Da Bassment, had to reflect their genius to the point where you could re-listen to that Jodeci album and recognize their unidentified fingerprints all over it. This kinship was mutually beneficial, but it was also authentic from the start. They all became so close that Tim and Missy affectionately started calling Aaliyah Baby Girl. It stuck.

There was also something else brewing. At twenty-three, Timbaland may have been young by music industry standards, but he felt too old to be taken by a sixteen-year-old. However, he was. In his 2011 *E! True Hollywood Story*, he admitted to having feelings for Aaliyah the moment he met her. "When I first met Aaliyah—it's time for the world to hear this; I'm gonna give a little secret—I was in love with her," he says in the episode, reconciling that she was just a "baby" and that he was "old." Well, at least too old for her. "I said to myself, 'I'm just gonna be her brother,'" he continues. "Oh man, I was fightin', I was fightin' a lot—a big war. But I loved Aaliyah." Timbaland kept his cool and made good on that promise to be her big brother and not cross a line that her previous mentor had crossed on the last project. He also later admitted, though, that he married his wife, Monique Idlett, for a very specific reason. "When I first met my wife, I knew I was going to marry her because she looked like Aaliyah," he explained. As for that "Sugar & Spice" song, it didn't make the cut on Aaliyah's project. It eventually became a song called "Candy" by R&B trio Tha Truth! Aaliyah, Timbaland, and Missy all recognized the inevitable chemistry that was brewing and were ready to jump into the studio and make magic together.

Once Tim and Missy returned to Ithaca, they had to tell the rest of the crew that plans had changed.

"In the middle of this Ginuwine album, Missy comes up to Ithaca and says, 'We ain't doing Ginuwine's [album].' I'm thinking, uh, yeah, we are," Douglass says with a laugh. "And she's like, 'Nah, we have this girl Aaliyah to do.'" Ginuwine already had his record deal with Sony (and his studio time was being paid for), yet Aaliyah was moved up on the priority scale. They struck a deal with Ginuwine that for every session given to Aaliyah that was supposed to be his he would later be compensated for those lost days. Ginuwine was cool with that deal. "I had to hide from Sony because they're waiting for their record," Douglass continues. "So I was like the guy in the middle. Sony was calling every day: 'How's it going? It's going fine.' Even though we're doing something else."

That "something else" was about to change R&B music forever.

CHAPTER FIVE: ONE IN A MILLION

Aaliyah's gonna show you how to turn this mother out.

—Aaliyah, "Ladies in da House"

Every superhero needs her theme music. . . .
The album was called *One in a Million*, but the title track was Missy and Timbaland's audition to work with Aaliyah. Together, they spent a week at Vanguard Studios. It was a culture shock to Missy and Timbaland, who weren't accustomed to using the old-school technology of the soulful Motown studio setups, where everything from the mics to the mixing boards was reminiscent of musical days past. Still, they holed up and got to work. A musical bond was forming, and the title track, "One in a Million," was proof of that.

"Tim and Missy had already done that song with her," Jimmy Douglass recalls of the track, "I guess to test for Barry Hankerson if they could do the album or they could do some songs." The song was still raw, and the beat ended up being re-polished once they all headed out to Ithaca, but it showed incredible promise and signified this new direction for Aaliyah. Aaliyah already knew that it was going to go places. "She immediately thought it was a hit," Missy recalled to *The FADER*.

"We didn't have to convince her; she was like, 'I'm telling you, this is hot.' I knew then there was a chemistry. She wasn't close minded. She was an artist that got it."

Once it was firmly established that they would all be working together, Aaliyah flew out to Ithaca with Missy to meet everyone at Pyramid Sound Recording Studios. Barry was still riding high on securing the deal with Atlantic Records and joined them there to lay some ground rules. It was the summer of 1995, and Aaliyah was ready to kick-start her career for the second time. For almost a year—from August 1995 to July 1996—Aaliyah cut close to sixty songs for her follow-up album.

"I'm seventeen now, so I've grown in a lot of ways, artistically and vocally," she said in an interview with MTV during the album's press run. "Before I went into the studio to do this album, I knew I wanted to showcase that . . . and really show my colors on this album. I was very confident in my convictions and what I wanted this time around."

The studio sessions were lengthy—sometimes for hours that would lead into the next morning—yet Timbaland compared it to being in a "funhouse," where musical experimentation went wild. Missy was autonomous ever since her Swing Mob days. "The way Missy constructed those records was she would write the song and she would actually go in and she would do all of the parts," Jimmy Douglass explains. "From soup to nuts, you know, harmony . . . that's how she writes songs. In her mind, she would orchestrate all the parts." They would then leave Aaliyah with Douglass to re-create the songs with Aaliyah's own personality. "They would let me kind of reconstruct what they had just done with Aaliyah," he continues. "And Aaliyah was fine with that. We would listen, track for track, and just replace, until it was the same arrangement—except that it was Aaliyah's interpretation."

In the July 20, 1996, issue of *Billboard*, reporter J. R. Reynolds penned a piece titled "Aaliyah Set Courts Broader Fan Base," discussing her diverse changes on the new album. "Aaliyah was more involved with *One in a Million* than she was on her first album," he writes, "taking co-writing credits and assisting in the creative direction on the project. 'I wanted to maintain my smooth street musical image but wanted to be funky and hot, yet sophisticated,' says the 17-year-old artist who has yet to sign a publishing deal." Her label even smoothed over the switch from R. Kelly to a semi-star-studded production lineup in the piece; as Atlantic Records' product development director, Eddie Santiago, told *Billboard*, "We wanted Aaliyah to keep growing, so we didn't want to have the same suspects on her new project." Aaliyah herself addressed the lack of R. Kelly's presence on *One in a Million* in her interview with MTV: "That was a decision that I made," she said in the interview. "I thought it would be best for my career and me personally to move on and really take control of this album." When the interviewer pried further about her previous personal ties to R. Kelly being the reason he wasn't a part of *OIAM*, Aaliyah continued, "Honestly, there were negative things that were said in the past, and that was one reason why I did feel it was best for me to move on. That was a rough period for me and my family—a very tumultuous time—but I'm a very strong person. I think it says a lot that I'm here today and I answer the questions."

There was a lot riding on this project. Aaliyah carved her own lane with her debut, regardless of who was behind the

wheel, and she blazed a trail for other female R&B acts to follow. Her next moves were going to either make or break her
career, but she was up for the challenge, complete with a new
record label behind her.

"I faced the adversity," Aaliyah told Gonzales in her *Request*
magazine interview. "I could've broken down, I could've gone
and hid in the closet and said, 'I'm not going to do this anymore.' But I love singing, and I wasn't going to let that mess
stop me. I got a lot of support from my fans and that inspired
me to put that behind me, be a stronger person, and put my
all into making *One in a Million*."

And that's exactly what she did.

The intro to *One in a Million* is a stark contrast to the one
from her previous album. Here, instead of her seductively scrib-
bling secrets into her teenage diary, a bell's toll is waking her
up, with Missy Elliott calling her name. "Aaliyah! Aaliyah!
Wake up," she utters with a laugh, adding, "You've just now
entered into the next level, the new world of funk." Her words
segue into "Beats 4 da Streets," a small ditty where Aaliyah
is basically announcing her arrival, as Missy sing-spells her
name, "A-a-l-i-y-a-h." Sure, on "Back & Forth" Aaliyah cooed
her name ("Ooh, it's the L-i-y-a-h"), but this was different.
From the door, the team circled around their star. It wasn't a
declaration of secret love, nor was it a rookie's big break while
the bigger star knowingly checked in to shine on his own. No,
this was an album titled *One in a Million* from an artist who
was, indeed, one in a million. The album reflects that from
beginning to end.

Thematically, *One in a Million* plays like a love story between
two age-appropriate young people. Girl meets boy, but boy has

another girl. Girl pushes boy away but still wants boy. Girl and boy finally get together; boy breaks girl's heart. While Aaliyah was getting older, there was a purity to this project; it was almost as if there was a stronger recognition of what it meant to truly date someone and fall in love as a teenager. There were all of the key elements there, from love to heartache. That was poorly inserted into her debut, as it was layered with secrets and misbehaving behind closed doors. Here those doors were flung open and the world had begun to see the angelic magic of Baby Girl.

The first taste of the project came in July 1996 when the lead single, "If Your Girl Only Knew," was released. The song is equal parts electronic and funky with hints of rock thanks to warbled bass-guitar licks. Timbaland's deep, impactful voice handles the ad-libs like they're their own bass lines while Aaliyah harmonizes over him. The song isn't directly about taking another woman's man. It's about criticizing a man for having a woman while trying to land another one, even though the other woman is into it. There's an underlying innocence to the song, while still remaining flirty and self-empowered. "I bet you like what you see," Aaliyah sings. "It ain't easy to get with me."

For the music video (released July 8, 1996), director Joseph Kahn stuck to the same monochromatic alternation aesthetic from her last album's visuals. They were a cool aspect that made sense. In the video, a motorcycle gang pulls up to the club. Aaliyah hops off the back of Ginuwine's motorcycle, gives a pound to her brother, Rashad, at the door, and enters. The scene is in black and white, where the only ones in color are Aaliyah and the man about to leave his girlfriend (played by Lil'

Kim). Throughout the video, Aaliyah's eyes are concealed again by dark goggles, until toward the end, where she opens them and they're in color, switching from blue to green. Other cameos in the video include Missy, Timbaland, and R&B group 702.

It was the perfect transition from "Back & Forth" into her new era. She didn't look like a completely different person, but the upgrade was evident. Aaliyah was noticeably older and more mature, her hair longer, and her clothes more fitted, while still baring her midriff and maintaining that tomboy chic look that she first arrived in. The song eventually reached Number One on *Billboard*'s Hot R&B/Hip-Hop Songs chart but was a slow burn. It was perhaps due to all of the bubbling acts simultaneously circulating that year.

A month later, *One in a Million* dropped on August 27, 1996. The cover was shot by photographer Marc Baptiste, who met Aaliyah prior, to shoot her for what would be *Seventeen* magazine's January 1997 cover. Baptiste got a callback to meet with Aaliyah and her family to discuss the album cover's concept. "She was very focused," Baptiste told *Vibe*. "She knew exactly what she wanted, how she wanted it." They shot the cover in the Canal Street subway train station in New York City, moving over to the then-rugged Brooklyn neighborhood of DUMBO. The front cover is of Aaliyah in a leather motorcycle-style jumpsuit, perched up against a subway station frame with her album title embossed on the pillar she's leaning against. The album is credited as executive produced by Jomo and Barry Hankerson; her father, Michael Haughton; and Craig Kallman. In her thank-yous, she thanks her "family, friends, and fans who supported me when the skies were not as clear as they are now!" She even wrote a whole song to her fans on the project, a short outro track called "Came to Give Love," which was produced by and features Timbaland.

One in a Million debuted at Number Twenty on the *Billboard* 200. R. Kelly did, unfortunately, remain a part of the narrative for this album run, mainly due to his sudden disappearance. "Kelly had no publicized input on this record, and Aaliyah fares well in his absence," Connie Johnson wrote in her *Los Angeles Times* review. "The 17 tracks offer no shortage of great material, ranging from the teasingly witchy 'If Your Girl Only Knew' to the gently poignant '4 Page Letter.'" Kris ex wrote in *Vibe* in 1996: "Jaundiced listeners will search to find Aaliyah's hidden messages to R. Kelly throughout *One in a Million*. But despite the ever churning rumor mills, Aaliyah has moved on past troubled waters."

In October, the second single, "Got to Give It Up," arrived with a music video, where Aaliyah sings into an old-school hanging dynamic microphone, while pivoting scenes to dance alongside a hologram of Marvin Gaye. By December, the title track was released. "One in a Million" marked the true turning point for Aaliyah. Initially, there was pushback from radio due to the sound. "[Radio] said they couldn't blend it in, they couldn't mix it in with records before it or after it because the cadence hadn't been done before," Missy Elliott told *Billboard* in 2018. "And so somehow, I think her uncle spoke to some people and they end up playing it. I know [Funkmaster] Flex was one of the first people to break that record in New York. . . . It was a headache at first."

While the song was warmly received by critics and fans in its ability to show Aaliyah seamlessly weaving through Timbaland's production—as she oozed sexy melodies over the beat—it was the music video that visually showed Aaliyah was on the verge of something entirely new and shape-shifting for the world of R&B. Aaliyah was dancing, *really* dancing.

The year 1996 marked a turning point in Black music. This year was the marker, where R&B and hip-hop had begun to blur their lines a bit more. In February, the Fugees released *The Score*, where the dynamic Lauryn Hill had the double duty of providing standout rap bars on the project as well as singing the phenomenal hooks, while bringing the trio to new heights with her cover of Roberta Flack's "Killing Me Softly." Meanwhile, in the spring Maxwell released his debut album, *Maxwell's Urban Hang Suite*, a project that oozed sexuality while also still playing the balancing act with what would later be christened "neo-soul." Hip-hop was in full swing by the summer, with Jay-Z's debut album, *Reasonable Doubt*, Nas's *It Was Written*, A Tribe Called Quest's *Beats, Rhymes, and Life*, and Out-Kast's *ATLiens* (the latter released the same day as *One in a Million*). Hip-hop and R&B's momentum would carry into the fall, even when rap music lost Tupac Shakur on September 13, 1996. The Roots released *Illadelph Halflife*, Mobb Deep brought *Hell on Earth*, 112 and Dru Hill dropped their eponymous debuts, 702 released their debut, *No Doubt*, while Ginuwine finally released that debut album, *Ginuwine . . . the Bachelor*, and Lil' Kim and Foxy Brown both emerged with their solo debuts in tandem, respectively titled *Hard Core* and *Ill Na Na*. There was a lot happening, but through it the lane was again wide open for Aaliyah to stand out. Since she had the foresight to work with producers and songwriters who straddled the line between hip-hop and R&B, her album was able to live in both worlds. During that time, it was the rappers who traipsed over to working with R&B artists in an effort to broaden their reach. Aaliyah worked in reverse, while still reaching that same end result. It was all a part of her process for change.

An important part of Aaliyah's next-gen transformation was shifting her style. Again, it couldn't be drastic; so many stars' attempts at reinvention often look exactly like that: reinventing an existing performer and turning them into someone else completely. Typically it happens with musicians when they're about to change their sound, so their hair, makeup, and dress will follow suit. That approach arguably lacks authenticity and feels more like a phase; with Aaliyah, there was staying power but also a need to create something striking visually, which had fans clamoring to look like her. Previously, her style was at the hands of her mentor—with a wardrobe filled with innuendos, like wearing a license plate with his state or a chain with his image still signifying his subtle dominance over her career. Now it was time to style an emerging icon on her own terms.

Her mother suggested she cover one of her eyes with her long hair, a "peekaboo" hairdo made popular by her mother's favorite movie star, Veronica Lake. Aaliyah would later use the name Veronica Lake when she checked into hotel rooms in homage to the actress and her iconic hairstyle. Aaliyah's favored eye to cover with her hair was her left eye, and even despite rumors still circulating that she was concealing a lazy eye, her fans quickly hopped on the trend and rocked an identical hairstyle for years to come.

Next, she needed a proper stylist who was all her own. She met stylist Derek Lee at a magazine shoot and within days asked him to join her team. Lee's first major styling came with the "One in a Million" (admittedly Aaliyah's favorite song on the whole album) video, where her evolution was quite clear. Her sunglasses came off, at least partly, only worn to accessorize and no longer hide. Her swooped hair still gave her an air of mystery, and in the video she's wearing a sterling silver monocle-styled eye patch in some scenes, which many felt was a pun on the rumors that she was hiding a lazy eye under her hair and her shades. In that same look, she's wearing a bra top that Lee purchased from a sex shop in New York City's West Village neighborhood on Christopher Street. "I went mostly shopping in the sex shops," Lee told *Nylon* in 2020. "That's why you see a lot of leather and stuff like that in there, because that was really my only option, along with the clothes that I already had, like the flight suit. And she loved it and she rocked it."

Her pants also fit differently, showing her slight curves and somehow striking a balance of femininity and androgyny. Her fingers were adorned with asymmetrically cut rings. She almost looked unreal; her beauty was in full view and her clothing accented what God had already given her. Derek made her soft yet tough. It was once again that "street but sweet" effect, only monumentally upgraded. From leather biker jackets and jumpsuits to all white loose jeans and cropped tanks, along with leather pants and bikini tops, this would become the "Baby Girl style" that fans and other artists would mimic for generations to come. It all started with this video. A remix was tacked on featuring Ginuwine, which had the whole team (Missy, Timbaland, and the others) front and center in the video. And then, of course, the dancing. Choreographer Sorah Yang provided the moves for Aaliyah, and her background in dance proved helpful in adding this new tool to her arsenal. It was all coming together masterfully, as Aaliyah was showing herself to be multidimensional and again being able to separate herself from the competition.

The director of the "One in a Million" video (and its subsequent remix video) was Paul Hunter. Hunter had also directed "Got to Give It Up" and the two would reconnect years later on "We Need a Resolution." The perfect picture came to life. The lights, the cameras, Aaliyah in action. With her new style coming through new lenses, everything changed. She was coming into her own, to the point where when anyone thought of Aaliyah this was the visual they conjured up.

Later, single releases off the album like the magical "4 Page Letter" continued her visual story, with a mythical element in her wardrobe to match the video's fairy tale "Once upon a time"–esque theme. That concept came from Aaliyah's brother, Rashad, who wrote a short story about Aaliyah that was sent over to the music-video director Daniel Pearl. Pearl, a friend of Barry Hankerson's, worked with Aaliyah as cinematographer on the "One in a Million" video and the remix video. They called him for "4 Page Letter," which became his directorial debut. "I was impressed from the beginning with her sophistication for her age," he told *Vibe* in 2016. "It's a very interesting blend of professionalism and innocence that she possessed that appealed to me." The "4 Page Letter" single also had another brother-sister connection, as the B side, "Death of a Playa," was the song that Aaliyah wrote together with her brother.

When "Hot like Fire" was released, she was already eighteen and very much leaning into her adulthood. The video is red themed, with Aaliyah donning a thin crisscross-strapped bikini top and red camouflage pants in some scenes while alternating with a fishnet top in other scenes. In the video Aaliyah still is styled true to form, and by this point any diversion would have been a stark contrast to the visual everyone was now used to. She's wearing red camouflage—custom designed by 5001 Flavors Clothing Co., along with mismatched Clarks Wallabees shoes, which her stylist felt was a nod to her Jamaican heritage (since Clarks shoes were big in reggae and dancehall). Her top was plain, and tempered the sexy "Hot like Fire" motif in a perfect way. Street but sweet. It arrived in tandem with the album's final single, the Diane Warren–penned ballad "The One I Gave My Heart To" (the radio single produced by pop producer Guy Roche); the music video (directed by Darren Grant) was more subdued than the others but still stylish.

The singles penetrated multiple charts. "If Your Girl Only Knew" topped *Billboard*'s Hot R&B/Hip-Hop Songs chart, while also hitting Number Five on the Hot Dance Singles Sales chart. "One in a Million" hit Number One on the Hot R&B/Hip-Hop Airplay and Number Two on both the US Dance Club Songs chart and Rhythmic. Both singles were also international successes, along with "Hot like Fire," which reached Number Three on the UK R&B chart, among others. "4 Page Letter" only reached Number Twelve on the US R&B/Hip-Hop Airplay chart, but it did reach the Top 10 on the UK's R&B chart, while also charting across Europe. "The One I Gave My Heart To" had even more international reach, charting in the UK, the Netherlands, Scotland, and New Zealand, while reaching the Top 10 here on *Billboard*'s Hot 100, Hot Dance Singles, Hot R&B/Hip-Hop Songs, and Rhythmic charts. Aaliyah proved she was multi-faceted and not your run-of-the-mill act who can only stay in one lane. Her reach was far and wide, and the world was starting to take notice.

Aaliyah took the sound that Timbaland and Missy were concocting and she ran with it, but what she also did was give it validity. They were on the brink of something, about to change how music would sound for generations to come, but they needed to house it somewhere. Aaliyah was that home. She was the physical embodiment of their style and their musical swag. The piecing of her together with them was indomitable.

When Craig Kallman called Aaliyah the "perfect package," he wasn't kidding. She had a strong team beside her: songwriters who understood that she wanted to be an adult yet remain girlishly flirty, producers who understood that the goal was to remain simultaneously classic and futuristic, and a stylist who understood that she wanted to accentuate her body through the use of clothing so that she wore the clothes—the clothes didn't wear her. Underneath it all, though, was Aaliyah . . . the natural born star.

It was time for her to officially cross over.

CHAPTER SIX: TOMMY GIRL

When I see Tommy Hilfiger, I think of Aaliyah.

—H.E.R., *i-D* magazine, 2020

One in a Million kicked off a new iteration of Aaliyah that was rooted in experimentation. Sonically, it was a no-brainer that working with both Timbaland and Missy opened up a whole new world of sound and style, but it was Aaliyah's stylist, Derek Lee, who provided her aesthetic to match that music. Her makeup artist, the late Eric Ferrell, was at the helm of keeping her makeup consistent—as he worked with Aaliyah from the beginning during her earliest "tomboy" years. He even maintained her signature thick eyebrows that later remained *en vogue* for women everywhere. At the heart of all of their curation, however, it was still Aaliyah who shone through. Gone were the days of simply acquiescing to a mentor and using her strong acting chops to be his puppet. No, now we were slowly learning about who the *real* Aaliyah was, and she exuded that on every song and in every outfit. It came as no surprise that the ingenue with washboard abs was destined for modeling. What was waiting to be discovered, however, was how one designer utilized Aaliyah's flawless figure as his canvas, as well as her personality and vibe within his clothes to set the visual standard for his clothing line to follow.

His name was Tommy Hilfiger.

Hilfiger cut his teeth in fashion in 1969, when he launched a store called People's Place with some friends in his hometown of Elmira, New York. The store grew into more locations throughout upstate New York, though they went bankrupt by 1979. In 1985, he started Tommy Hilfiger, his own eponymous line dedicated to "classic, American cool" menswear. By the nineties, Hilfiger was embraced by hip-hop, once the fashion trend "urban preppy" took off. There was also an allure to the Hilfiger designs that spoke to hip-hop beyond the growing rugby shirt and windbreaker trends happening within the culture. Tommy utilized color schemes differently. He paired bold hues with subdued ones. There was rarely a timid earth tone in his designs, though something about bright yellow sewn beside navy blue just popped.

Tommy Hilfiger's clothing line became something of a hip-hop fashion staple at a time when designer clothes were slowly entering the rap fashion purview, but in an unconventional way. The juxtaposition of street rappers in preppy clothes ran rampant, which offered designers like Hilfiger the opportunity to slide right in and corner a market that was previously uncharted, at least for them.

What was once the uniform for preppy white guys who were into sailing or horseback riding (the names and logos of Nautica and Polo are proof alone of that) traveled over to the other side of the tracks and landed on the backs of drug dealers turned record-label owners and rappers. It was the loudest secret that these clothing designers weren't pleased with the new "street marketing team" for their clothing lines but loved their deep pockets. After all, the brands each carried significant price points for shirts, jackets, and jeans, yet in the minds of executives there was no guarantee that poor Black kids could play the long game with their clothing and keep their bottom lines healthy for years to come, like their previous audience. And once *that* audience saw the new adopters of those brands, they may be less likely to sport them. It made sense but didn't make it any less disturbing.

Hip-hop's relationship with fashion is pretty extensive. It started in the late 1970s and early 1980s, when the preteen and teenage hip-hop pioneers left their bedrooms and congregated in the parks that split up the South Bronx housing projects for outdoor jams in the summertime and packed roller rinks, clubs, and event halls once the weather chilled. Hip-hop culture was built on fashion. In fact, the documented "birthdate" of hip-hop (August 11, 1973) is celebrated because of a fashion fundraiser. Hip-hop's founding father Kool Herc deejayed his sister Cindy Campbell's back-to-school party at 1520 Sedgwick Avenue in the Bronx, where she charged at the door in an effort to pay for her new school clothes.

Crews during the seventies and eighties had matching jackets sewn with their names on them and would often dress in the same outfits when they were onstage performing. Groups like Salt-N-Pepa were twinning in their 8-ball-style leather jackets and spandex pants with bamboo earrings, an eighties staple accessory. The legendary Daniel "Dapper Dan" Day became known as a Fashion Outlaw when the Harlem native took a printing machine and counterfeited overpriced logos of designer fashion houses and plastered them, head to toe, on articles of clothing. That need to be fashionably cutting edge remained a prominent theme in hip-hop after decades of fashion evolution. As the top preppy designers (Ralph Lauren's Polo, Nautica, and Tommy Hilfiger) were luring in the hip-hop crowd while simultaneously scared of it, rumors started circulating that there was widespread objection to rap artists in their clothes.

Tommy Hilfiger was the first to come under fire, when the designer and his brand were rumored to have expressed a disapproval of people of color wearing his clothing. It was a gradual snowball that had begun to develop when a further rumor stated that Hilfiger allegedly said he wouldn't have made his clothing "so nice" had he known it would be worn by POC. A boycott campaign had taken off from there, and then another rumor fueled the fire when Hilfiger apparently appeared on *Oprah* and defended his stance about not wanting POC to wear his clothing. This era predates YouTube or even a sophisticated internet, so really no one was on hand to pull up this fictitious episode or even create a social media post denying those claims. It then traveled through nearly every minority community, where Jewish people and Latinx people alike were told that they were also on the "Do Not Wear" list for Hilfiger. The rumors lingered on for years—over a decade in fact. Hilfiger eventually really went on *Oprah* in 2007 to address it, though like he told "Godmother of Fashion" Fern Mallis during their interview as part of 92Y's Fashion Icons series, "Some people may still believe it."

There was really no merit to the origin of those claims; Tommy Hilfiger hadn't even appeared on *Oprah* during the time the rumor originated. The only real damage control was to continue with smart collaborations that not only showed the brand's diversity but also dismissed any idea that there was a preferential person in his fabrics.

That same year, 1996, Tommy Hilfiger expanded its brand into women's fashion. By August, Tommy's women sportswear line landed in four hundred department stores within the United States. The next move was to fully immerse the brand into music, capturing a whole new consumer. There were already a few moments that foreshadowed his entry into the adjacent industry. In 1994, rapper Snoop Dogg landed his first performance on *Saturday Night Live* and was wearing a red-and-blue-striped Tommy Hilfiger rugby, which many point to as a major pivot for hip-hop fashion. Snoop was dressed for the performance by Tommy's brother Andy Hilfiger, who was the director of public relations for Tommy Jeans. It was also the shift where Tommy Hilfiger became the go-to uniform for true school rap fans.

Tommy Hilfiger secured his next hip-hop moment, when he custom designed a shiny silver suit for Sean "Puffy" Combs's performance at the 1997 MTV Video Music Awards. That suit signified what many hip-hop historians refer to as the hard switch—where in a post-Tupac and post-Biggie world hip-hop became diluted by the mainstream—known as the "Shiny Suit Era."

Hilfiger's portfolio also included rock, as he dressed the legendary Rolling Stones for their 1997–1998 Bridges to Babylon Tour, after Tommy partied with Mick Jagger in the Caribbean. Everyone from Sheryl Crow to Gwen Stefani and Treach from Naughty by Nature has also worn Tommy Hilfiger in public. The real impetus behind the music came from Andy Hilfiger.

Andy would scour the hip New York City nightlife scene in the nineties in search of the next big partnership. Andy loved music and working with musicians, so the partnering really meant something to him. He later even started his own record label.

The ads for Tommy Hilfiger boasted these "coming of age" lineups of young models and actors, where their success was foreshadowed by their placement on these ads. With hip-hop, though, it was less about the artists' appearance in these campaigns and more about them being dressed in Hilfiger as walking advertisements. The goal was to find someone who could fluidly do both.

Hilfiger added another hip addition to his team, Kidada Jones (the daughter of Quincy Jones and Peggy Lipton), who styled for Hilfiger in the past. In 1997, she still held an unofficial post as both a talent scout and a consultant for the company. "Me and Aaliyah met at a Tommy Hilfiger fashion show that I styled in about '93," Jones told *The FADER* in 2008. "She had really small feet and so did I and she didn't have shoes for the show, so I remember loaning her my shoes. Then we met again on the Tommy Hilfiger photo shoot when we were both in the ad." They immediately connected and later became best friends. "Her mom allowed me to be her guardian for a little bit," Kidada continued. "I was a few years older, so when she went to Europe I was the guardian—which was a complete and total nightmare. I'll keep it mild, but it was just young fun and maybe I didn't really understand the boundaries. We got in trouble quite a few times, but she was the funnest friend." They even had plans one day of launching their own clothing and accessory line called Dolly Pop.

Kidada and Aaliyah reunited professionally in 1997. That was the year Tommy Hilfiger made a game-changing decision to have Aaliyah included in his spring line marketing campaign, at the behest of Andy and Kidada. As always, the talent was handpicked in the hopes that their celebrity would later become a check point in these ads, but with Aaliyah he saw something bigger. Tommy Hilfiger *needed* Aaliyah.

In the spring of 1997, Tommy Hilfiger launched his "Next Generation Jeans" campaign. The group of young celebrities who were a part of the campaign included a pre–*Almost Famous* Kate Hudson, producer Mark Ronson, Kidada Jones, and of course Aaliyah.

By this point, Aaliyah was a full-fledged music star. *One in a Million* was out for nearly a year, so she had not only proven there was no sophomore curse, but she was even bigger than before. And again, a growing tastemaker in the fashion world. So with her natural beauty and body that could wear any outfit, modeling was also an inevitable foray. She was a longtime Tommy Hilfiger fan and wore the clothes on her own, but Atlantic Records reached out to Hilfiger gauging their interest in working with Aaliyah, and Andy readily put her in their ads. Aaliyah wasn't the tallest—she stood at five-seven—but with washboard abs and a dancer's physique, she had the luxury of being able to wear baggy clothes and tight clothes and still look amazing in both. She was undoubtedly the star of the campaign, but the costar was definitely that memorable outfit she was in.

Many will clearly remember her notorious Tommy Hilfiger uniform. Aaliyah wore a tube top with the infamous Tommy flag of half-red, half-white, and a navy blue trimming that partially framed the logo. Her bottom half included loose denim with one red and white leg and one navy blue leg. "Tommy" is stitched from hip to ankle on one pant leg, "Hilfiger" on the other. They're slung low enough to reveal the thick waistband of Tommy Hilfiger boxer shorts that she's wearing underneath. A unisex Tommy belt completes the outfit. Her campaign video was shot by Mark Ronson, where Aaliyah is gracefully dancing as she voices over the video in her lightly delicate tone, discussing her parents and where she gets her traits from. It was a sweet clip where she was able to both honor her family and show while also showing yet again why she was so incomprehensibly magical. There was also this air of self-love, since she's answering the hypothetical question of *Why are you so fly?* with *It's in my genes/jeans.*

The print ads became legendary; Aaliyah has her hands up and is tilting to the side, angled beside Ronson, who was perched behind two turntables. Another ad showed Aaliyah shyly standing behind the turntables herself, with one headphone cupped on her ear and propped by her shoulder, as she attempts to scratch a record and push the crossfader. Once the ads appeared in magazines, they sold out of all twenty-four hundred of the limited-run jeans and immediately requested five thousand more from the Tommy Jeans factory. "After we started working with Aaliyah, we put a lot of that stuff [she wore] into the line," Andy Hilfiger told *Complex* in 2016. "Tommy Girl was [previously] very preppy; it had a lot of plaids and was very schoolgirl. But then we added this whole Aaliyah look to it, which really gave it some new legs."

By the fall, Tommy Hilfiger handpicked Aaliyah as the face of his fall 1997 campaign. His entire women's line that year was designed with Aaliyah in mind. Before Aaliyah even endorsed a stitch of the designer's thread, both Tommy and Andy knew that she was setting trends with her style. The way Aaliyah combined men's clothing with women's, the way her clothes fit her, the way she carried herself in them . . . it was transformative. So the Hilfiger brothers used their clothing to reflect her existing swagger—a combination of men's fits with women's, compliments of their Tommy Jeans line.

Aaliyah's look became iconic in almost record time, and the impact has lasted for decades.

The ads appeared not only in magazines like *Vibe* but also in the metal doors inside of high school lockers, on the walls of fans' bedrooms, at the front of fashion marketing boardrooms, and glued to the cardboard of personal (and professional) vision and inspiration boards. Further, while Tommy Hilfiger did a strategically impressive job of having Black men openly support his brand, he didn't have Black women. Aaliyah became a reference point for young girls who never saw themselves in a Tommy Hilfiger ad, especially Black- and Brown-skinned ones. If they couldn't see themselves in an ad, how could they possibly see themselves in his clothing? What Aaliyah accomplished was she bridged the gap between Hilfiger's ultra-preppy reputation and his desire to reach the cool kids, the inspirers, and yes, the "urban" crowd.

Above all, it showed Aaliyah truly as a growing style icon. Aaliyah wasn't dressed in Tommy Hilfiger, Tommy Hilfiger was dressed in Aaliyah, and that became clear with this one casually fly outfit. It was more than Aaliyah bearing her abs and no sunglasses, revealing the true essence of her beauty. She looked comfortable in her skin. For so long she was hidden by the styling bells and whistles. Sure, they looked wonderful on her, but this clean look showed that underneath it all, Aaliyah was still very much a star. This was also one of the first times a female R&B artist was a model for a designer fashion brand and received such a massive endorsement. Aaliyah broke down doors previously shut for women and in doing so created a legendary moment in fashion history that rendered her untouchable.

"What Aaliyah really did was show this style, the sexy but sporty-chic style. She brought this swagger, this sexiness. It was just incredible," Andy Hilfiger told *Complex*. "I give Kidada a lot of credit, because she had such a vision. She and Aaliyah were on the same page. And Aaliyah loved Kidada and would listen to anything she said."

It's the reason why twenty-three years later during an episode of ABC's prime-time comedy *Grown-ish*, the character Zoey (played by Yara Shahidi) wears Aaliyah's exact Tommy Hilfiger outfit for a costume party on the show's 2020 season finale. When R&B singer/songwriter H.E.R. was asked that same year by Tommy Hilfiger to design a capsule collection, she told *i-D* that when she recalls her memories of Tommy Hilfiger as a child "I always think of Aaliyah!" When recording artist Lolo Zouaï secured her own brand ambassador deal with Tommy Hilfiger, Aaliyah was also at the front of her mind. "She was bringing a style to women's fashion that was also masculine," Zouaï says. "'I'm working with Tommy Jeans, because to me, I was like, "'Okay if someone as iconic as Aaliyah wore this then it's like why not continue that legacy?'" Zouaï has a line on her song "Blue," off her 2019 critically acclaimed album *High Highs to Low Lows*, that even references Aaliyah. "I feel like her voice and her style and everything was just so one of a kind," she continues. "There are not that many artists that come around in the world that are like her, that completely change the music industry. She definitely did that."

And that's what Aaliyah did: she was the person who for years to come remained the face of a brand that seemingly struggled to understand what their perfect face looked like. While there's no real perfect paragon who could speak to every person in one outfit, Aaliyah came damn close. Even outside of Tommy Hilfiger, Aaliyah represented something: the unapologetic tomboy who didn't compromise comfort for cutesiness. Karl Kani even circled back in 2020 to re-create her look on the cover of *Age Ain't Nothing but a Number* in his line's black hoodie, using rapper Coi Leray as the muse. Hip-hop legacy clothing brand Cross Colours also released a capsule collection in 2020, featuring designs with Aaliyah's image on everything from shirts to slides. While her image is readily painted and stitched across clothing nowadays, worn by stars like Halsey and everyday fans alike, it really comes down to how Aaliyah wore her clothes, which in turn changed generations' perceptions of what qualified as womenswear. Aaliyah proved that women could wear anything they wanted.

Grammy-nominated artist Rapsody composed an ode to Aaliyah's tomboy style, with her song aptly titled "Aaliyah," where she rhymes, "When Aaliyah was alive, it was cool to be a tomboy. Tommy boy fly." The song was the centerpiece of her 2019 critically acclaimed album, *Eve*, where each track is titled after a groundbreaking Black woman. The song is an ode to being that proud tomboy, something that both Aaliyah and Rapsody embody. "That was the very first song I did [for *Eve*]," Rapsody explains. "I had been wanting to do a record about being a tomboy. And I have written it over and over again, but it never was the right time. I could never express it the way I wanted to." When she finally did and thought of a title for the song, only one name came to mind. "And it was at that moment, I named it 'Aaliyah,'" Rapsody continues. "I was like, I should do an album and just name songs after women. So she was the first one I did. I wanted people to know that Aaliyah had a crazy big influence on me and she taught me how to be sexy and be myself at the same time."

On Halloween 2020, rapper Kash Doll dressed as Aaliyah for Halloween in her signature Tommy outfit, and she has replicated other styles of hers in the past. The fellow Detroit native is a die-hard Aaliyah fan who says Aaliyah influenced her whole career. "That was my idol growing up," Kash says. "I knew that she was from Detroit, and it just made me feel like, 'She's so pretty and so chill with a tomboy swag.' She was so smart and so sweet, and it made me feel like, 'Dang, I could do it! I could do that.' She gave me inspiration. She never really tried too hard. She was just her." Kash even appeared in Las Vegas in 2019 for the unveiling of Aaliyah's wax figure at Madame Tussauds, posing beside the wax figure in photos and playing games with Rashad in the museum's Virtual Room. The figure is dressed in another iconic look of Aaliyah's from her "Try Again" video.

It all started with her Tommy Hilfiger campaign, where she was given the space to openly be herself stylistically and in turn created a mainstream safe space for other young girls to be themselves as well.

"We created a new look with Aaliyah, and that look is still popular today," Andy Hilfiger continued. "Now, I see all kinds of companies doing the whole bandeau tops with the under-wire waistband, and we did that first." And just like that, with just a few hints of authenticity and flair, her style became immortal. It came at just the right time, when her music was aligned with her fashion and both were entering the world of film. She was edging forward from the Blackground family and becoming everyone's Aaliyah, but they had no idea just how big she was about to become.

CHAPTER SEVEN: BABY STEPS

Sometimes I'm goody goody. Right now I'm naughty naughty.

—Aaliyah, "Are You That Somebody?"

By 1997, Aaliyah was growing in popularity, yet she still craved some regularity. She attended Detroit High School for the Fine and Performing Arts when she could, only now with a bodyguard. "I'm in independent study, where I have a tutor that travels with me, so I don't feel the pressure of having to go back home and get up at eight in the morning and go to different classes," she told MTV. "I can go into my school from twelve to four, so I have some normalcy in my life—so I can see my friends, be in the environment—but I work at my own pace." It was her senior year, and given that she didn't have much of a high school experience, she wanted to get what little out of it that she could before it was gone completely. That meant showing up for events without making a scene, though how could she possibly not? Aaliyah was all over the radio, in every magazine, her music videos were played on every network, and her style was consistently imitated by her adoring fans. There was no way to escape that, even for just a night. On top of that, being known for her unbridled authenticity meant she wouldn't just show up; she would show up on her own terms.

Initially, Aaliyah's plan was to wear a pair of baggy jeans for her high school prom back in Detroit. She opted at the last minute to wear a powder-blue pants suit, with a crop top. Naturally, her decision to even wear pants to the prom caused a commotion. Girls back then were not only expected but basically instructed to wear dresses to any "fancy" events. But Aaliyah was Aaliyah, and if she was going to do the prom, she was going to go all out. But no commotion that night was greater than superstar Aaliyah showing up to her high school prom while she was dominating R&B music. Aaliyah graduated from high school at the start of the summer that year with a 4.0 GPA and even had hopes to one day attend Spelman College in Atlanta, Georgia. Her career had other plans for her.

20th Century Fox was in the process of releasing the animated film *Anastasia*, about an eighteen-year-old orphan with amnesia, looking to put the pieces of her life and memories back together. The film has a star-studded lineup of voiceover talent, including John Cusack, Meg Ryan, Kelsey Grammer, and Kirsten Dunst, among others. In the film, the song "Journey to the Past" (written by Lynn Ahrens and composed by Stephen Flaherty) is sung by actor and recording artist Liz Callaway, though with the soundtrack release Fox Music wanted someone with a bigger name and a wider reach to sing the song. The head of Fox Music, Robert Kraft, chose Aaliyah for the job.

Kraft connected with producer Guy Roche to work with her again and change the shape of the song to fit a broader audience, while also remaining true to Aaliyah's R&B sound. "Although she came from a hip-hop background musically, her character, smile, and looks exuded something very, very sweet and gentle, very kind and peaceful," Roche told VICE's *Broadly* in 2017. "Not to mention the tone of her voice was perfect for the song." Ahrens and Flaherty returned to the song to change up some lyrics and the composition to tailor it for Aaliyah. "After seeing the movie, I was very excited," Aaliyah said in an interview during the recording process of the song. "I mean, it's a great opportunity for me as an artist. Even when it was first brought to my attention before I even saw the movie, I was familiar with the story." She said the team wanted to change it up a little bit, while preserving the "magic" of the song that was reflected in the film.

In August 1997, Aaliyah was bound for Toronto to meet with Roche and record the song. "Her career was on the up," Roche told *Broadly*. "It felt like, every time we met she had just gotten off a plane, [gone] straight into the studio, got right into work mode, and delivered the song beautifully, between interruptions for interviews. Then [it was] on to the next plane."

In the music video, Aaliyah travels through various past and present cityscapes, while also being inserted into animated moments from the film, which takes place in both Russia and France in the mid-1900s. Through this single and its visuals, Aaliyah once again was connecting two different audiences together. The video found significant airplay in network rotation, from BET to VH1. It was a genius move on behalf of Fox to make her the face of the soundtrack. Aaliyah was a star, but more important she was beloved, which gave the song wings to fly from the Disney-style dedicated crowd to R&B lovers who adored their princess. The result was a win-win.

The song was nominated for an Oscar and a Golden Globe

that following year, for Best Original Song, losing to the soundtrack giant "My Heart Will Go On" from the film *Titanic*. Still, Aaliyah made history at nineteen as the youngest artist to ever perform at the Oscars. She also wore a dress, which alone had fans shocked. Her date for the Academy Awards was her brother, Rashad.

This wasn't her first appearance on a soundtrack, but it was a springboard for what was to come. Within a few short months, a new opportunity appeared that not only took Aaliyah to the next level but also proved that when talent comes together to make magic there's no time stamp on their genius.

It was the baby coo heard round the world, and its birth happened in less than a day of labor.

In June 1998, Eddie Murphy starred in a reboot of *Doctor Dolittle*, the 1967 cult classic film about a doctor with an innate capability to speak to animals and understand their responses. The film boasted a star-studded cast of animal voiceovers, including Ellen DeGeneres, Chris Rock, and John Leguizamo. As part of the film's release, a soundtrack arrived in tandem, released through Atlantic Records. But it needed a hit, and the way to get there was to hit the hit makers.

Timbaland and the gang were fresh off the stage one night when he got a call from Barry Hankerson. Atlantic wanted Timbaland to produce the lead single off the *Doctor Dolittle* soundtrack; Aaliyah would perform it. Hankerson already told the label that they had a song ready, so by the time he called Timbaland the deal was "etched in stone," per Tim. This was 4:00 AM in New York, but the team was out in Los Angeles, making it 1:00 AM there. The track had to be delivered by 11:00 the following morning. Naturally, despite Hankerson's grandiose gesture to the label that landed them this coveted soundtrack slot, there was no song recorded. Timbaland immediately pushed back, but the hefty price tag of over $400,000 for the track (to be split between Aaliyah and Timbaland) was enough to get them into the studio to create something. Anything. So they headed to the Village Studios on the west side of Los Angeles to begin working on a song that—unbeknownst to them—would propel Aaliyah into soundtrack royalty.

By this point, Aaliyah was working with another songwriter in the crew, Stephen Ellis Garrett, better known as the late Static Major. While Static was also a graduate of the Swing Mob, he and his group Playa were fresh off the release of their debut album *Cheers 2 U* that March. Static's singing and songwriting came into focus when he co-wrote Ginuwine's "Pony" in 1996 (with Ginuwine and Timbaland), while also singing background vocals on the hit single. He and Aaliyah were already putting some songwriting concepts together for what would become her final album, just a few short years later. Since he was already actively penning songs with Aaliyah, he took the songwriting reins on this fast-turnaround track.

Static, Timbaland, Aaliyah, and engineer Jimmy Douglass were all in the studio that late evening, figuring out how to flip this song in record time. Just a few hours earlier, they had no idea this song was even supposed to exist, yet here they were, attempting to develop some quick concepts.

Timbaland nailed the beat on the second try.

It all came down to the drums. While Timbaland introduced a keyboard note and manipulated guitar sounds to guide Static's writing (like a songwriter creating a song with his acoustic guitar), it was the thuds of the ricocheting bass line that made the beat come alive. On top of the bass line were blips and beatboxing; Timbaland later returned to the beat to give it layers once the song was written.

The concept of the song wasn't hard for Static Major to write at all.

"Are You That Somebody?" is a song about love that is cautiously optimistic, yet it's hidden from the rest of the world. The song places Aaliyah in the position of spotting the object of her affection but preferring to keep it a secret and wondering if the other person is down for the same. There's even a part where she's asking him to come through on a late-night creep but still keep it between the two of them.

Static Major's vocals can be heard singing on the hook with Aaliyah. His falsetto fits hers like a glove, and with good reason:

You can't tell nobody
I'm talkin' 'bout nobody

In this case, art imitated life.

"You're dealing with Barry's niece," says Static's former manager Tim Barnett. "And it was like, man, you know, don't tell nobody."

Static's mother, Edith Garrett Raymond, confirmed to *Vibe* in 2008 that Aaliyah and her late son were dating. They started around 1997 and continued into 1998. "They were definitely an item," she said. "Aaliyah was crazy about him." And while the song cloaks their romance in secrecy, they were pretty open to Static's mom and apparently Aaliyah's own parents.

"He brought Aaliyah to my wedding," Edith continued.

"That was a big deal because [her parents] didn't let her go places."

While Static laid down the lyrics in the studio that evening, the song had been brewing. He originally wrote it *to* Aaliyah: "Girl, I've been watching you like a hawk in the sky. . . ." And since their relationship was hidden from her uncle (and seemingly everyone else in the camp but their parents), the "hush-hush" nature of asking if she was down was a sly way of asking her out.

It was cutesy, but endearing.

Aaliyah wasn't a fan of the song on the first listen, despite the autobiographical undertone. Still, she recorded it, and of course it was perfect. "Now, her voice was the icing on the cake," Timbaland said in his MasterClass segment on creating the track. Considering the slim turnaround, the song had to be written, produced, recorded, mixed, and mastered all in the same night. Once Aaliyah's vocals were laid down (along with Timbaland's and Static's), Timbaland came back to put on the finishing touches, which were some more beat layers and his now-infamous "Dirty South" intro. Then came a last-minute addition.

After re-listening to the hook, Timbaland paused and headed to his CD collection.

"Literally we were done and about to print the mix and [Tim] said, 'Wait, one more thing,'" Jimmy Douglass remembers, "and out comes this baby sound. Everybody else was gone; just me and Tim were left when he did that."

The sound was of a satisfied baby, not quite laughing but showing emotion. Many believed it was actually clipped from a home movie of Aaliyah as a baby, but it wasn't. It was later revealed that it's a sample from a sound called "Happy Baby" off a 1964 album called *Authentic Sound Effects*, volume 8. How and why did Timbaland even choose that for the song?

"Because he's Tim?" Douglass says with a laugh. It was unorthodox and a little weird, but something only Timbaland could pull off. It strangely worked. Aaliyah thought the sound was "so cute." It was also the first time she was referred to as "Baby Girl" on record, thereby birthing that term of endearment to be used by the rest of the world, all from a track with a baby sample.

"Many times during the record-making process, the creators do things that ain't as big a deal as the public perceives it," Douglass continues. "That was one of those moments. We had a morning deadline and had to finish and suddenly a baby appears. And the rest, well, is history."

The song was a hit, though its success was contingent upon factors that set it apart from other popular songs that arrived during that time. For one, "Are You That Somebody?" wasn't initially released as a single to record stores. In the late nineties, retail singles were the norm, especially when dictating a song's success. "Are You That Somebody?" was only available on the *Doctor Dolittle* soundtrack, meaning fans had to buy an entire album in order to grab that one song. It leaned heavily upon the radio for its push, though moving units were historically the driving force behind charting on *Billboard*. However, concurrently, the *Billboard* charts decidedly altered their charting practices to allow for those songs with only radio airplay to hit the Hot 100. The perfect timing of this switch allowed the song to chart when it previously couldn't have.

The song pushed through the charts, cracking the Top 25 on the *Billboard* Hot 100 (at Number Twenty-One), while hitting the Top 10 of the US Mainstream Top 40 (at Number Six) and topping both the US R&B/Hip-Hop Airplay and US Rhythmic charts. It also charted around the world, reaching Number One in New Zealand, while hitting the Top 10 in the UK Dance and R&B charts, as well as Canada and the Netherlands. The song also earned Aaliyah her first Grammy nomination for Best Female R&B Vocal Performance at the 41st Grammy Awards. In the May 30 issue of *Billboard* magazine that year, Larry Flick wrote in his "Singles" column that "Aaliyah is on the road to becoming the new queen of soundtrack hits." His words foreshadowed where Aaliyah would later go with other songs, like "Try Again" off *Romeo Must Die*.

"Where most divas insist on being the center of the song, she knew how to disappear into the music, how to match her voice to the bass line—it was sometimes difficult to tell one from the other," Kelefa Sanneh wrote in 2001 for the *New York Times*. "This new approach helped change the way popular music sounds; the twitchy, beat-driven songs of Destiny's Child owe a clear debt to 'Are You That Somebody?'" Music critic Simon Reynolds called "Are You That Somebody?" "the most radical pop single" of 1998.

A remix was later released, featuring various members of Tha Supafriendz crew, including rappers Lonnie B, Danja Mowf, and Mad Skillz. There was something endearing about Aaliyah always willing to put lesser-known talent on, the way others had done for her.

The music video was another vital piece to the equation. Directed by Mark Gerard, the video takes place in a cave in

Los Angeles's Griffith Park. The video opens at dusk, with a motorcycle gang of guys entering the secret cave through a magical force field, as Aaliyah and her girls are waiting for them to arrive. Aaliyah has a hawk perched on her forearm (like the "hawk in the sky") as scenes alternate between dance sequences directed by Aaliyah's famed choreographer, Fatima Robinson.

During Timbaland's rap, he's flanked by the members of Playa, which included Static Major, who played the back despite being the lyrical mastermind behind the song.

Toward the end of the video, Aaliyah's whole style switches up. Throughout the video, she's in her usual casual garb, with cutesy pigtails that layer the top of her crown. But then all of a sudden, she flips it over to a flamenco dance sequence in a dress with high slits on either side and heels. It was almost like there was a visual switch from young girl to young lady all within the dance and outfits of this one video. It was a bit of a hard sell for Aaliyah, though.

"The only time that I'd say she needed some convincing on was in the video for 'Are You That Somebody?'" stylist Derek Lee recalled to *Vibe* in 2016. "That is where we did the skirt and the heels for the end of that video. I had all that stuff made, and I brought it because she was still kind of [iffy] on it, but Fatima [Robinson, choreographer] was like, 'No, you need to do that; you got to do it.' And she was like, 'Okay, if you think this is the right time then let it be the right time,' so that was the only time that she was [iffy] on something." Lee had the outfit custom designed for her in that scene, as well as another where she's wearing a red Gucci bathing suit top adorned with red Swarovski crystals. Everything was very specific and very intentional—every dance move, every stitch of fabric that she wore, including the skirt.

While wearing a skirt was simply not her thing, she had done it for the Oscars this same year. Though there it felt more like "get dressed up; you're at the Academy Awards!" like a child dressing up for a wedding. With "Are You That Somebody?" a pivotal scene in the video couldn't have been accomplished in baggy pants and sneakers or else the moment would have been lost. The flamenco dance routine called for it, and so Aaliyah did it. The result was a game changer. Not only did fans recognize there were different dimensions to Aaliyah's style, but this was something of a turning point for her. She was no longer the young girl in categorically "boys'" clothing. She was coming into her own and growing up.

The video became the most played across networks like MTV, The Box, and BET in a relatively short amount of time. It was mainly because of everything happening all at once, musically and visually. The beat, the lyrics, the dancing, the costumes, the "baby in the background" as Mad Skillz says on the remix, and, of course, Aaliyah. To think, this song might have never happened had Barry Hankerson not pretended prematurely that it had. "We came through before the night ended," Timbaland recalled in 2017. "And we came *through*, boy."

At the 1999 Grammys the following year, Aaliyah was nominated for Best R&B Vocal Performance, but she lost to Lauryn Hill's "Doo Wop (That Thing)" off *The Miseducation of Lauryn Hill*, which swept the Grammys that year.

The landscape of hip-hop and R&B was dramatically different from when Aaliyah had first started. Lauryn Hill was at the top of her solo game in 1998, dominating in both worlds of rapping and singing, while also becoming a commercial smash. Likewise, there were plenty of other acts moving through the pipeline. The staple stars like Mariah Carey, Usher, Faith Evans, Janet Jackson, and Whitney Houston were actively releasing projects and singles during the 1998–1999 season, along with Aaliyah's earliest competition—Brandy and Monica, who tag teamed on the massive hit "The Boy Is Mine." Jennifer Lopez flipped the switch from acting to singing, releasing her debut single, "If You Had My Love," as newer artists like Mýa were entering the scene, along with Erykah Badu, whose entry came in 1997 thanks to her artistically eccentric debut, *Baduizm*. Even Ginuwine released his hit single "So Anxious" during that time period, as R. Kelly was knee-deep in his redemption tour, collaborating with Celine Dion on "I'm Your Angel" in 1998 and "If I Could Turn Back the Hands of Time" in 1999. He also collaborated with Puffy on the single "Satisfy You." A lot was happening at once in music.

However, this was also the era where R&B groups came back into formation. Dru Hill, Total, 112, even BLACKstreet were climbing up the charts, though this was also the moment when Destiny's Child was coming into focus. Their self-titled debut album dropped in 1998, and as fast as that arrived, so did 1999's *The Writing's on the Wall*. This was the album that would bring the group into stardom. Missy Elliott is featured on the project (on the song "Confessions," which she co-wrote and coproduced). She and Timbaland also wrote and produced the track "Get on the Bus," off the *Why Do Fools Fall in Love* soundtrack, later added to the international release of *The Writing's on the Wall*. Aaliyah choreographed Destiny's Child's music video for "Get on the Bus." It's not to say that this group or any other artists were a direct threat or competition to Aaliyah, but there was more traffic in her lane now. Further, by 1999, it had been three years since *One in a Million* was released.

Meanwhile, her team was diversifying their respective portfolios. Missy and Tim were on the aforementioned Destiny's Child project, while also moving further into their artistry as actual recording artists. In 1997, Missy released her debut album, *Supa Dupa Fly*, which altered her course in music. Debuting at Number Three on the *Billboard* 200, the project showed that Missy could not only craft hits for others (mainly Aaliyah), but she could also give herself some real hits. Her style was abstract, melding together hip-hop and R&B in almost a Warhol-esque way. Aaliyah supported with a feature on the album cut "Best Friends." In 1999, Missy followed with *Da Real World*, where Aaliyah appeared on "Stickin' Chickens" with Da Brat. Both projects were produced entirely by Timbaland. Missy released the projects on her own vanity label, The Goldmind Inc. Goldmind was the imprint Missy secured when she signed with Elektra, as CEO Sylvia Rhone not only wanted Missy on the label, but she also wanted her to find more talent. Missy's artist Nicole Wray released her debut album, *Make It Hot*, under Goldmind, with the title track produced by Timbaland. Everyone from Aaliyah to Ginuwine, Timbaland, and Playa were in the title track's music video.

Timbaland, in turn, released his first project with Magoo, *Welcome to Our World*, in 1997 through Blackground. Aaliyah sang the hook to the project's first single, "Up Jumps da Boogie" (also featuring Missy), while also collaborating with them on the album cut "Man Undercover." She also appears in the videos for "Up Jumps da Boogie" and "Luv 2 Luv U."

Timbaland's solo album *Tim's Bio: Life from da Bassment* dropped in 1998, with Aaliyah and Missy on the song "John Blaze."

Playa's aforementioned *Cheers 2 U* came in 1998, and Aaliyah guested on that project as well, on the song "One Man Woman." She appeared on Ginuwine's song "Final Warning" off his 1999 album, *100% Ginuwine*.

Aaliyah was spreading her own wings beyond her core team, as well. In 1997, she jumped on a remix for Brooklyn rap outfit Boot Camp Clik's "Night Riders." Boot Camp Clik was the quintessential nineties boom-bap-rap crew, and Aaliyah's appearance on their song was a big move in combining the worlds of mainstream R&B and street-leaning independent hip-hop. Initially, Aaliyah was slated to be on the original single release, but by '97 her career was on fire, and so was her schedule, so the song was released without her. She kept her promise, though, and hopped on the remix. "I wrote that hook with her in mind, with a real soulful vibe," rapper and Boot Camp de facto leader Buckshot remembers. "When I put that track together, people thought I was crazy. It was the first time Boot Camp was going outside of what people knew Boot Camp was—these hard, street dudes, wearing Timbs in the streets in fatigues. Now we're doing a track with Aaliyah and a guitar in the background." Aaliyah was the cousin of Boot Camp Clik member Tek (of the group Smif-N-Wessun), which is how the opportunity came about. The remix was produced by Grammy Award–winning producer 9th Wonder. "She went in and she did it on the first try, and that was it," Buckshot continues about working with her in the studio. "Great singers are like that."

Aaliyah then collaborated with Nas on his song "You Won't See Me Tonight," off his 1999 project, *I Am* . . . . She also grabbed some more soundtrack spots that same year with the song "Turn the Page" from the *Music of the Heart* soundtrack, along with the song "I Don't Wanna," which first appeared on the *Next Friday* soundtrack at the end of 1999 and appears again on the *Romeo Must Die* soundtrack in 2000. The latter track was perhaps one of the slicker business moves pulled by Barry Hankerson, whose reputation was continuously growing as the most difficult part about working with Aaliyah. Family and business were beginning to mix and get muddy.

The track "I Don't Wanna" was written and composed by a team, including Jazze Pha, Johntá Austin, Kevin Hicks, and Donnie Scantz. Hicks and Scantz also produced the song. When the opportunity to work with Aaliyah presented itself, a company called Noontime Music jumped into the race and met with Blackground in New York. They had several songs to "audition" for Hankerson & Co.; "I Don't Wanna" was one of them. Scantz, a relatively unknown producer, was left behind in Atlanta, yet put together the song before the NYC trip. He was working back at the company headquarters with another Blackground artist and songwriter, Tank. "Nobody knew who did the track," Scantz remembers. "I get a call while I'm in Atlanta with Tank. They loved the joint."

Johntá Austin joined in to write the first verse, Jazze Pha the second verse. The following day after recording "I Don't Wanna," Jazze cut another track, "Come Over," with Aaliyah, which was given to the group Changing Faces instead, with Aaliyah's version released after her passing. "That was the most angelic and effortless piece of work I have ever done, and it wasn't even work," Jazze told Ed Lover on his *C'mon Son!* show in 2016. Jazze described working with her as "magical," with some setbacks. "You know how God works, and the devil is always right there," Jazze continued. "I ain't gonna say no names, but somebody almost messed up the whole shit." Per Jazze, Aaliyah's mother, Diane, was there in the studio with them and everyone was talking for hours like old friends. "When Aaliyah comes in, she nicknames everybody. She called me Fuzzy, because 'every time I see you I get warm and fuzzy,'" Jazze says. In the midst of the banter, one of the studio workers interrupts Diane's speaking to remind everyone that it's time to get to work. "Her mom got up and walked out of the room. Then, Aaliyah's phone rang, and she got up and walked out of the room. Two hours later, neither one of them was there." Jazze called Jomo, met with him, and apologized to Diane. "She had never heard our music; she didn't care about it," Jazze adds. "Aaliyah was all upset, because she was like, 'Aw, Mom! He didn't mean it. Let's work!' Whatever she said made everybody like, 'We can't go to the studio until Momma says it's okay.'" It was smoothed over and they were finally able to work, but more business matters piled on.

"From what I know, [Noontime's] business deal with Blackground soured and the shit went all the way south," Scantz remembers. "Blackground was like, 'Nope, none of them records y'all did with Aaliyah? None of them coming out!'" They eventually mended fences with Noontime, but at this juncture it was a no go. Cut to the *Next Friday* soundtrack, where the song somehow made its way to the hands of the soundtrack's A&R. Noontime owned the licensing, and so a bid on the track was placed. There was a massive price tag by then for an Aaliyah track. "This was the first record that I sold and jumped me into the game," Scantz says. "Noontime sold that record to Priority Records, because Priority was licensing the soundtrack to *Next Friday*." Meanwhile, Blackground circled back and "put the highest price on Aaliyah," Scantz continues. "Blackground was like, 'Oh, y'all just gonna feature Aaliyah like that on the record? We need $200,000.'" Blackground was paid; Priority bought the track for $43,000. "After *Next Friday*, Blackground was like, 'Hold up, we gonna buy the rights, because that $200,000 paid Aaliyah; we gonna own the rights now.'" Blackground got the licensing back from Priority and also put the song on the *Romeo Must Die* soundtrack. So in essence, the label managed to pay their artist with someone else's money while in turn buying back the song to make money of their own. It was a diabolical genius ploy, though all shrewd business moves aside, Scantz said that song changed the course of his career thanks to Aaliyah. He went on to work with other big-name acts like Jagged Edge, Chris Brown, Pitbull, and Miguel among many others.

"I did have one time that I had the opportunity to get an acknowledgment from her for making the record and it was in passing," Scantz says, as the two met at an industry event and Aaliyah thanked him for the song. "But my life was forever changed after that instance because it accomplished something for me that I knew that I wanted to do from the beginning, which was work with Aaliyah. I felt like she was the greatest gift that we had that had ever so much more to give us. But she gave us the greatest she had while she was here. I'm happy to be a part of that story."

There were a lot of guest features happening for Aaliyah, with little movement on her own album. She was already working on some things with Static, but there was no formal release in sight, where she could show significant growth and once again display her constant evolution. For most, it's a cause for concern, and fearing their own relevance was hanging in the balance, especially during that era of music.

It was a time of major experimentation for both male and female artists. Gone were the days of fitting one specific cookie-cutter classification, and enter the landscape of "originality is King/Queen." The more unclassifiable you were, the better. That was Aaliyah's superpower, but now everyone was in on the secret. Sure, there were still none like her, which always gave her the added advantage. Not a single artist out during that time period had anyone saying, "They remind me of Aaliyah," though even years after her passing that phrase remains reiterated. Still, despite having no third album in sight, Aaliyah was appearing on others' projects to still keep her name out there, since for many in the music industry a lengthy absence means you've retired. The competition *was* getting thicker, however, and her own team was even changing. But there's a thing called faith, and Aaliyah had plenty of it, given where she'd come from before. So instead of Aaliyah deciding to quickly hop back in the studio and slap together another project, she kept her cool and took her time. She didn't race to the studio. In fact, she did the exact opposite.

She headed to the silver screen.

CHAPTER EIGHT: ROMEO MUST TRY

Look, I don't know how it is in China, but in America
if a girl is kicking your ass you do not have to be a
gentleman.

—Aaliyah as Trish in *Romeo Must Die*

A aliyah demanded she perform her own stunts.
"I wanted the audience to be like 'wow, she actually got up there and is kicking some butt,'" she told CNN in 2000. It was a tall order when you're filming a movie that involves kicks, jumps, and fight scenes, but she was up for the challenge. It was also her very first movie role, so she wanted to go big or go home.

The film was *Romeo Must Die,* an action film based loosely upon the Shakespearean tragic love story *Romeo and Juliet.* Where Shakespeare had Capulets and Montagues at war in Verona, Italy, *Romeo Must Die* had two rival gangs in Oakland, California: one being Chinese and the other Black. Both families are battling over the same "turf." The film is steeped in both martial arts and hip-hop, as Jet Li makes his English-speaking debut here as Han Sing (the son of a rival gang) and the late DMX continues his track record from nailing his role in *Belly* just a year before *Romeo Must Die* went into production, playing the role of Silk, a club owner caught in the cross hairs. Aaliyah plays the Juliet to Jet Li's Romeo; her character is Trish O'Day, the fiery yet good-hearted daughter of Isaak O'Day, played by Delroy Lindo.

It's a modern-day love story–slash–action film, with a twist. The concept came from producer Joel Silver, who along with fellow producer Jim Van Wyck wanted to create an American action film that didn't feel dated. Silver's track record in that arena was solid; his résumé includes the *Lethal Weapon* and *Matrix* franchises, the first two *Die Hard* films, and the first two *Predator* films, among many others. Silver had just released the first *Matrix* within two months of starting production for *Romeo Must Die*, along with *Lethal Weapon 4*, which costarred Jet Li. Silver wanted to bring Jet Li further into the American action film industry, while also experimenting with new ways to convey martial art fight scenes—which included the application of X-ray vision, similar to the spacey effects found in *The Matrix*. *The Matrix* also borrowed from the Kung Fu movie technique called wire fu, where fight scenes are wire assisted, using pulleys, and shot to create these dramatic action moments. *Romeo Must Die* also utilizes this, though it's arguably more fitting here, since Jet Li was actually a martial arts star—particularly in Wushu, which is Chinese Kung Fu.

Aaliyah met with Lorenzo di Bonaventura (then a studio executive at Warner Bros. Pictures) and told him her vision for her very first acting role. Di Bonaventura then introduced her to Silver. After a screen test, she landed the role. Her acting was impressive from the start, as Silver later cast Aaliyah for the role of Zee in *The Matrix Reloaded* following this one, as well as *The Matrix Revolutions*. Cinematographer Andrzej Bartkowiak also made his directorial debut with *Romeo Must Die*, which kicked off a track record of other action films, including two more with DMX—*Exit Wounds* and *Cradle 2 the Grave*, the latter of which also stars Jet Li. The screenplay was written by Eric Bernt and John Jarrell.

Hip-hop and martial arts have a long-standing history. Rappers often recall growing up in households where grainy Kung Fu flicks were playing, which first introduced them to the art of physical battle. Berry Gordy's 1985 film *The Last Dragon* reinforced that connection on the big screen, though hip-hop artists turn toward old Kung Fu movies like 1972's *Five Fingers of Death* as early inspiration. Then, of course, Wu-Tang Clan jumped into the nineties with their own brand of martial arts–inspired hip-hop, even renaming their Staten Island stomping grounds as Shaolin. Later hip-hop artists like Migos and Kendrick Lamar have also sent nods back to martial arts; the latter affectionately referred to himself as "Kung Fu Kenny," a callback to the *Rush Hour 2* film (which was another fusion of hip-hop and martial arts).

With *Romeo Must Die* there was a combination of traditional fight scenes, mixed with high-speed chases, violence, a few categorically gory scenes, and yes, a romance—though the latter was more implied than enforced. There was a sixteen-year difference in age between Jet Li and Aaliyah, and while that large gap wasn't a focal point of the film, it did seem to affect their on-screen romance. The two never kiss on screen. There were a number of factors that were "blamed" for this, though it was really all speculation. Some felt it was the age difference that made the romance seem less desirable (and an unfortunate throwback to Aaliyah's past), while others have speculated that racism toward Asian actors deemed them undesirable and unsexy to anyone outside of Hollywood, so it was best to imply that the two were in love rather than physically express it. On top of that, having an Asian man and a Black woman in a relationship on-screen was also rumored to be less appealing, had it played out as visibly romantic for the audience. (There was a kissing scene filmed, though it happened right after Jet Li's father in the film commits suicide, so it was written off as an insensitive moment to wedge in a kissing scene that was allegedly deemed unpalatable.) Regardless of the motive behind there being no love scene, there was still considerable chemistry between Aaliyah and Jet Li in the film. Aaliyah was a natural at acting, and considering her emergence in almost every facet of entertainment prior to this moment, all signs proved that Hollywood was next for her. She had roots in entertainment since she was a kid, so this was merely a progression of what she already created over the years.

Her stunts weren't over the top, but at least she did them herself, which included one scene where Jet Li's character uses Aaliyah's body to fight a female nemesis since he wouldn't strike a woman. She high kicks and twirls against his body, while still somehow looking like she's dancing. Aaliyah went through one month of training for the one action scene, since again she turned down a stunt double. The scene was rehearsed over and over until they were ready to shoot, which in and of itself took three days. Martial arts weren't a foreign concept to Aaliyah, either. "I used to take [martial arts] when I was seven or eight," she said in an interview during the film's press junket. "It sparked my interest again." The idea of turning the scene into a martial arts dance was Jet Li's. "I am so glad I had the chance to work with Aaliyah," Jet Li told *HelloBeautiful* in 2020. "She's charming, beautiful; it was a great experience in my life."

Filming started in early May of 1999 in Vancouver. DMX was brought on when both Aaliyah and Joel Silver paid him a visit. "When I was on tour her and Joel Silver came to my dressing room to see if I wanted to be a part of the movie," DMX told *Billboard* in 2011. "Most people would have their people call, but she came herself. I'm like, 'Is this a trick question? You have to ask me if I want to be in a movie with Aaliyah? Hell yeah.'" He then met the cast and crew in Vancouver to start filming. He described her presence on-screen as "sexy but kind of gangster."

Scattered throughout the film are little winks to Aaliyah's fans, only further proving that the film was really intended for her fan base. In one scene of the film, there's a toy orangutan, which was actually a real-life gift to Aaliyah from her late grandmother Mintis that she carried with her. In the record-store scene, a Lil' Kim *Hard Core* poster is in the window, along with a poorly placed poster of R. Kelly's album *R*. There are also moments throughout the film where either Aaliyah is dancing to her own music at the club or, again, in the record-store scene her song is blaring through the speakers as Anthony Anderson's character, Maurice, exclaims, "This is my shit right here!" He later goes on to look for Trish and refers to her as "your Aaliyah lookin' ass."

The film did well globally. With a $25 million budget, *Romeo Must Die* made over $18 million the opening week of its release (March 22, 2000). Domestically it made $55,973,336 and internationally $35,063,424, raking in over $91 million in combined sales.

Despite critics feeling that Aaliyah and Jet Li lacked significant romantic chemistry on the screen, Aaliyah's performance was favorably reviewed. Elvis Mitchell of the *New York Times* wrote: "*Romeo* is a come-on, with cooing Hip-Hop songs popping up whenever Aaliyah, who's a natural, glides across the screen." Mitchell also predicted the success of the film, based upon that hip-hop element. "Dreary as it is, *Romeo* is bound to be a hit, thanks to its well-selected and wall-to-wall Hip-Hop soundtrack—particularly good songs by Timbaland and, yes, Aaliyah— that's so pervasive *Romeo* might as well be a musical," Mitchell continues.

The *Romeo Must Die* soundtrack became a moment for hip-hop, due largely to the number of Aaliyah tracks on the project. It arguably served to sate fans as they anxiously waited for her third album to arrive. The soundtrack was released under Blackground and featured Timbaland, Magoo, Playa, Ginuwine, and other acts like Destiny's Child, Joe, Mack 10, B.G. of the Hot Boys, and Chanté Moore, among others. Aaliyah's songs helped propel the album up the charts, as it reached Number Three on the *Billboard* 200 and Number One on the US Top R&B/Hip-Hop Albums chart. It also made its mark overseas, touching places like Australia, Austria, the UK, Switzerland, New Zealand, and Germany—all within Top 20 charting positions.

Aaliyah brought some hits with her. She and DMX continued their creative momentum for the soundtrack on the song "Come Back in One Piece." The track is a hip-hop love song, where Aaliyah lightly pleads with DMX to come back home safely ("in one piece") when he's done running the streets.

They arguably have more romantic chemistry than her and Li in the song's music video (directed by Little X), where Aaliyah went to DMX's stomping grounds to film it. "We did the video in Mount Vernon and Yonkers. I got to bring Aaliyah to the hood," DMX continued to *Billboard*. "Not many people can say that."

The international double A-side to "Come Back in One Piece" was the aforementioned "I Don't Wanna," which beat the DMX-assisted track, as it reached a charting position on *Billboard* at Number Five on the US Hot R&B/Hip-Hop Songs chart (Number Thirty-Five on the *Billboard* Hot 100, Number Twenty-Two on the US Rhythmic). "Are You Feelin' Me?" wasn't released as a single, though it was later filed under Aaliyah's deep cuts and also appears in a pivotal scene in the movie.

And then, of course, came "Try Again."

The track at its core was designed for empowerment, as Static Major wanted to create an inspirational song. Where the hook says "dust yourself off and try again," it originally said "you can be a fireman." The track was about living out your dreams and making them come true. "You can do anything; that's what he had written," Jimmy Douglass remembers. "And then Barry was like 'that's kind of cool, but you gotta put some love in there, man. Otherwise it ain't going anywhere.' So Static restarted and changed it into 'dust yourself off and try again.' And then he made some of the metaphors about love instead. Get knocked down in love and just getting back up. And there's a hit record."

Much like "Are You That Somebody?," Aaliyah wasn't in love with the song at first listen. But once she got into the studio and added her own subtleties to it, she became more used to it.

The song was chosen as the lead single for the *Romeo Must Die* soundtrack, so Aaliyah was forcibly made to feel comfortable with whatever would happen with the song and wherever it would land. Little did she know. . . .

✿

"Try Again" catapulted Aaliyah to another level. It was more than just Timbaland's little ode to Eric B. & Rakim's "I Know You Got Soul," where he opens the track with the line "It's been a long time, we shouldn't have left you . . ." over the hazy synths of the intoxicating beat. It was more than the transformative meaning behind the song—where what was once a cut listing all of the possible occupations you could become evolved into a melody about telling someone to "keep trying" if they really want you.

It was Aaliyah, front and center, yet still remaining elusive.

By this point she was a pro at tackling Timbaland's beats, knowing when to fade in and to fade out, even when she was simply repeating the same lines over and over again until we all understood. " 'Try Again' helped smuggle the innovative techniques of electronic dance music onto the American pop charts," Kelefa Sanneh wrote for the *New York Times*, "and it established Aaliyah as pop music's most futuristic star."

Years later, producers from all genres still seek to find that creative balance that Timbaland and Aaliyah struck on "Try Again." Electronic producers are in search of ethereal female voices to glaze over their genius beats while allowing their sound to remain the star of the show. Likewise, singers actively seek out producers who will elevate their sounds by hugging their vocals with pleasant noises to make hits that are no longer their sole responsibility. In both of those regards, Aaliyah actually failed. She was never an accessory to the production; her star power was a force of nature. Even when she *tried* to let something other than her shine, it was nearly impossible. It was a humble glow, but a glow nonetheless; and while "Try Again" was once again a miracle within a soundtrack, it was yet another building block for what was to come for Aaliyah's rise to the top.

While the track made history in its sound, it also made history on the charts. "Try Again" was released on February 22, 2000, and by the week of March 18 it made its debut on the *Billboard* Hot 100 at Number Fifty-Eight. By the week of June 17, it reached the top of the chart, making it the first single to crack the Number One slot through radio airplay alone. It also reached Number One on the US Rhythmic chart, and made the Top 5 on the US Mainstream Top 40 and the US Hot R&B/Hip-Hop Songs. Globally, it reached the Top 5 across the UK charts (even getting to Number Two on the UK R&B chart) and Top 5 in Norway, Portugal, the Netherlands, Germany, Iceland, Denmark, Canada, and Belgium, as well as Top 10 and Top 20 across other territories. Danette Chavez of *The A.V. Club* said that the song "serves as a far better legacy for Aaliyah than the movie from which it sprang."

The music video was directed by Wayne Isham and is a combination of the futuristic vibes of the song mixed with re-created scenes from the movie, along with clips of some actual scenes. Jet Li makes a cameo in the video, shadowboxing through a hall of mirrors, with Timbaland in the cut mouthing lines and beatboxing against those same mirrors.

And then there is Aaliyah.

"I knew 'Try Again' was going to be a dance video, and she was going to wear one outfit for the entire thing," Derek Lee recalled to *Nylon*. "So it had to be really strong, and really her." The goal was to take her signature style of a bra top or midriff and baggy pants and completely elevate it. He chose to do that with a Dolce & Gabbana crystal bra top, complete with a matching choker and belt. Her pants were loose, but not sagging, with chains affixed to either side of her rotating hips. Her hair is pin straight and parted down the middle; her eye makeup is dark, shadowy, and dramatic. The look became so iconic that it was chosen as Aaliyah's outfit for the 2019 unveiling of her wax figure at Madame Tussauds in Las Vegas. Celebrities like Kim Kardashian even replicated the look on Halloween in 2017. There are moments throughout the video where Aaliyah is dancing but also a part where she mimics a fight scene. Since she was already a master of wirework during the filming of the movie, she even climbs the side of a wall while guided by Jet Li in the music video.

In September 2000, Aaliyah took home the MTV VMAs for Best Video from a Film and Best Female Video, beating out pop titans Britney Spears (for "Oops! . . . I Did It Again") and Christina Aguilera (for "What a Girl Wants"), respectively. It was proof of the song and the video's reach. To win against pop darlings showed Aaliyah had become one herself. She even flew twenty-two hours with her brother from Australia during her *Queen of the Damned* filming just to show up at the award show ceremony. It was well worth it. She was clad in her memorable Roberto Cavalli yellow-and-black zebra-striped dress, with a fur-fringed slit that revealed her one leg. Aaliyah was evolving in so many ways.

While "Try Again" was a hit, it still served as a reminder that a singer was acting. That wouldn't be for long, since her next role was geared to be the one that would allow Aaliyah to make the seamless move from music to film. "I wanna do films in the future where I don't do any music," she told MTV Europe Select in 2000, "and then I'd like to do it again."

CHAPTER NINE: TAKE IT PERSONAL

I'm a very mysterious person, and when you first
meet me I don't really think you know where I'm
coming from. It takes a while to get to know me,
I think it's because I take my time to get to know
people. You're gonna get someone who's affable,
who's nice; but you're not gonna get the whole
picture of Aaliyah for a while.

—Aaliyah, *Teen People*, 1999

Aaliyah originally started working on the *Aaliyah* album in
1998, cutting some preliminary tracks in the studio. It was
two years after *One in a Million,* so the timing was ideal. However, with Aaliyah's growing film stardom, her long-awaited
third album was put on pause to focus on her new career
extension. Songs like "Are You That Somebody?" and "Try
Again" clearly kept her afloat musically, so by 2000 the world
was more than ready for her to get back into the studio and
start working on her album again. By then, however, a few
things had changed.

In May 2000, the announcement was made that Aaliyah
would be moving from Atlantic Records to Virgin Records. It

wasn't the most surprising move; the *Romeo Must Die* soundtrack was a joint release in March of that year through Blackground and Virgin, with co-financing through Warner Bros. Records (which is under the same umbrella as Atlantic). In two months' time, news circulated that Aaliyah was "so impressed" with how Virgin handled the *Romeo* rollout that she decided to make the label her new home and pushed Blackground into pursuing a joint venture. By August 2000, the deal was finalized, for an estimated $15 million. In the deal announcement, HITS Daily Double also noted: "In addition to the $15 million, Blackground is also expected to receive new business cards and several lifetime subscriptions to AOL."

❦

Timbaland was mentioned in the release as dropping his project in February 2001, but that never happened. He dropped his collaborative follow-up, *Indecent Proposal*, with Magoo in November, three months after Aaliyah's passing. A shift started happening. Business with Blackground was souring for everyone, primarily for Missy and Timbaland. When the time came to record Aaliyah's third album, Timbaland and Missy weren't going to be a part of it at all. The plan was for Aaliyah to record the project while she was filming *Queen of the Damned*, which involved the team heading out to Australia. With Missy and Timbaland seemingly removed from the equation, Aaliyah had begun forming a new circle through the static, pun fully intended.

Enter, again, Static Major.

Stephen "Static Major" Garrett was born in Louisville, Kentucky. Raised in the Church, he met his two friends named

Jawaan "Smokey" Peacock and Benjamin "Digital Black" Bush in high school. They formed the group A Touch of Class in 1990. By '91, Static had already dropped out of school but remained with the guys. Jodeci was on tour and had a stop in Louisville, and Smokey's mother managed to get them backstage. They sang Jodeci's song "Stay" for DeVanté while backstage, and DeVanté gave them his pager number. He also later renamed them Playa. After some time, Static started to get cabin fever within the confines of Louisville. He wanted out. Badly. So he reached out to DeVanté, who brought Playa out to New Jersey, where they first met Timbaland and Missy, along with Ginuwine and Magoo. They signed to Swing Mob shortly thereafter and were all holed up in the toxic upstate compound with everyone else. While there, Static helped Timbaland piece together Ginuwine's "Pony" track, while simultaneously contributing to Jodeci's album, like everyone else.

Static had a gift that few singers, songwriters, and producers possessed. He was able to really emulate the artists he was working with. It was almost as if he wore them while making their music for them. When he helped write and produce "Pony," he also sang on the song so similarly to Ginuwine that it was almost as if you had no idea where Ginuwine ended and Static began. He would later bring that superpower to other artists' projects, most notably Lil Wayne's Grammy Award–winning song "Lollipop" in 2008. That same year, while shooting the music video for "Lollipop" in Las Vegas, Static wasn't feeling well. He flew back home to Louisville, leaving his flight in a wheelchair when they landed, and was later admitted to Baptist Hospital East. He was diagnosed with a disease called myasthenia gravis, which is an autoimmune disease that causes neuromuscular issues within the body's skeletal system, igniting heightened levels of fatigue. It was recommended that he have a procedure done, where a catheter is inserted through either the neck or the arm to filter the blood, much like how kidney patients do with dialysis. The blood was supposed to be filtered of its autoantibodies, and when it was inserted Static said he immediately felt something was wrong. When the nurse attempted to remove the catheter from his neck, Static went into a state of respiratory distress, convulsed, and bled to death. He died on February 25, 2008, at the age of thirty-three. The rumored cause was an aneurysm, though his family suspected malpractice, given the success rate of this procedure in any other instance. Even his doctor said he was supposed to make a full recovery within a day. A year later, his wife, Avonti Garrett, sued the hospital, a case she later settled outside of court.

His passing was another grim example of a real talent not being able to truly realize the depths of his gifts while on earth.

Sparks flew when Static first met Aaliyah, in more ways than one, and while "Are You That Somebody?" was their cute secret love letter that turned into a giant billboard for the world to admire, Static still lived in Timbaland's shadow when it came to really helping Aaliyah shape her sound. That was until Timbaland wasn't there.

Static Major was at the helm of Aaliyah's third album. As he had already dated Aaliyah and remained her good friend, there was a different kind of chemistry happening. While Aaliyah and Static were about four years apart in age, it was an entirely different dynamic from her last creative relationship that turned personal. Aaliyah was of age, and the lyrics Static wrote for her were based more on building upon her growth than revealing some forbidden love. Her parents had made the move to start monitoring her lyrics now, so in the end they had the final say on a lot of what was created for Aaliyah. But in Static's hands, they shared a commonality. Their creative intimacy allowed for the lyrics to be even more personal to Aaliyah.

"He was able to write for her so well because he knew her language," Static's mother told *Vibe*.

Their sessions were different from ones she'd had in the past. Here she would sit with Static and discuss her life and he would write to her thoughts. He didn't have to improvise and imagine what she might be going through, nor did he create a world for her where she would come in and make it hers. She was telling him what her vision was, and in turn he was putting it all together *with* her, not *for* her.

"It's different from the last LPs because I'm older. I'm more mature," Aaliyah said in her behind-the-scenes interview for the album. "I think that's very evident on the album, so it really showcases Aaliyah and who she is right now."

Aaliyah also started working with other songwriters and producers, where Static was primarily the conduit, though it was still a Blackground experience. Durrell Babbs, better known as Blackground R&B singer Tank, came through to help write for the project, along with Static's Playa partner Benjamin Bush, known as Digital Black. More Blackground producers joined in too, like "J. Dub" Walker and Stephen "Bud'da" Anderson. Rapture Stewart and Eric Seats (known collectively as Key Beats) had worked on the *Romeo Must Die* soundtrack and jumped in now for Aaliyah's new project. Together they all joined forces to create a new iteration of Aaliyah and, through their collective efforts, a project that would not only solidify her stardom but also serve as the perfect accompaniment to her Hollywood takeover. The new team was ready to work, with Aaliyah as the boss.

The first step was to create enough tracks Stateside to bring overseas. Static wanted to make sure that they didn't reach the new continent empty-handed, so a month prior to heading over to Australia the newly assembled team gathered in Sony Studios in New York and got started. "On that particular album, we collectively just wanted to make the best possible album that we could," Rapture told website *YouKnowIGotSoul* in 2011. "It was really like a family type of thing, there wasn't any hostility recording that album, and that's why the album came out the way it did. No one was competing to try to outproduce somebody else." There was also the idea that everyone was valuable and a vital piece to the puzzle. "Everybody had their own style to bring to the table," he continued, "so that made it a collective effort from everybody because we knew each person was going to bring fire to the project, so it wasn't even an issue."

The only real competition was ensuring that each producer and songwriter was represented, since they were working with limited real estate. It was only one album, but for everyone involved it was a chance to really shine. Aaliyah had market value that some hadn't experienced before; being a part of the project really meant something, and everyone there knew it.

With the work they had previously done in New York City, a blueprint was laid so that Aaliyah could easily record once she got to Australia. "And so when we got there, it was like, okay, she can film the movie during the day and we would go to the lab at night," manager Tim Barnett remembers. "And so we all stayed in the Como [Melbourne] hotel right there on Chapel Street. And it was crazy too, because she had just signed that new deal with Virgin. She was doing the *Matrix* movies, and then she had did *Romeo Must Die*, she was doing *Queen of the Damned*." A lot was going on. Chapel Street is the Australian equivalent to Melrose or Rodeo Drive. "Our money was worth double over there anyway," Barnett says, "and we're over there on *Aaliyah's* budget!" The team stayed over the course of a few months, had room service three times a day, and even took in some nightlife while creating what some consider to be Aaliyah's magnum opus. They recorded in Melbourne's Sing Sing Studios, which was within walking distance of their hotel.

"It just really gave Static more reign," Barnett adds, though he made it clear that Aaliyah was the leader. Even when she would defer to Static, he would push her back into the lead. "It was so dope just watching the chemistry that those two had," Barnett continues. "And watching Static produce her vocals and say, 'Oh, nah, nah, nah, you should do it like this,' or, 'Try it like this.' Static really pushed her to make it her record. Make it Aaliyah's record." The team was comprised of songwriters and producers would move from room to room throughout the studio, bouncing ideas off one another. It was almost a replication of what Static experienced with Swing Mob and Da Bassment, only here there was far less competition, much more camaraderie, and the end result was to make sure that Aaliyah had the greatest masterpiece possible. "To be honest, it was surreal," Bud'da also told *YouKnowIGotSoul* in 2011. "We got to bond on different levels because we were in another country and you guys are all you got." Aaliyah was on a rigorous schedule where she was filming, then recording, and taking some time here and there to decompress, but really she saw the finish line in front of her. There was an album and a movie to be made and she was going to do both concurrently, and they would both be game changing. With the album in particular, she already knew that she was holding all of the cards in making this project her most personal one yet.

It's the reason why she chose to name the album *Aaliyah*, because for the first time she really felt like this album was specifically about her and *for* her. Much like the meaning of her name ("The highest, most exalted one. The best."), she wanted the album to be held in the highest regard. "I wanted the name to really carry the project," Aaliyah continued in her behind-the-scenes interview. Static left Australia in November, and Aaliyah stayed with some of the other team to finish up; Barnett made sure she stuck to the studio routine that she and Static had created during her movie filming. They returned Stateside around Christmas Eve.

A few of the tracks were in the running to be the first single. "Loose Rap" (featuring Static) was one of them, and what became her final single was also in the lead for the first. "A lot of us was like 'Rock the Boat' could have been it," Barnett remembers. " 'Rock the Boat' could have been the first one." There were a few reasons why it wasn't. For one, the suggestive nature of the song didn't sit right with the label as Aaliyah's first single, coming back out after a lengthy hiatus. Granted, she was grown, but starting right out of the gate with very vivid wordplay about sex through lines like "work the middle" just didn't seem like the best course of action for her triumphant return. Second, Barry was adamant that the first single be

Timbaland's, regardless of their current situation. Third, this would be the third time in a row that Aaliyah had a total team switch on her project if Timbaland was nowhere to be found. That wasn't a part of Aaliyah's brand, where she would purposely use an entirely different team with every album, since they publicly preached about their sense of community. Moving into the second project, it was obvious why she needed a new environment, but for the third project it would look suspicious, indicative either of problems at Blackground (which was true) or that Aaliyah was difficult to work with (which wasn't true). Timbaland had to be a part of it somehow, to save face, for Aaliyah's sake.

While Timbaland was still reluctant to get involved with the third album, Aaliyah was the one to convince him to do it. Out of love for her (and not allegiance to her uncle) he finally agreed to have a part in the project. "Right after the New Year, we flew to New York and we did 'We Need a Resolution' with Timbaland," Barnett says. "We did 'More than a Woman' with Timbaland, and we did 'Don't Know What to Tell Ya.' We did those three joints because Barry and them wanted Tim to have the single. You know how it goes in the industry." They reconvened at the beginning of 2001 at the studio in New York City's Manhattan Center to bring Timbaland back into the fold. However, things had drastically changed. All of her trust was now placed in Static Major. "We'd be in the studio, me and Aaliyah, and she would listen to me," Jimmy Douglass remembers. "Like, you know, it's kind of producing the vocals that are already down, but I'm producing how it should work, right? And how it should sound, doing whatever we need to do." Things changed this last go-round. "When we get to this last moment, she suddenly doesn't have the confidence in me to want to do that anymore," he says. "And I felt it. And I felt a little bit, not slighted, but I was like, 'Whoa, what's going on here? Like it's just me and you.' No. Static had to come. And he had to sit there and do what I normally do with her, which is direct her." Timbaland only produced his own tracks and wrote his rap on "We Need a Resolution"; Static wrote Aaliyah's part. The last Timbaland contribution also included Missy by proxy. It was "I Care 4 U," a song that wasn't new but reworked for the project. At first it was in consideration for *One in a Million*, but then they decided against it.

"That song we actually had about two years before with some young kids that Barry Hankerson had signed to his label Blackground, and it never happened," Douglass adds. "They never got released or whatever, but that track Missy had written." The song was a perfect ballad for the *Aaliyah* project, since it needed one. So the beat was flipped and parts resung to be retrofitted for the album, becoming one of its strongest ballads, where Aaliyah is professing her love to someone emphatically, yet impressively still maintains her swagger.

Before Timbaland agreed to come on board, "Loose Rap" was going to be released as the first single, but then the decision was finalized for "We Need a Resolution" to be the official single.

I'm tired of arguin', girl.

Timbaland repeats that line over and over in the opening of "We Need a Resolution." The production uses a woozy Middle Eastern–style sample borrowed from John Ottman's "Tricks of the Trade." Art imitates life in the song, as the lyrics from both Timbaland and Aaliyah reflect a very obvious argument—which, like Timbaland says, they're tired of. It becomes a volleying of bars: Aaliyah coyly asks if he slept on the wrong side of the bed, because she's catching a bad vibe from him and is urging him to speak up. Meanwhile, Timbaland has had enough of the back-and-forth. Sure, the song was packaged as a lovers' quarrel, but really it was them saying to each other "we need a resolution." It was money; it was egos; it was fame. It was also Blackground, and Aaliyah was caught in the cross hairs of that war, as both an artist, part-owner, and family member.

But even through the storm, they worked together for one more go-round and made some hits.

In addition to "We Need a Resolution," Timbaland produced bonus track "Don't Know What to Tell Ya," where he also utilizes a Middle Eastern–style sample (this time from "Batwanness Beek" from Algerian singer Warda Al-Jazairia). The song talks of Aaliyah refusing to be tied down by a controlling relationship, as she compares it to incarceration. The final Timbaland offering is the potent "More than a Woman," which became Aaliyah's battle cry even after her passing. Again, he uses a Middle Eastern sample, from Syrian artist Mayada El Hennawy's song titled "Alouli Ansa." That Middle Eastern sampling continued to appear in Timbaland's catalog. He added a heavy Punjabi bhangra sound for Missy's "Get Ur Freak On" in 2001 and collaborated with Indian hip-hop artist Rajé Shwari for his *Under Construction II* track "Indian Flute" with Magoo in 2003. Other artists followed suit with that new avenue for sampling. Even with their final collaborations, Timbaland and Aaliyah changed the game one last time.

Timbaland's contributions to the *Aaliyah* project were important, and when placed alongside the rest of the work it made a well-rounded album. The crux of the project was changing Aaliyah's narrative. For so much of her album work, there was a younger, flirtier vibe to her songs. The love songs were more about longing (and sometimes secrecy) than actually having a real relationship. With *Aaliyah* it was different. She was discussing themes that can happen in actual relationships outside the fantasy of it all, and working with a team who bonded so tightly after their trip to Australia made it all the more personal for everyone involved.

The aforementioned "Loose Rap" was futuristic meets melodic, as Aaliyah pushes back on her man offering lip service. Some even took it as a diss track against her haters. The same fluid style of Key Beats' production also appears on the erotic "Rock the Boat," "It's Whatever," and "Those Were the Days." They adapted to a Timbaland style of production on tracks like "Extra Smooth," "U Got Nerve," and the hidden track "Messed Up." Bud'da gave her the ballad "Never No More" and "Read between the Lines," while pushing her to her creative limits on the electro-rock-inspired "I Can Be," where she's accepting the position of being the other woman. J. Dub brought a similar vibe on "What If," while bringing another mid-tempo ballad on "I Refuse." Aaliyah was like a chameleon; she became every track on the album. As a huge Nine Inch Nails fan, she wanted to show she had a rock edge. She and Trent Reznor even talked about working together. *Aaliyah* would have been the perfect kickoff for that new sound.

The album was a combination of romantic and explorative, where the lyrics noticeably matured, yet Aaliyah sang them like they were autobiographical. The music was equally a part of her. It felt like, for perhaps the first time, this was a project specifically made for her. Yes, on her first and second works she did what it was that she's the best at doing: interpretation. Aaliyah could take a piece of music and immediately make it her own. Here it felt like the music was her own from the start, and in turn she made it ours.

The packaging of the album—from the liner notes to the physical CD—was red, so it became known as "The Red Album." The ultimate goal with the Red Album was to bring Aaliyah to the next level of her life. It was a coming-of-age project, as she was now an adult experiencing adult things at an adult's pace.

Reviews for the album recognized that there was a shift in Aaliyah's sound. "*Aaliyah* provides a missing link between hip-hop and electronica," journalist Sal Cinquemani writes in his review for *Slant Magazine*. "Following in the footsteps of some of today's biggest icons, Aaliyah has learned how to align herself with A-list producers without losing her individuality and, instead, makes the sound her own." BBC writer Daryl Easlea wrote: "*Aaliyah* is a fascinating work; it shows a 22-year-old artist truly finding her direction, delivering well-tailored material with élan." The review from *The A.V. Club* recognized that she was escaping the shadow of her mentors, finally. "A show-business veteran at 22, Aaliyah has often been over-shadowed by her collaborators," writes Nathan Rabin, "but her strikingly assured third album establishes the young over-achiever as a major artist in her own right." The project was widely regarded as experimental, showing how Aaliyah was tinkering with new sounds and styles and formulating a whole new blueprint for herself. In the wake of her passing, it became more of an unfortunate example of unrealized potential, where Aaliyah was just warming up for a bright future ahead of her.

But there was something far greater to glean from the *Aaliyah* project. Through every album, Aaliyah's songwriters and producers were regarded as the geniuses who helped define her sound, yet through three projects she worked with predominantly three different teams. The only true constant was Aaliyah, and her eponymous project solidified that reality for everyone.

It was Aaliyah who was the genius all along. She was the thread, woven through the projects, bringing the fabric of the work to life. It was more than just having the right people in her corner, writing her songs and producing her beats. The magic of *her* touching that music was what captivated the audience. These weren't songs that could have been handed off to just anyone. No, it was Aaliyah's ability to take a song and run with it. She accomplished that with her first project and her second, and it was finally understood that she was the true star of the show with her last.

The positioning of the album alongside its peers was something to behold, mainly through the progression of Aaliyah's influence over other artists. In 2001, we witnessed an influx of R&B and hip-hop-leaning albums from both new and established acts. Mary J. Blige delivered *No More Drama*, as Jennifer Lopez was on her second album, the more rap-infused *J.Lo*. Alicia Keys made her big debut with *Songs in A Minor*, as well. There were countless "comeback" albums in the mix too, yet where *Aaliyah* was positioned marked both a cause and an effect of sorts. So many artists by 2001 had borrowed notes from the Aaliyah playbook over the course of her career—either by

incorporating dancier more electronic blips into their inter-
pretations of R&B or through female artists fully embracing
a tomboy-chic style as they sang their songs. There was also a
fusion with hip-hop that Aaliyah perfected through her work
with Timbaland and Missy, where you didn't necessarily need
a rap feature, but you could immediately tell the essence of
the song had strong hip-hop roots.

The Red Album posthumously took home several awards.
In 2002, Aaliyah won Favorite Soul/R&B Female Artist and
Favorite Soul/R&B Album at the American Music Awards. A
year later, she won Favorite Soul/R&B Female Artist again.
In 2003, she also won Top R&B/Hip-Hop Artist, Female at
the Billboard-AURN R&B/Hip-Hop Awards. She also won a
MOBO Award, an NAACP Image Award, an NME Award, a
Soul Train Award, and two Soul Train Lady of Soul Awards.
She was also nominated for three Grammys.

Most of the album's visuals were unfortunately rolled out
posthumously save for the first single. "We Need a Resolution"
is sectioned off into parts, where in some scenes Aaliyah is
spacey and futuristic and in some parts she's even levitating.
In others she's keeping it street, and of course there are the
unforgettable scenes where she is wrapped in a python, a testament to her love of snakes. "We wanted an exclusive peek
into her life, so the idea there was to create a sense that every
room, every scenario, that you're looking at something that
only certain people can see," director Paul Hunter told *Vibe*
in 2016. "It's almost like if you've ever seen a celebrity in the
airport, they're going into a first-class lounge, or they're going
into a private hallway; they sort of slip past you. The idea was
to have this experience where we create these rooms that felt

like they were exclusive." Timbaland is in the scenes where he's rhyming and ad-libbing, though he and Aaliyah never share any camera time. Her makeup was dark and commanding, like she was already winning the argument with her face. "The whole look we did for the 'We Need a Resolution' video came from stuff that I saw on the runway from Alexander McQueen and John Galliano," Eric Ferrell told *Vibe* in 2016. "Every idea I brought to [Aaliyah], she was like, 'Well, why don't we do this too?'"

The remaining videos were spaced in their rollout following Aaliyah's passing. The first that came was "More than a Woman." Director Dave Meyers was introduced to Aaliyah through Damon Dash. "I just remember Damon telling me I better make his girlfriend look good," Meyers expressed to *Vibe*. Meyers directed videos for Dash's Roc-A-Fella Records, primarily Jay-Z—most prominently "Izzo (H.O.V.A.)." In working with Aaliyah, Meyers explained how she approached him with almost a vision board for the video's concept. "She was pulling tears out of magazines and sharing those with me," Meyers says. "It was a little bit more of how she wanted to present herself and I built the world around her with the motorcycle and the lights and the dance." In the video for "More than a Woman," Aaliyah is dancing inside of a motorcycle, proudly donning her boyfriend's Roc-A-Fella chain throughout. The scenery is like the inside of an engine, complete with gears and coils, that doubles as a dance floor where Mark Ronson is deejaying. Other cameos include Kidada Jones and her sister, actor Rashida Jones (who was dating Mark Ronson at the time).

The video was released concurrently with the release of "Rock the Boat" as a single. While bittersweet at its best, the

"Rock the Boat" video was released in Aaliyah's honor. Hype Williams's bright beachy visuals were a reminder of Aaliyah's light and her ultimate place in the sun. From dancing on boats to the Bahamian beach side, she looked peaceful and happy. The final video didn't feature Aaliyah at all. It was for the posthumously released single "Miss You," which started as a song for Ginuwine. "We played her a couple of tracks and that particular track happened to kind of pass by. [Aaliyah] was like, 'Wait a minute, back that up. I want to hear that again!'" producer and songwriter Teddy Bishop recalled to *YouKnowI-GotSoul* in 2012. "We played it for her and she was like 'I want to cut this record,' and we were like 'Well, this is Ginuwine's record.'" Aaliyah wanted to cut the record for herself. "She got on the phone, called him, and said, 'Hey, I know you cut this record already, but I would love to cut it.' Ginuwine, because he was a part writer on the song, it benefited him anyway . . . Ginuwine told her to cut it and we cut it on *Aaliyah* and it went on to be a number one hit." In the video, artists like Lil' Kim, Missy Elliott, Tweet, DMX, Quincy Jones, Queen Latifah, Jamie Foxx, and many others all lip-synch the song in Aaliyah's honor. A remix by Jay-Z followed, where he lists the people in Aaliyah's life who all miss her, including Dash, Kidada, her brother, Rashad, and many others.

Aaliyah had a mission with the Red Album, and despite her untimely passing, her vision was realized. From every visual, every lyric, every piece of music, her goal was to give her fans a deeper understanding of herself. She was an artist on the verge of something great. After setting trends for years, Aaliyah was on the path to icon. She got there, though not in the manner that anyone had planned.

CHAPTER TEN: THINGS FALL APART

I enjoy every second of my fame. If I could start my
life all over again, I wouldn't change anything. Honest.

—Aaliyah, *Die Zeit Online*, July 2001

It was right after she turned twenty-two when Aaliyah started having a series of dreams. They weren't enough to rattle her into agoraphobia and keep her in her room, but they were impactful enough to make her bring them up to a complete stranger. And that wasn't like Aaliyah, at all. Through the duration of her career, her mysteriousness was her handshake. She was vague, probably due to her turbulent beginnings, often conducting interviews with this invisible veil in front of her. She was still charming, she was still demure, and she was still sincere. However, she was still guarded. As she grew into her own, her interviews became increasingly more intimate. You started to feel like you were just getting to know her; much like her music.

So during her final round of international press, Aaliyah sat in a hotel room in Paris and divulged to a German reporter what she had been feeling for the last month or so. The publication was *Die Zeit Online* and the writer's name was Dagmar

Leischow. For forty minutes on a sofa, Leischow sat and heard what many would continue to dissect for decades to come. Aaliyah was reserved at first, but once she let the words out they just kept flowing. She settled right back into the dream she was repeatedly having, along with all of its ebbs and flows.

In the dream, it's dark. Aaliyah is being chased and she's scared, but then all of a sudden she takes flight. She describes it as "swimming in the air." She feels free and weightless. "Nobody can reach me. Nobody can touch me," she continues. Then she starts to talk out of concern for the dream. What does it even mean? Anxiety kicks in, as she thinks it means she's becoming jaded and wants to "fly away" from her career, so to speak. She started to explain to the reporter how she doesn't feel that way, almost trying to convince them both that this wasn't the case. She goes on about her childhood, how the idea that she never got to be a kid was a total fallacy. She felt like a normal little girl, with some minor (read: major) modifications. She went on to discuss with the reporter her earliest beginnings, onstage with Gladys Knight, preparing for what she felt was her destiny: to be famous. "I worked towards this dream. Hard. Very hard. I took singing lessons, I took part in school performances," she admits. "I did everything I could to become a good entertainer. Because a pretty appearance doesn't make you a star."

But fear is one hell of a poison, and coupled with being shy it can be a prison. "I preferred to take refuge in my dreams," she continued. That dreaminess about her followed her from childhood to adulthood, as she also admitted she kind of stares off into space when she's around family and friends, thinking of something else beyond what is within her reach. "Where am I?" she hypothetically asks the reporter. "No idea. Probably in higher spheres." Sometimes she doesn't even know herself, basically joining us all in the enigma that is Aaliyah.

Back to the dream of flying.

Aaliyah is in Egypt. She walks the same sand-dusted ground that Cleopatra and the Pharaohs once walked. Egypt was one of her travel goals. She wanted to visit there, ever since she was a child, often burying her head in books about Egypt. When she bought her New York City apartment at 25 Central Park West, she decorated it in Egyptian iconography. Once she became a star, the goal was to bring her career closer to Egypt. She was aiming for a role as Cleopatra but settled on almost getting there, playing the Kemet-turned-Egyptian vampire queen Akasha in *Queen of the Damned*. Still, she wanted Cleopatra. Aaliyah wanted a lot of things.

She wanted to get married, to have a family. The man she would marry would "be strong, as an Egyptian warrior," she continued, making her dreams yet again come full circle. She also wanted to finally enroll in college. Her major? Egyptology.

After this interview—which wasn't published until a week after her passing—many surmised that Aaliyah had a premonition. She realized something was going to happen to her. Recurring dreams for nearly a month might make anyone else overtly cautious, refusing to step on cracks, walking around ladders, and paying heed to other superstitions. And as Aaliyah went through her dream in detail, it seemed as though she started with unease but allowed the story to unfold, and she eventually landed on peacefulness. She discussed the future after that. She mentioned her Dolly Pop clothing and accessory line that she had planned with Kidada Jones (which was slated for production the following year). She mentioned more music, more movies. Egypt had to wait, because there were other dreams she had to fulfill.

But God had other plans.

Two weeks before Aaliyah died, she was happy. *Really* happy. She was headed to the Hamptons by helicopter with her boyfriend of one year, Damon Dash. While Aaliyah had previously been loosely involved with his Roc-A-Fella business partner Jay-Z, it was Dash who won her heart. The two met through one of Aaliyah's best friends, model Natane Boudreau. "I introduced her to her great love, Damon Dash," Boudreau told *Vogue* in 2016. It seemed as though Dash and Baby Girl were perfect for each other. She chipped away at his tough exterior and opened his heart, while he created a safe place for her to explore her edgier side. Aaliyah was a lady but knew how to hang with the fellas. "We were in Dame's house one day, when he had the big mansion, I believe in Alpine [New Jersey], and it had the movie theater at the bottom," rapper Jim Jones remembers. "[Dame] had one of the first edits of the *Paid in Full* movie, and me and Cam['ron] went over there to watch it. Him and Aaliyah were there. I had maybe a half an ounce of weed, and [Aaliyah] kept tellin' me, 'Roll up, n***a, you smokin' that or what?'" Jones was shocked. He ended up smoking nearly the entire half of an ounce of weed with Aaliyah while she watched *Paid in Full* with the guys. "It blew my mind," he continues, unaware that the Princess of R&B was not only a weed smoker but a champion one at that.

"She damn sure was. She smoked with the best of them," Jones punctuates with a laugh. Aaliyah fit right into Dash's life, and he fit into hers. They had plans to get married; Aaliyah wore a Roc-A-Fella chain around her neck. Even Dash's demeanor became noticeably different. "I'd known Damon for years," Jimmy Douglass remembers, from working with Jay-Z. "He was a bit of a difficult person, and he wasn't kind." After he met Aaliyah, things changed. "I'll never forget this. One day, I'm in the Manhattan Center studio—[Aaliyah] is on the microphone out in the booth—and Dame comes in and he goes, 'Hey, man, what's going on?' And I looked at him like, 'Huh? What the fuck?' and then [Aaliyah] comes out of the booth and she goes, 'Hey, darling,' or whatever. And I go, oh shit, he's in love. Holy shit. It softened him up. Now he's Mister Friendly 'cause he found love."

The couple spent their Fourth of July weekend in 2001 in the Hamptons for the Bad Boy versus Roc-A-Fella softball game. Aaliyah is sporting a Rocawear tee, along with Dame's cousin, actress Stacey Dash, and Natane Boudreau. Aaliyah and Dame look as happy as can be together.

On August 11, the couple was in that helicopter, back in the Hamptons. Journalist Touré was on assignment shadowing Jay-Z and he wrote of how Aaliyah was hugging a black pillow and nuzzled into Dame's shoulder as she fell asleep on the helicopter ride. Touré observed her while he was there observing Jay, equally taken by her ability to remain sweet yet still sexy. "Throughout the weekend, she was quiet but not quite shy, quick to flash her wide, bright smile, quick to laugh at Dash's jokes and quick to dance with him in the middle of the living room when Michael Jackson's *Off the Wall* came on," he wrote of Aaliyah for *Rolling Stone* following her death. "On Sunday, she slept hours longer than everyone else, on a bed strewn with rose petals. She and Dash seemed very much in love." While she was in love with Dame, she was also in love with her life. Her eponymous album was on the charts, she was finishing up her role in *Queen of the Damned* and had begun preproduction for her roles in the second and third *Matrix* films. This was everything she had manifested. It was the moment in time that she had dreamed of, and everything from the past only made her strong in her present. The future looked bright.

On August 21, 2001, she sat down for her last interview with BET's *106 & Park*. She was coming off the high of holding the biggest contest ever for BET, where a fan took home $20,000 and a Cadillac Escalade. She talked about never having a car before. For the years leading up to her passing, she moved back to the city she was born in, New York City, so a car wasn't really necessary. Aaliyah spoke of her favorite videos she had done, from "One in a Million" to "Are You That Somebody?" and was preparing for the road ahead. She handed the Cadillac keys to the lucky winner and then headed back to her place to prepare for her flight to Miami. "Me, Aaliyah, and Missy were supposed to meet up," Lil' Kim remembers. The girls were going to convene at Aaliyah's before she left. Kim was running late, so she called Missy to tell her. "So Aaliyah grabs the phone from her and was like, 'If you don't get your ass here . . . I have so much to talk to you about I have so much to tell you. I really need you, I need my sister,'" Kim continues. "But Aaliyah never stressed how much she needed me to be with her until that night. I just couldn't understand it." Kim hurried to get there, but arrived too late. Aaliyah already left for the airport. "It fucked with my soul, because I'd never see her again," Kim adds with remorse.

Aaliyah was bound for Miami.

She had questions about her safety the moment she laid eyes on the airplane taking her to the Bahamas from Miami. For one, she hated flying; and even further, she hated the idea of boarding a tiny aircraft. She was anxiety ridden about that initial trip, as the flight felt unnecessary and downright dangerous. But Aaliyah was a team player and didn't want to disappoint anyone. Getting there wasn't a problem; it was returning that proved to be the impossible.

"There is no chance that if I was there we would have been on that plane," Damon Dash told *The Real* in 2016. "It would have never happened that way."

Both Aaliyah and Dash were in Miami a few days prior, but for different reasons. Aaliyah was shooting some preliminary footage for the music video to her upcoming single "Rock the Boat," while Dash was with Roc-A-Fella Records crew State Property along with his son Damon "Boogie" Dash II and a few of his nephews. While there, Aaliyah was going to record a song with Roc-A-Fella's State Property crew rapper Freeway when plans changed all around. She was going to come back from the Bahamas and then hit the studio. "When Aaliyah died in that plane crash, she was on her way to come meet me and Freeway to do a remix for 'More Than a Woman,'" Just Blaze confirmed to Fuse in 2012. "We got a call saying, 'She just got on a plane. She'll be at the studio in an hour or two.' Then, twenty minutes later, people are on the radio saying that she died. We didn't believe because we had literally just got off the phone with her people. We got confirmation a few minutes later that it was true."

The director for the "Rock the Boat" music video, Hype Williams, made the call to move the filming over to the Bahamas.

Dash had to fly back to New York because he had a court date pending and his son had a football game. He couldn't join Aaliyah on the next leg of her work trip. On his way heading back to New York, he and Aaliyah had an exchange on their BlackBerrys about her last-minute Bahamas trip.

She didn't want to go to the Bahamas. She didn't like the looks of the airplane heading there. Dame pleaded with her not to go. She had to. There were enough label issues and contractual obligations happening where Aaliyah knew that this wasn't an instance where she could fold her arms and be defiant. Well, she could have, but that wasn't in her nature. She wanted to keep the peace. This was one of the only times her family hadn't been traveling with her. Her mother was having a medical procedure done and couldn't be present for the shoot. There was no one around to understand the energy around Aaliyah's concerns and effectively advocate that she not board that flight.

The Bahamas are a frequent spot for filming, especially for footage that is geared toward creating an "out to sea" effect. Many film directors opt to shoot there, since certain areas are less crowded, beautiful scenery is within close proximity everywhere, and the cost to shoot is often less expensive. There are also many options for shooting, considering you can hop from island to island in an effort to nail the perfect shot.

The Abaco Islands are a collection of small islands that sit within the northern extension of the Bahamas. They are east of South Florida. An air taxi ride from Miami to the Great Abaco is about an hour and a half. Aaliyah reached the Abaco Islands safely, traveling in a bigger aircraft, but she would never make it back.

The shoot for "Rock the Boat" started on August 22, 2001, in Miami and concluded in the Bahamas on August 25, 2001. On August 22, the crew had a long day, nearly twelve hours of shooting green-screen footage at the Miami Broadcast Center. From there, they headed to the Florida International University campus, filming underwater shots in a campus pool until 4 AM August 23. In the finished product the shots are beautiful and free-flowing, where Aaliyah looks like a mythical mermaid. During the filming, however, Aaliyah's anxiety got the best of her when it came to breath control underwater. "I'm trying to get it done quickly," she says on camera for BET's ALL ACCESS, who followed her throughout the shoot. "I don't know how long I can last under there." The shot involved intricate details at the floor of the pool, where an entire set was down there waiting for her, along with a blue screen to add other underwater imagery to the video. Aaliyah was supposed to use a breath regulator to stay under the water longer, but she struggled with quickly training herself to breathe through it, once she got farther beyond the shallow waters. *I can't do it, I can't do it*, she's seen mouthing from a distance in a panic. It was not going to happen so easily. She finally completed the shots holding her breath for extended spurts in a nearly fifteen-foot pool. "It was worth it," she says afterwards. "We got some really pretty shots out of it." Following the mildly traumatic underwater scene, the crew moved forward to shoot the next batch of footage in the Bahamas. They flew later that day from Miami to the Treasure Cay Airport in Abaco, staying at the Treasure Cay Beach, Marina & Golf Resort for the next few days. Choreographer Fatima Robinson was there, and two-thirds of her glam squad known as Eric, Eric, and Derek or The Dream Team: stylist Derek Lee and hair stylist Eric Foreman. The second Eric, makeup artist Eric Ferrell (who died in 2020), was on tour with Macy Gray and didn't make it to the shoot. His replacement was Christopher Maldonado. Foreman's business partner Anthony Dodd was also there.

On the morning of August 24, Aaliyah was up at 3:00 AM on the beautiful island, doing her hair and makeup to prep for her 6:00 AM call time. She watched the sunrise kiss the ocean in the distance as her makeup was touched up. She was urging everyone around her to see the beauty that she was witnessing. "It's beautiful; did you catch that?" she tells the cameraman, making sure he pans the camera away from her for a split second just to capture the view on film. "It's so pretty," she continues.

The next day, August 25, Aaliyah and her team were bound for Marsh Harbour to film the remaining shots for the video—out to sea, dancing on a stage built into a seventy-two-foot catamaran (known as the *Fat Cat*) that cut through the crystalline turquoise waters of the Bahamas. The shots were epic, and Aaliyah was ecstatic, lip-synching for the video shots but in between takes singing like a songbird, just out of pure joy. She was in paradise and had created visuals for a song that was as smooth as the calming waters she was gliding upon. It was all so perfect. "I live out my dreams of being an artist through Aaliyah," choreographer Fatima Robinson tells the cameraman. "'Cause she's on my same vibe." The shoot was a wrap, and everyone agreed it was seamless, the kind where once it's over, people feel as though a bond was formed. Aaliyah asked the crew if she could take some time in the water by herself. She hopped on a Jet Ski, and all alone (with two men guarding her from a distance) she traveled to the center of the sea and just sat there, gazing. She wanted that moment, to bask in her place in the sun and in solitude. After that she ventured back to land to conclude her trip. Some of the crew opted to stay behind and take an extra day to enjoy the island. The remaining crew, Aaliyah included, decided to head back that late afternoon, flying out this time from the Marsh Harbour Airport.

The Abaco Islands are small and tight-knit, but tourism is definitely a real stream of income. A young man named Kingsley Russell was part of his family's business, where his mother worked at the airport and his father and stepmother had a taxi and hospitality business. His auntie also drove taxis and worked in hospitality. Kingsley was only thirteen at the time, but when a celebrity landed in Abaco and used his family's business he would be the luggage carrier, because that meant he would get the best tips. Kingsley's auntie Annie Russell was the person who picked up Aaliyah at the airport when she first arrived. While waiting in the taxi line, Annie conversed with a member of Instinct Productions and the two got along. She was then brought on to secure drivers and equipment handlers for the duration of the trip, while also assisting in scouting spots for rehearsals and filming. Annie spoke with South Florida's *Sun Sentinel* a week after Aaliyah's passing about the experience. "She had money, but it didn't spoil her," Annie remarked. "She acted as if she knew you for a long time. She was a nice person."

Kingsley's stepmother, Louise McIntosh, was one of Aaliyah's taxi drivers throughout her Bahamian trip. She even cooked conch stew for Aaliyah on request. When Aaliyah first arrived at the resort, Kingsley was there to grab the luggage. He was there again in the taxi ride to the airport for the flight back to Miami. "When we were on the long road stretch to the airport, I was talking to her," Kingsley says. She was kind; his little sister Diamond sat in the back with her, and Aaliyah called her Little Sis. His cousin was there in the van too, and everyone was asking Aaliyah questions. "She was talking about her life and her career," Kingsley adds. "I asked any question I could fit in, in between my cousin and my sister." Kingsley then asked her how he could be famous like her one day. "Please don't be a singer . . . or a rapper," she advised. "Write a book. Become an author instead." He took that advice and later started writing his own sci-fi novel because of her. "She was so nice and so happy," Kingsley expresses. "She was smiling the whole time . . . until we got to the airport."

When Aaliyah reached the Marsh Harbour Airport and saw the tiny plane waiting for her, she didn't want to board it. It was significantly smaller than the one she had arrived in. The check-in for travel at the airport is outdoors, covered by a series of huts. She returned to the taxi van, flustered, just as Kingsley was arranging her luggage outside of the van. "I know she was speaking to her entourage and they were going back and forth with the pilot," he says. "I guess they had this argument with the pilot, but she didn't want to get on the plane." Lining the airport are taxi drivers, waiting for passengers to drive into the island. "We heard the taxi officers—everyone that was inside the hut where they were all chillin' and waiting for the planes to land—they were all talking about the luggage and all of the heavy stuff." Everyone was in the airport whispering to one another. "They were like, 'How are they gonna put this girl on this little plane with all of this heavy stuff when the plane is overweight?' Everyone was telling them that the plane was overweight and [Aaliyah] was on board with that. [The airport staff] *and Aaliyah* had the common sense that the plane was overweight. She was getting frustrated because she was getting nowhere in the argument." Kingsley also overheard from other baggage handlers that Aaliyah was even told the luggage was lessened so the plane was now safe, when that wasn't true. Aaliyah was still concerned. She complained of a headache and went back to the taxi van. She got on the phone with her boyfriend, per Kingsley, who he later learned was Damon Dash.

While speaking with Aaliyah, Dash echoed his previous sentiment from before: don't go. A private G4 jet was slated to come get her and her team the following day (Sunday, August 26), but as the summer was coming to a close Aaliyah had several packed weeks leading into the fall ahead of her, including presenting at the MTV VMAs a few days after Labor Day weekend. This would be one of her last weekends to spend with Dash. It was confusing for her, and she was emotional. As she sat in the taxi van, spiraling, she put her head down. She said she wanted to take a quick nap; then she dozed off.

"So we came out of the car and my stepmom, I remember, put the air conditioner on full blast," Kingsley continues. "Someone from her entourage opened the door and woke her up; I think they were talking to her and asking her what was wrong." Aaliyah advised them that she had a headache, reiterating again that she didn't want to get on the plane.

Then Aaliyah was handed a pill.

"We went to go to the food stand to get her a cup of water and we brought it back. That's when she took the pill and fell back off to sleep." This time, however, it appeared that she fell immediately into a deep sleep and not just dozing. It was almost suspicious, but young Kingsley wanted the scoop on what was going on inside of the airport. "Me and my cousin went back in the airport because we wanted to finish hearing the stuff that was going on," he continues. People were bickering, demanding that the plane get off the ground to "get her back on time to where she needed to go" and saying how people "were going to get fired for slowing down the process." Aaliyah and her team had arrived at the airport around 4:00 PM, and there was a lengthy wait for takeoff. They were supposed to be heading for Miami at 4:30, so everyone was growing agitated at the multiple delays, despite the glaring safety violations. "There are varying reports of arguments between Aaliyah, her entourage, and the pilot overheard by baggage handlers at the airport," the Abaco Islands local paper *The Abaconian* reported on September 1, 2001.

They all attempted to board the plane after nearly two hours of waiting, when the pilot allegedly again advised that there was too much cargo and too many passengers. By this point, emotions were high, and the team (outside of Aaliyah) grew adamant to board, even when the baggage handlers also pointed out that there was far too much cargo for the plane to fly safely.

Then the argument abruptly ended. The pilot ultimately agreed to continue forward with the flight. "They just started loading all of the stuff onto the plane," Kingsley says.

Meanwhile, Aaliyah was still knocked out, unaware of what was going on. "They took her out of the van; she didn't even know she was getting boarded on a plane," Kingsley reveals. "She went on the airplane asleep." Whether she had any moment of consciousness, where she acquiesced to her team's desires despite her own concerns, remains a mystery.

The aircraft that attempted to fly Aaliyah home (a Cessna 402-B twin-engine plane) can carry anywhere from six to ten passengers, factoring in cargo and the weight distribution of the people on board. The aircraft is only able to take off at a weight of 6,300 pounds. An empty Cessna 402-B itself weighs 4,117 pounds alone, with the fuel weighing in at 804 pounds. Considering a significant number of the team flew on board (Aaliyah, seven of her team members, and one pilot) with their luggage and equipment in tow, they were pushing the limits of the bodies allowed on board, even without factoring in their luggage and heavy equipment. *The Abaconian* also reported that there was "no indication that any of the luggage was weighed before it was loaded on the plane." The baggage that managed to be salvaged weighed 574 pounds—that's not including one piece of luggage that was lost in the marsh. The remaining weight allowed was around 805 pounds. Aaliyah's bodyguard, Scott Gallin, was 300 pounds himself. That left a little over 500 pounds remaining among seven individuals. Meaning, around 70 pounds per person was the maximum weight. Survival was impossible, given those numbers. Investigators have surmised that the plane was carrying a weight that was 700 pounds beyond its authorized capability.

It was arguably the perfect evening for flying, with nothing but clear skies, as the plane was scheduled to head from the Marsh Harbour Airport to Miami's Executive Airport in Opa-Locka. The engines prior to takeoff were inspected and appeared to be working fine. Everything was a go. The plane traveled down the runway and hit the air at 6:45 PM, though not for long. Within a minute's time, the airplane reached a height of 200 feet off the ground. Spectators have said that the plane made it to the air and quickly took a left turn for the worse, nose-diving and crashing beneath bushes, facing 180 degrees from its direction at takeoff. Gasoline was spilled everywhere, igniting a fire all around the remnants of the airplane. One of the engines, the right one, appeared to be in flames while the plane was still in the air. Kingsley and his cousin didn't see the crash, but they heard it, as they were sitting and eating in the airport. He saw people running with fire extinguishers to head to the site, and that's when he learned of the crash. He was told to never speak of the incident.

The plane was left in torn-up parts, some pieces still ablaze, others completely disintegrated. Charred seats were ejected from the plane, and bodies were flung everywhere, while some were still stuck inside. The pilot was found dead in his cockpit. Aaliyah's bodyguard, Scott Gallin, was found alive, saying he was thirsty and asking about Aaliyah's well-being. He was her bodyguard since high school. He was also saying that he wanted to see his son. Gallin died around ten minutes into his flight to a Nassau hospital. One of the other passengers, hair stylist Anthony Dodd, was still alive yet badly burned and was successfully transported to a hospital in the Bahamas, Nassau's Princess Margaret Hospital, but he passed away after 3:00 on Sunday morning. Another unidentified passenger was found alive and severely burned, screaming in agony. That person barely survived being transported before passing away shortly thereafter.

And almost twenty feet away from the wreck lay Aaliyah.

She was still in her seat, with her seat belt on, coiled up on her left side. She looked as though she were hugging herself, her head affixed between her legs. Her hair was burned off from the flames, and she was covered in burns, with signs of massive head trauma. Aaliyah had a weak heart, so while the autopsy report confirmed that condition, there was also speculation that she suffered a heart attack during the short flight. Her body was so severely burned and in such a state of shock that her survival would have been "unthinkable."

An icon was gone, at just twenty-two years old, due to the crash of a plane that should have never taken flight.

The mortician at Marsh Harbour who was called to collect the bodies and wrap them in fire blankets and body bags advised that it was terrible to witness. "I've been on some gruesome ones," mortician Ernest Scott told investigative journalist Daniel Hopsicker in 2009, "but this one was bad." Bahamian investigators on-site initially chalked the crash up to engine failure, despite the dual engines passing inspection prior to takeoff. It was also deduced that the overloading of cargo and people on the flight could have contributed to that engine failure.

There were so many moving parts to the crash, and it took years for the pieces to come together. Even now, still, there are inconclusive fragments to the story. Yet the end result is still the same. Aaliyah didn't make it home, and neither did the eight other people on the flight with her.

Those on the flight included her bodyguard, Scott Gallin, age forty-one. Then there was Douglas Kratz, who was the director of video production at Virgin Records. He was only twenty-eight. Gina Smith, who was Aaliyah's product manager at Blackground Entertainment, was only twenty-nine. Keith Wallace was forty-nine and a manager for Blackground. Two of Aaliyah's hair stylists—Anthony Dodd, thirty-four, and Eric Foreman, twenty-nine—died along with makeup stylist Christopher Maldonado, thirty-two. The pilot, Luis Morales III, was thirty.

And Aaliyah Dana Haughton, age twenty-two.

There's something especially dismal about musicians dying in plane crashes. From Buddy Holly and Ritchie Valens to Patsy Cline, Otis Redding, and Stevie Ray Vaughan, artists who die during this travel are typically headed to do something to continue their art or returning from it. It's not to say that drugs and gun violence and disease aren't devastating ways for a musician (or anyone for that matter) to die. It's just that these individuals died in the name of doing something they loved: music. Aaliyah was no exception, but knowing how desperately she didn't want to board that plane makes her untimely death even more hurtful for those she left behind.

News of Aaliyah's plane crash broke in the wee hours of the morning on August 26, 2001. Headlines were to the point and heavy: "Aaliyah, Singer and Actress, Killed in Plane Crash" (*New York Times*), "Pop Star Aaliyah Dead in Plane Crash" (ABC News), "Aaliyah Killed in Plane Crash" (MTV). The news cycle had a way of making it more real with its pointed verbiage. It stabbed.

When the news broke, rapper Ludacris was on stage in Anaheim, California, for Power 106's Powerhouse back to school concert, which included him, Ja Rule, Nelly, OutKast, and many others. As his performance was about to finish, a person jumped to the stage and whispered in Luda's ear. He paused. "Hold up. This is serious," he said. "We just found out R and B singer Aaliyah was killed in a plane crash." The crowd (and Ludacris) stood there in shock but held a moment of silence for her. All of the artists backstage were shaken up when they heard the news. Ja Rule was up next to perform, and he got on the stage numb and in disbelief. He had just been with her right before she passed, but they didn't get to really connect. "The last time I saw Aaliyah, it was too quick," he now recalls. "We were both doing *106 & Park* and I was rushing to the stage. Someone from my camp was like, 'Yo, Ja! Baby Girl is here. You wanna holla at her real quick?' and I was like, 'Yo, I'll see her when I get offstage when I get back.' I didn't get to see her after that. She had to rush to the stage. They were moving us around really quickly. So I didn't get to really see her. It was just a quick hi; we didn't even get to kick it. And that was the last time I had seen her. It was like, damn, I took for granted that I would see her again."

While most reported on her passing from a place of honor and sympathy, one radio DJ did not. HOT 97 morning show shock jock Star (of Star & Buc Wild) announced Aaliyah's death by playing plane crash noises and people screaming in the background. Morning show co-host Miss Jones stormed out of the studio after he did that. What followed was an onslaught of angry responses, from both HOT 97 listeners and artists. Rapper Q-Tip called in to say that the station was losing his support; it was rumored that Jay-Z also threatened to lead a major boycott. Fans of Aaliyah took to the internet, posting Star's personal information, as well as a major petition to have him removed from the station called "No More Star." Veteran journalist Davey D also watched the fans work firsthand. "The Star incident has reached such heights that I saw the petition being passed around at a candlelight vigil for Aaliyah right here in Oakland, 3000 miles away," he wrote on his site DaveyD.com. Star was ultimately suspended from the station, and while he had played countless tributes to Aaliyah earlier on in the show, one swift act of recklessness negated all of it. The moment spread from coast to coast; the next day he apologized to the fans, along with Damon Dash. It was a heartless joke to chase, but the way Aaliyah's fans mobilized was comparable to a modern-day assembly of any fan hives for artists like Beyoncé, Taylor Swift, or Nicki Minaj. Still, despite Star's tasteless move, many other celebrities and artists all spoke of Aaliyah—each with an anecdote of how she touched their lives.

Mariah Carey wrote about how she felt about Aaliyah's passing while in the midst of enduring her own well-documented emotional setbacks in her 2020 memoir *The Meaning of Mariah Carey*: "When we got to LA my anxiety and disorientation was intensified by the tragedy of Aaliyah's sudden and horrific death. Just a few days earlier she had told the press, 'I know this business can be difficult, it can be stressful. Much love to Mariah Carey. I hope she gets better soon.' The entire music industry was rocked by her death, but the R & B and hip-hop community was devastated. She was indeed our little princess."

There was an outpouring of grief that followed from the music and film industries alike. That Monday (August 27), MTV VJ John Norris held a news brief on *Total Request Live*, where Timbaland called in on the air. He was beside himself and could barely talk. "She's like blood, and I lost blood," he said, fighting through tears. "Me and her together had this chemistry. I feel like I've lost half of my creativity side." DMX released a statement for MTV to air, where he described her as "a down-to-earth sister with enough energy to put anyone on a cloud." Jive Records even released a formal statement on behalf of R. Kelly; MTV simply (and appropriately) regarded him on air as the producer of her first album: "R. Kelly is deeply saddened by the tragic loss of Aaliyah. His thoughts and prayers are with her family during this time of grief." Puffy was hosting *TRL* that day and was still grieving to the audience. "She's just one of those individuals that would light up a room," Puffy told the audience and Norris. "She's one of those individuals that was very down-to-earth. She doesn't really feel like 'Aaliyah,' like a big superstar. She always felt like just a beautiful person, like a special individual that whenever you was around her, she treated everybody the same—whether it was a fan or a person on the street, or me." His words followed with a montage of Aaliyah's best MTV moments, complete with Carson Daly naming her pet snake on air Boots. "Biggie's death hurt my soul, but Aaliyah's? That took my soul for a long time," remembers Lil' Kim.

Everyone who spoke on Aaliyah's passing had their own personal reference point to speak from. Sure, there was the mention of the bright future she had ahead of her, the unrealized potential, the stardom that she was just beginning to embrace in both the music and film worlds. But above all, the greatest takeaway they all made sure to impress upon was who Aaliyah was as a human being, and oftentimes that part of a lost celebrity's persona gets removed from the grief cycle, though not here. The focus was on how kind she was, how she always managed to smile at anyone she met. How she lit up a room and made it her unspoken mission to brighten up people's days.

Tameka Foster, who styled Timbaland and other Blackground artists during Aaliyah's time, described her as exuding an "angelic vibe," even while on earth. "It's funny, when you see people that have passed, you kind of realize like, 'You know what? She was always different,'" Foster remembers. "I always believe that people who die young are angels. I think that they're just on earth for that limited time. Aaliyah always had that spirit, that aura." Above all, Foster remembers Aaliyah's smile. The loss was compounded by the fact that she was so bright and never known to be foul to anyone. Plus, she was just so young.

Aaliyah's family and both of her record labels each released statements announcing her passing to the public. While they honored Aaliyah's life, they also referenced the various team members who also passed during the plane crash. "Aaliyah's family is devastated at the loss of their loving daughter & sister," the official Haughton family statement read. "Their hearts go out to those families who also lost their loved ones in this tragic accident." Blackground wrote: "Blackground is devastated with the loss of our Queen. The example she showed young people will be sorely missed and we hope her short time on earth will be an inspiration to young people all over the world. We are equally distraught by the passing of our Blackground family members Gina Smith and Keith Wallace. Their hard work and dedication were an invaluable contribution to the success of Aaliyah and Blackground. Our prayers go out to all the families."

Virgin Records also chimed in with a statement, saying:

"The worldwide Virgin family is devastated by the news of this terrible and tragic accident and our hearts and thoughts go out to all those families who lost loved ones. Aaliyah, one of the world's brightest and most talented stars, will be mourned by all who loved her and loved her music. Her depth and versatility as an artist was matched by the passion and devotion she had for her craft. We extend our deepest sympathies to the family of Virgin staff member Doug Kratz. Doug was an extremely dedicated and talented professional, whose enthusiasm, energy and spirit will be missed by everyone who worked alongside him every day."

On August 31, 2001, Aaliyah was laid to rest. The funeral took place at the Frank E. Campbell funeral home, located on Manhattan's Upper East Side. It's known as the Funeral Home to the Stars," where everyone from The Notorious B.I.G. to Joan Rivers, Prodigy of Mobb Deep, Jacqueline Kennedy Onassis, Robert F. Kennedy, and even Greta Garbo had their respective services held. Hundreds of fans surrounded the funeral home that day to honor Baby Girl. Celebrities in attendance included Jay-Z, Sean "Puffy" Combs, Lil' Kim, Mike Tyson, Busta Rhymes, and many others.

Rashad Haughton's eulogy for Aaliyah at her funeral was beautiful and poignant. He spoke about losing his sister but also the other passengers who were on board the flight. He compared life to the pages of a book, where collectively they make up a person's whole journey, yet it's through the individual chapters where anything can happen—from happiness to sadness, pain, love, all of it. We can reread those pages as our memories. "God has decided that Aaliyah's book is done," he said, "and now she can sit by his side and enjoy flipping through the pages of her life and finally learn the meaning of the mystery we are all still living here on earth." The two were inseparable. Where you saw Aaliyah, you saw Rashad. They were more than siblings; they were confidants, best friends; and as her brother bravely addressed the congregation, he spoke of the hope that his angel will visit him in many ways throughout his days.

"Baby Girl, I will see your smile in every sunrise and feel the warmth of your touch in its rays. I will remember how your tears cleansed my soul in every raindrop and your kiss like the wind on my face," he continued. "When the birds sing I'll hear your angelic voice resonate through the sky. I'll look at the moon and stars and see the twinkle in your eye, I'll walk the earth knowing that you are everywhere. Looking down from heaven, waiting for your big brother to get there. Hold her for me, God. Amen."

Aaliyah's mother, Diane, released twenty-two doves into the air outside of the funeral home; each dove represented one year of Aaliyah's life. Aaliyah's dove tattoo on her lower back in honor of her late grandmother meant even more now, since she was joining her in heaven. Aaliyah's casket was brought by carriage to the St. Ignatius Loyola Roman Catholic church. The repast was held in Midtown's Cipriani, where thousands of fans showed up outside, flooding the streets. Concurrently, fans on the West Coast in Los Angeles held their own memorial under the billboard for Aaliyah's *Aaliyah* album that sat on Sunset Boulevard. Other pocket cities across the country held their own tiny ceremonies to honor Aaliyah's life, including back home in Detroit where her high school was filled with flowers, photos, and stuffed animals. Her final resting place is in the mausoleum at the Ferncliff Cemetery in Hartsdale, New York. To date, fans still gather every year on both her birthday and the anniversary of her passing to remember a life cut short.

At the MTV VMAs a week later—the event where Aaliyah was scheduled to appear—a short memorial took place during the ceremony. Janet Jackson opened, reiterating what Aaliyah said when her grandmother passed: "One day we will be together again." A fan's letter was read, and then Missy, Timbaland, and Ginuwine took to the stage to honor Aaliyah. Ginuwine called her "one in a million," as Timbaland advised, "Your music will always live on through me." Missy, still in shock, said, "I love you, Aaliyah, and you're forever missed." Rashad, near tears, closed out the moment. Other artists honored Aaliyah throughout the night, including Usher, who wore an Aaliyah T-shirt to present Destiny's Child with the VMA for Best R&B Video.

Even though nearly two weeks had gone by, everyone was still shaken and so confused as to what had happened. Plane crashes are a semi-frequent occurrence in the stories of superstars, but again something with Aaliyah's felt even more inconclusive and open-ended. She was later honored at the BET Awards in 2002, alongside Lisa "Left Eye" Lopes of TLC, who died tragically in a van accident in Honduras on April 25, 2002.

Investigations for the plane crash continued on for years, coupled with various lawsuits that arose in connection to the disaster. With every new dissection of the days/hours/minutes leading up to the crash, new information surfaced that only added to the devastation and confusion. Within days of the crash, it was revealed that the pilot had a criminal record of drug possession in the past. In fact, it was within two weeks of his piloting the plane that Luis Morales III brought a plea of no contest in a Broward County, Florida, court for four felonies, one of which included the possession of crack cocaine. Because there was no guilty plea but an acceptance of sentence, he was sentenced to three years' probation without conviction. A conviction would have inevitably suspended his pilot's license, though despite the license not yet being revoked under the rules of the Federal Aviation Administration (FAA), he was not authorized to pilot the plane. The charter plane company, Blackhawk International Airways, issues certificates for each flight, where a single pilot's name is listed. The certificate for Aaliyah's flight did not list Morales as the authorized pilot. In addition, an autopsy report almost a year later revealed that Morales had cocaine in his urine and alcohol in his stomach when he took flight.

There were a series of misfires in scheduling this trip altogether that left many bewildered when later putting the pieces together to get a clearer picture. To start, the gear, wardrobe, video equipment, and luggage that was flown from Miami to the Bahamas already came with a major warning that there was a weight overload on flight. In addition, the plane that they were using to deliver the cargo was far bigger than the one they attempted to return the passengers and cargo in.

Scheduling the shoot was also done haphazardly. Prior to the Bahamas being chosen as the location for the shoot, Jamaica was also on the short list, along with a different location in the Bahamas outside of Abaco. The clear weather in the forecast led to the hasty decision to move forward with Abaco. Plans weren't even finalized until a week before the shoot was scheduled. Hype Williams's production company,

Instinct Productions, worked with Atlantic Flight Group to handle the travel arrangements, which included brokering the other flights that would carry the cargo as well as flights for the team/talent. Atlantic was working with a company called Sky Limo to charter their planes and Pro-Freight Cargo Service to organize the cargo shipments to the Bahamas for the "Rock the Boat" shoot to continue after the Miami footage was filmed.

In the midst of the hastiness, there was a reckless desperation to cut corners wherever possible. It became clearer and clearer that none of this should have happened at all, right down to the change in location for the video shoot and ultimately right down to the plane taking flight against the aviation guidelines. "These people didn't need to die," Eddie Golson, owner of Pro-Freight Cargo Service, told the *New York Times* in 2001. "This all could have been avoided if they had just followed the rules." During the process for securing the cargo, Golson wasn't given clear calculations as to how much cargo would be packed on one flight, and he was coerced into allowing for some overloading, despite regulations. Once the weight of the cargo came in at 15,000 pounds, it was obvious that multiple flights had to be chartered. After delays in the cargo arriving at the correct destination (they were incorrectly scheduled to arrive in North Eleuthera, over one hundred miles away), everything eventually reached Treasure Cay, the part of Abaco where they were supposed to be. Sky Limo was then advised last minute that the plane scheduled to bring Aaliyah and her team back would not be needed until a day later. The plane Sky Limo had could safely bring everyone back and they were planning to do so until plans had changed. Enter Black-hawk, who was then called to fill in for the newly scheduled

Saturday flight. Instinct Productions later alleged that they had no idea who Blackhawk was or who called upon them for the replacement.

The owner of Blackhawk, Gilbert Chacon, had a criminal record for fraud—including bankruptcy fraud, where he was a player in a $400 million insurance scam with another charter company. A company called Skystream was named as the owner of the Cessna 402-B, with the address of Skystream being listed as Chacon's home address in Pembroke Pines, Florida. Chacon was also known as a reckless pilot (and could have possibly originally been listed on the certificate). Morales started working for Blackhawk a few days before the flight. He had very little previous experience and this flight would be his first . . . and last. An FAA representative later advised that there was no record of this aircraft (with its tail number N-8097W) being scheduled for flights within ten days of the crash.

Three weeks following Aaliyah's plane crash, the FAA inspector responsible for clearing the flight committed suicide.

After the August 25 crash, Gilbert Chacon vanished. He popped up in September to pay back rent to the airport where he rented space for Blackhawk, out in Lantana, Florida. He told the airport manager all about the crash and in the midst of the conversation made claims that Morales was qualified to fly the plane. When the lawsuits inevitably arrived, Chacon was represented by a Fort Lauderdale attorney named Michael Moulis, who was a former FAA prosecutor known for defending charter companies that had violated rules and even caused more crashes comparable to the one involving Aaliyah and her team. Moulis died in 2020. The pieces to the puzzle remained scattered.

Speculations still arose as to why Blackhawk was even cho-sen for the rescheduled flight and who made that call, consid-ering another company had already been chosen to take the team home. The belief they landed on was that Blackhawk was less expensive, so in an effort to cut costs *someone* went with a cheap, disreputable company, which ended the lives of nine individuals, the real precious cargo on the flight. Fighting to jam-pack people and luggage into a smaller and cheaper plane was a move that resulted in catastrophe. Virgin Records was taken to task for cutting those costs when it involved safety, yet again, no one knows who made that final call.

This wasn't the last time there would be money-related issues with Virgin attached to this disaster.

A mortuary located in Nassau, Butlers' Funeral Home & Crematorium, was hired to prepare Aaliyah's body as well as those of the other passengers to be sent back to the States rather quickly. Virgin Records executives Ken and Nancy Berry requested that due to Aaliyah's celebrity status, her prepara-tion be prioritized. Within three days of her death, her body was already prepared and flown on a private jet back to New York City. The cost to prepare Aaliyah and the rest of the bod-ies was in excess of $68,000. It was a verbal deal but a deal nonetheless. Weeks had gone by and no payments were made. Then, Mariah Carey's film *Glitter* was released in September and was a box office failure. Virgin Records took a financial hit and both Ken and Nancy Berry were cut from the label. The label then decided that since neither Ken nor Nancy was still working at the label, Virgin was no longer responsible for the incredibly costly funeral home bill. The Haughtons, as well as the families of the other fallen passengers, all claimed that the financial responsibility was supposed to fall on the label, as agreed upon. The label denied that responsibility, perhaps in an added effort to recoup from *Glitter* in the most dishonorable way possible. After a year, the funeral home was still fighting for their payments.

It was R&B singer Maxwell who reportedly paid for Aaliyah's funeral.

In November 2001, a criminal investigation was begun by the U.S. Department of Transportation, where records were taken from Blackhawk's offices as well as from the home of Chacon—his home address being listed as the same location as Skystream's offices.

In 2002, the Haughton family filed a multi-defendant lawsuit for wrongful death and negligence. The family named everyone from Instinct Productions to Hype Williams, Gilbert Chacon, Blackhawk, Skystream, Atlantic Flight Group, and Virgin Records among others. The only company not named was Blackground. Other suits followed involving Scott Gallin's family, as well as Anthony Dodd's and Eric Foreman's. The attorney in the latter suits described the charter company as "fly-by-night" and said Virgin Records "put profits over people." He posed the question: "Do you think that type of transportation would have been provided for Madonna?"

Other artists even spoke out about the nature of the crash, speculating that Aaliyah's team was partially responsible. Singer Mary J. Blige was very vocal about her speculations surrounding the crash. "I don't even know what to say," she told *106 & Park* years later. "I just know that, that was a murder." She went on to specify that it was a "spiritual" murder, saying, "I could go deeper. For a lot of people I would really have to bring proof." She also expressed to Oprah for *O, the Oprah Magazine* in 2006 her suspicions about whom Aaliyah surrounded herself with and related to the fogginess. "She was surrounded by people who weren't telling her the real deal," Blige advised. "We weren't close friends, but I'd talked with her a couple of times. I very well could've been the woman on that plane." It had many questioning their own mortality but also the notion that a simple switch involving luggage could have ensured that everyone would have survived.

In essence, Aaliyah would still be here.

Aaliyah's wrongful death suit lasted for years in conjunction with the criminal investigation. In September 2003, the Haughton family settled their lawsuit with Chacon, Blackhawk, and Skystream for an undisclosed amount. They also agreed on both sides to keep the details of the settlement completely confidential. By November, a coroner's inquest was opened where the devastating details of how Aaliyah died were revealed by the coroner, Dr. Giovander Raju.

Within two months of the Haughtons settling, Blackground Entertainment opened their own wrongful death lawsuit against Instinct Productions. The suit goes into detail, stating that the relationship between Blackground and Instinct was "long, close, trusting, and professional" and that Blackground had faith that they would keep Aaliyah safe. The complaint was amended to reflect that there was a breach of contract on Instinct's behalf, where neither Aaliyah nor Blackground failed on their part of the agreement and that there was no misconduct. However, there was on Instinct's end, as part of the agreement involves transporting Aaliyah safely and accordingly. Blackground also highlighted the damages they faced following Aaliyah's death. Instinct attempted to have the suit dropped, stating that Aaliyah was an employee of Blackground and therefore they couldn't sue for negligence from a third party when it involved injuring (or in this case killing) an employee. However, in 2004 the courts ruled that Blackground could, in fact, sue. Aaliyah owned 10 percent of Blackground Entertainment and per the judge was its "chief asset," stating "growth and prosperity were primarily the result of its efforts to successfully develop and nurture Aaliyah's career." The following year, however, the tune had changed when the lawsuit was unanimously dismissed by a panel of judges in the Manhattan appeals court. "The concept that a person is a property asset of another is, of course, abhorrent to modern-day thinking," wrote the judges in their dismissal. "Courts almost universally reject the antiquated proprietary view of the master/servant relationship."

In the state of New York, only the next of kin can sue for wrongful death, and since Aaliyah's family had reached their settlement back in 2003, Blackground jumping in to sue for their own damages was nothing short of "frivolous."

There really is no adequate settlement to this case. A tiny plane was overloaded, operated by an unauthorized, inexperienced pilot with cocaine and alcohol in his system, hired by a charter company known for countless ills within the aviation industry. Despite the plane's taking flight on a clear day, the crash was a perfect storm. What remains a mystery is what was the pill that Aaliyah was given to keep her unconscious when she boarded? Was she drugged? There were rumors that the short-lived survivors on the flight mentioned Aaliyah was asleep at takeoff. Could that deep sleep have been achieved synthetically, or was she really just tired with a headache from fighting to not board the plane that she inevitably boarded? Again, what was in the pill? It could have just been an aspirin, but it could have been more, but as Kingsley Russell remarked, the goal was to find a way to get Aaliyah onto the plane when she actively did not want to board it.

Many have later speculated that it was her uncle Barry who orchestrated this whole catastrophe. After all, she was getting bigger than Blackground and might one day leave the label. Hankerson's track record for violence only added fuel to the fire. In 2007, Hankerson was sued for stalking his ex-girlfriend Kyme Dang, including buying (and renaming) the hair salon where she worked, spreading a rumor online that she had AIDS, and blowing up her car in front of her home. In 2012, Blackground agreed to pay Dang $4.6 million, but they never did and she sued Blackground in 2015 for the debt. It would seem highly unlikely, though, that Barry Hankerson would have his own niece killed, especially given the lengths he went to in protecting her in the past. But in the absence of facts, assumptions run wild, leaving space for mind maps that lead to nowhere.

The truth of the matter is that no dollar amount can bring Aaliyah back, no conspiracy theory that this was all planned or determination that this was predetermined by the universe and evidenced by Aaliyah's recurring dreams. No, this was a total nightmare, derived from a star's story that was supposed to have a happy ending. After all that Aaliyah had endured in her twenty-two years, she at least deserved that much. The only solace is that she did leave the planet happy. She achieved everything in her career that she sought out to do, and while there was still so much more to be done, she had made her mark. It was so impactful that little did she know that she would continue to change the world, even after she departed from it.

At the end of her MTV *Diary*, a month before she died, Aaliyah had this to say: "Everything is worth it. The hard work, the times where you're tired, the times when you're a bit sad. In the end, it's all worth it, because it really makes me happy. And I wouldn't trade it for anything else in the world. I've got good friends, and I've got a beautiful family, and I've got a career. I am truly blessed, and I thank God for His blessings every single chance I get."

CHAPTER ELEVEN: LIFE AFTER DEATH

I wanna be seen as an entertainer. When I'm dead
and gone, I want my name to be uttered among the
legends. I want to be remembered as the girl who
did it all.

—Aaliyah, *Honey* magazine, November 2001

"Unfortunately, we weren't talking when she passed. She
wasn't talking to Timbaland, I think her and Missy fell out
as well, but we still had love," Ginuwine told Premier Live TV
in 2020. "It's just the business and when you're young, people
can separate you and you don't know how or why. You just are."

All wasn't well on the home front with Blackground at
the time that Aaliyah had died. It seemed as though it wasn't
specific to the people but their experiences working with the
label. Artists, songwriters, producers (sometimes all of those
titles were within the same person), anyone working within
the Blackground family, had begun to take umbrage at the
fact that they were not being paid appropriately, if at all. With
Aaliyah being the niece of the label head, it made the situation
all the murkier, since how do you defend the creative rights of
those around you while remaining loyal to your family? Power

struggles would seemingly seep in as well, since you're now dealing with a whole team of artists, each thriving in their own ways and now being told to suck it up. Resentment is inevitable.

It was Lauryn Hill who said, "It's funny how money change a situation," and she was right. What was once that "family unit," that "crew," that "posse," those "Supafriendz," was then dismantled in the absence of a paycheck. And while Aaliyah and Timbaland both willfully publicized their dissention on "We Need a Resolution," no one really caught on that they actually *were* in an argument. But tensions were running high, ballooning to the point where they popped once news hit that Aaliyah had passed away. Then things changed. Resentment swiftly transformed into regret. Like most stages of grief, there's disbelief and numbness, before reality sets in, along with inevitable guilt. If the crew was at odds when Aaliyah died, then perhaps this terrible event could bring them back together.

"What touched my heart one time is Missy called me and she said she had a dream and she said she woke up crying," Ginuwine reflected. "I was like what happened? She was like, 'It was about Baby Girl and she told me to tell you that she's not mad at you and that she forgives you.' Dude, we bawled crying, because I always had that empty space in my heart. Do you understand what it feels like to have someone that you love and get caught and they were in a plane accident? Dude, that is horrible. *And* you are at odds? *And* you can't fix it now? Man, that hurt me to death. . . . My heart was just broken."

While everyone was hit hard in their own way, it seemed that Timbaland was hit the hardest.

"Well, Tim . . . it devastated him," Jimmy Douglass says.

"He kind of lost it for a while. He kind of just removed himself for a minute. Of course he and Missy were devastated. Static was devastated." Douglass recalls working with Timbaland in the studio during 9/11, which was just a few short weeks after Aaliyah's passing, and it seemed like the magnitude of that event barely moved Timbaland given the grief he was going through. "[Aaliyah] was like . . . if you were to look at it like a chessboard, she was one of his most important pieces that he had."

There was a magic to Timbaland and Aaliyah working together, yet its potency wasn't fully realized until after she passed away. In her absence, it was clear just how vital she was to the equation. Her career was never viewed by the sum of its parts; rather, it was defined by whom she was working with and how that respective collaboration manifested in her output. It was always this game of chicken versus egg: Was Aaliyah the main ingredient or the producers/songwriters she was working with? Taking Aaliyah out of the equation, the answer became glaringly apparent, for Timbaland. It's not to say that Timbaland didn't move on to become one of the most legendary super-producers that hip-hop, R&B, electronic, and pop music has ever known. However, he continuously lacked that one-on-one kinetic frequency that he plugged into the moment Aaliyah entered his world. We watched his attempts with other artists in earnest. It could be argued that Tweet was the first, despite her arriving earlier than Aaliyah under the Swing Mob umbrella. Then there was Justin Timberlake, whom Timbaland first mentored on his solo debut album, *Justified*, in 2002. By 2006's *FutureSex/LoveSounds*, the two were exclusively working together on the project (with Timbaland's production protégé Nate "Danjahandz" Hills), but it still didn't fully feel like he found his new Aaliyah. He tried it again, working with Nelly Furtado on 2006's *Loose*, as well as cultivating younger talent from Ms. Jade to Tink. And while all of his collaborative projects were groundbreaking in their own ways, they still didn't match what he created with Aaliyah.

Timbaland fell into a deep depression for nearly a decade, fueled by the loss of his muse but also the loss of who many have surmised to be the woman he was truly in love with and lost while they were at odds. He expressed the depths of his grief on the song "Hold On" with Magoo featuring Wyclef (off 2003's *Under Construction, Part II*), where he discusses his pain: "I go through a lot, since my Baby Girl's not here," he says on the track, as Wyclef urges him to "hold on."

Missy also mourned through her music. On her 2002 album, *Under Construction*, she is joined by TLC, as they both grieve their respective losses (Aaliyah and Left Eye) on the song "Can U Hear Me?" The song opens with a voicemail from Aaliyah's mother, Diane, about where Missy can send flowers, as Missy later sings about checking in on Aaliyah's family. "Aaliyah, can you hear me?" she sings on the track. "I hope that you're proud of me."

Static Major recorded an unreleased song called "Aaliyah, Aaliyah," featuring vocals from Aaliyah herself, but the song was pulled from the internet. On it, he sings, "Aaliyah, Aaliyah. Said I miss you, baby. It ain't the same without you, Aaliyah." The devastation was layered, especially as more content was rolled out that Aaliyah had been preparing prior to her death.

On February 22, 2002, *Queen of the Damned* was at long last released into theaters in the United States, six months after

Aaliyah's death. Directed by Michael Rymer, the movie lived at the intersection of music and vampire films and was theoretically perfect for Aaliyah's first major role for a number of different reasons. There's of course the plot line: loosely based on Anne Rice's Vampire Chronicles series (it borrows pieces of her novel *The Vampire Lestat* and of course *The Queen of the Damned*). The vampire Lestat (played by Stuart Townsend) is asleep for years and years, before suddenly being woken up by the loud guitars of a rock band. He then goes on to become the band's lead singer, writing songs that are drenched in darkness but almost leave bread crumbs of clues as to who he really is.

And then there's Akasha, played by Aaliyah. In vampiric history, Akasha is the first vampire ever to be born. She's from Uruk, which in modern times is now Iraq, and her husband was Enkil—the King of Kemet. Kemet eventually became Egypt. In the film, Akasha was also asleep and in the same way Lestat was awoken so was she. Only it was Lestat's music that woke her up.

Considering Akasha became queen of what was later known as Egypt, there was a connection for Aaliyah that she was drawn to, given her aforementioned Egyptian fascination. That and the musical theme that is threaded throughout the movie is another tie that made this film make so much sense for her. The underlying hard-rock theme was new territory, and she doesn't even appear on the soundtrack. But songs like "I Can Be" off the Red Album and her growing love of motorcycles and leather also in a way pulled this all together.

The film received lukewarm reviews but was met with decent box office success, given the budget to make it. *Queen of the Damned* carried a $35 million budget, with nearly $45.5 million in box office sales (around $30.3 million domestically, $15.1 million internationally). Many vampire film fans held it to the standard of 1994's *Interview with the Vampire*, which was a box office smash—taking in $223.7 million in combined box office sales. It was one of the major breakout roles for Tom Cruise, and many had hoped the same would happen for Aaliyah. There was room to accomplish that, but her time on-screen was limited. Aaliyah had technically finished the film, though her scenes were more minimal than anticipated. In fact, she doesn't even appear until much later in the film, and again her time is brief. Her brother, Rashad, had to go back in after her passing to speak over some lines for some scenes. Akasha spoke in a thick Egyptian accent, and at times Aaliyah was difficult to understand. Since Rashad had a similar-sounding voice, he was able to repeat the lines, and their two voices were merged together.

Critics' reviews about Aaliyah's portrayal of Akasha reflected what many already knew: that she would have made a perfect Hollywood starlet in her ability to become the role. In her first scene in *Queen of the Damned*, Akasha enters the nightclub called the Admiral's Arms and annihilates everyone in her path. Her entry, the way she slithered through the room, was one of the most anticipated scenes in the entire film—enhanced by the unfortunate circumstances that happened months before. The magic, however, that Aaliyah revealed in that character was something to behold. She knew how to elegantly combine being a horrific queen vampire with still remaining sexy. While Akasha is supposed to be this dominating intoxicating force, having Aaliyah in the role only made that magnetism greater.

"She was spot-on perfect as the Queen of the Damned," one film blogger wrote in 2002 for Ain't It Cool News, as the blogger had never even heard of Aaliyah until the film. "Her initial scene in which Akasha enters a vampire bar and kills everyone in her path was visually stunning and drew raucous applause. She clearly cared a great deal about doing a good job with this role and it shows. She seems to move in slow motion, catlike. She is mysterious, electric."

Robert Gonsalves from eFilmCritic.com wrote: "Whatever life there is to the movie is what she brings to it; she had star presence, and her eagerness to play a glamorous villain in a big-budget horror movie gives her scenes a lift the film sorely needs." Andrew Manning of *Radio Free Entertainment* agreed, writing: "Aaliyah steals the show as a villainous vampiric vixen in an otherwise ludicrous waste of a story."

Aaliyah was regarded as the best part of the movie, just like with *Romeo Must Die*, only here it was a greater shift from the world she had known. Her previous role was a little closer to who she was, though in this role it was a little closer to what she ended up being, which was immortal.

Vampire film and book fans are a tough crowd by design. They hold their transformative works to a standard, an incredibly high one in fact, where the demand is that the fictional element still somehow feel non-fictional. Not to mention, there is an onus placed on accuracy, where the books must match the films and any other adaptations. There can't be gaps in the narrative (which was a huge gripe with *Queen of the Damned* versus Anne Rice's *The Queen of the Damned*). At the same time, the viewers want to be taken away, brought to another dimension where the paranormal is the norm, simultaneously transfixed by what the underworld has to offer. Without knowing them or the depths of their commands, Aaliyah spoke to them.

It was exactly what Aaliyah would have hoped for; having those unaware of who she was see that film and say, "Whoa, who is *that*?" It's the same reaction most had and still have when they first experience her music, being totally taken, shocked, and awestruck. Her ability to captivate had officially jumped from the CD to the silver screen. The hope for what was to come would include her *Matrix* franchise role as Zee (her scenes were later refilmed with Nona Gaye), keeping her in a somewhat similar lane before diversifying. In 2011 the late Whitney Houston revealed that she wanted Aaliyah to star in the remake of the film *Sparkle* about the Supremes. "This was [Aaliyah's] movie," Houston told *Access Hollywood*. "When we brought it to her, she was so enthusiastic about it and she wanted it, to do it so badly. She was our Sparkle." Her passing caused Houston to shelve the project.

"Unfortunately . . . it just didn't go that way," Houston added. "I put it down. I said, 'My Sparkle has gone to a better place'; then we just left it alone." The film eventually was released in 2012, starring Jordin Sparks. There were so many more films for Aaliyah to appear in, so many more characters for her to portray. The real tragedy is that for those who experienced Aaliyah for the first time through *Queen of the Damned*, it was inevitably their last.

Fans, new and old, started demanding more.

As everyone knew full and well that there was plenty of extra music that could be released in the wake of her passing, the hum on the streets was "Where was it all?" Much like Tupac Shakur,

Aaliyah was a studio fixture, constantly cutting tracks, which at this point would be cherished by her fans, even if they were the roughest of demos. To sate fans, the *I Care 4 U* compilation album was released on December 10, 2002. The project featured most of Aaliyah's hits—spanning from *Age Ain't Nothing but a Number* tracks like "Back & Forth" all the way through to her soundtrack work. Songs like "All I Need," "Come Over" (with Tank as a guest feature), and *Aaliyah* digital bonus track "Erica Kane" were added for good measure, as well as "Miss You" and some behind-the-scenes footage and digital extras. The project reached the Number Three spot on the *Billboard* 200, along with topping the US Top R&B/Hip-Hop Albums chart, while hitting the Top Five on various charts across Europe. It became Certified Platinum in the United States and Gold across Europe. *I Care 4 U* was just the right amount of promise, where fans could embrace it as a "greatest hits" album, yet feel confident that more music would come.

On May 10, 2005, the second (and final) compilation album, *Ultimate Aaliyah*, was released in the UK, Australia, and Japan. Like *I Care 4 U*, the project was a double disc, with the first disc being again a rehashing of the greatest-hits track list (titled as such) and the second disc (titled "Are You Feelin' Me?") adding some more soundtrack B sides, like "Are You Feelin' Me?" from *Romeo Must Die*. Songs like "Messed Up" (a hidden track on the US *Aaliyah* release) were also added, along with some of Aaliyah's guest features like "Man Undercover," "John Blaze," and "I Am Music." Timbaland's dedication to Aaliyah, "Hold On," closes the project. The project didn't chart incredibly high, especially when most of the songs were already released on *I Care 4 U* and the myriad of projects that featured the other songs. As any Aaliyah fan can attest, there was no need for a second housing for any of the songs, since most fans already had the entire catalog.

It was during this time period that promoting Aaliyah's legacy first came into question. Aaliyah was only growing in popularity, even in her absence. New fans started sprouting up, searching for more ways to continue their fandom. However, they were in store for a moratorium that would feel like it would last forever.

CHAPTER TWELVE: PLEASE DON'T STOP THE MUSIC

It ain't gonna work because Aaliyah music only
works with her soul mate, which is *me*.
— Timbaland, REVOLT interview, 2013

On December 8, 2009, Blackground Records released the final project under its record label: Timbaland's third album, *Shock Value II*, the follow-up to 2007's *Shock Value*. What followed was a moratorium on all releases that subsequently found the label defunct yet not formally bankrupt. There's been speculation that if Hankerson filed for bankruptcy he would then surrender ownership of his Blackground catalog, which is why he has yet to do it. However, given his absence from the music business for years, he also lacked the financial stability (and willingness) to pay to have his artists' catalogs uploaded to streaming platforms. It's become a sore spot for every artist involved and the fans who love them. For Aaliyah, Hankerson had multiple roles. Not only was he her record label head, but he executive produced all three of her albums; he was responsible for handling her royalties and her publishing. He was also the man holding on to her masters, as during her transition from Jive to Atlantic, Barry was able to gingerly claim ownership of her work thereafter.

In the wake of Aaliyah's death, however, Hankerson spiraled, and his business was put on hold. One by one, his artists sued him. Toni Braxton—who at one time was managed by Hankerson and later a part of his label—sued in 2007. The heart of the suit was that Braxton felt Hankerson used dirty business dealings to cleverly lure her away from Arista Records to Blackground, while he still managed her. This caused her to ruin her relationship with Arista, though Hankerson alleged that she was dropped from the label over low record sales. Per Braxton, he initially wanted $1 million to only partially free her from her contract, to which Braxton retorted that she was owed over $10 million in losses for going to Blackground to begin with. The 2007 lawsuit also explained that Barry wanted a return on a $375,000 advance; he denied all of those allegations. They eventually settled outside of court. Two years later, Timbaland sued Hankerson over lack of funds for his projects and for also negatively affecting his career as a producer. JoJo sued in 2013, following a long haul of conflicts with Blackground—which included shelving her third album with Blackground for over half a decade and refusing to release her from her recording contract, which was signed by her parents in 2004 and should have ended in 2011. It was settled outside of court, and by January of 2014, JoJo was finally freed from her contract and inked a deal with Atlantic Records. Producers have also filed suits for dirty dealings, and rarely anyone who has participated in anything Blackground related has had a pleasant word to say about the experience.

Artists like Missy Elliott and Ginuwine have been able to

survive unscathed, since neither was signed to Blackground, so they didn't fall victim to the label's pregnant pause, which halted all releases and operations. Timbaland was able to salvage two projects thanks to their being tied to his imprint Mosley Music Group—the aforementioned *Shock Value* and *Shock Value II*. But his projects with Magoo unfortunately have no streaming presence. He isn't alone, though some have found ways around it. JoJo rerecorded her entire Blackground catalog in 2018, which allowed it all to exist on streaming platforms in its new form.

Blackground eventually partnered with an independent music publisher called Reservoir Media, and in 2012 Hankerson sold them part of Blackground. Aaliyah was the bargaining chip, as her masters were included in that deal. Reservoir's CEO, Golnar Khosrowshahi, told *Complex* in 2016 that they planned to pin the Aaliyah release to the tenth anniversary of her passing, but the milestone came and went. There was recorded material left as well. Aaliyah had several songs and parts of songs recorded before she died, over a dozen in fact. It was Hankerson's job (and, if you ask the fans, his obligation) to find a producer who could piece these all together. Since his relationship with Timbaland soured, it would seem impossible for Tim to want to get involved; Missy too. In the same interview with *Complex* in 2016, Reservoir COO Rell Lafargue blamed the lack of new material on Barry's complicated and long-term grief over losing his niece. "Barry can't be in the room when the new music is playing," expressed Lafargue.

It's because of Khosrowshahi and Reservoir that Aaliyah's music had been licensed to newer artists and had doubly kept her relevant. A sample of Aaliyah harmonizing was used on

A$AP Rocky's 2012 hit single "Fuckin' Problems" featuring 2 Chainz, Drake, and Kendrick Lamar off *Long. Live. A$AP.* The track was co-written and coproduced by Noah "40" She-bib. Drake also coproduced under the name C. Papi (he later referred to himself as Champagne Papi). The original sample came from Aaliyah's vocals mixed under Tank's for "Come Over," later repurposed for another posthumous track called "They Say (Quit Hatin')," pieced together with fragments of another unreleased song. Chris Brown was able to credit Aaliyah as a feature on his 2013 track "Don't Think They Know," which was taken from her cut with Playa's Digital Black (with the same title) and also included previously unreleased takes from their recording session. T-Pain even acquired vocals from Aaliyah for a song called "Girlfriends."

The one artist who is probably the most affected by the fickle ways of the presumed estate is Drake. Aaliyah recorded a song in 1999 called "Enough Said," but it was never finished. In 2012, Drake completed the song with Noah "40" Shebib and Blackground in turn uploaded the song to the label's strangely present Soundcloud account. Drake was simultaneously tapped to be the artist who would finally get to create the posthumous album that everyone was waiting for. He made it public, and "Enough Said" announced its arrival. The sixteen-track album was supposed to arrive at the close of 2012, including previously unreleased tracks and vocals of Aaliyah's that would be reimagined into songs with Drake and 40.

Drake and 40 were arguably the perfect pair to handle this project, as outwardly die-hard Aaliyah fans with Drake even sporting a tattoo of her on his body to boot. However, it was 40 who was first approached by Blackground to work on the project. Knowing Drake's shared fandom for Aaliyah, 40 brought him on board. Both Drake and 40 laid the groundwork for the album's arrival.

Months later, Timbaland and Missy Elliott vocalized that they would not be taking part in the project. In an interview with Angie Martinez for HOT 97, Martinez asked both Timbaland and Missy to clarify, as the rumor mill suggested they were a part of the project and then not a part of it. "40 called me, he was like, 'Man, this was not supposed to be . . . it came to me in a different situation,'" Timbaland explained. "It wasn't even about an album, what he was explaining to me. So I didn't know; when everybody would call me, I was kinda like, 'I don't wanna hear that mess.' So stayed out of it until he actually called me . . . but we really removed ourselves from that. I didn't wanna hear nothing about it." Timbaland continued to say that 40 told him he initially only anticipated doing one record and then an album followed. This would explain why Blackground planned to release an album of unreleased songs, along with fragments of vocals that they anticipated would be sewn together by Drake and 40. Still, Timbaland was confused, and from his conversation with 40, it seemed that 40 was confused as well.

When Angie asked if the call came asking them to formally be a part of it, would they do it? Missy advised: "Well, my response would be a little different because I have to respect her family. She has a mother; she has a brother; she has a father that she's very close with. And until they come and say, 'We're ready to do another Aaliyah album,' then I don't really wanna step over and try to get into that." Missy added that while fans like herself would love to hear another Aaliyah album, a time stamp can't be placed upon her family's grief. "Until they come and say, 'We're ready to do an Aaliyah album,' I just feel like moralistically and respect-wise," Missy continued, with Angie completing the thought, "you don't want anything to do with it." Missy's response was, "No."

Timbaland further took umbrage at it a year later, challenging both Drake and Chris Brown for using Aaliyah's vocals in an effort to create whole new songs. "In music, people always say, 'I [wanna] do a song with Aaliyah.' It would never work. Chris Brown got a record, it won't work. Drake can go do a record with Aaliyah. It ain't gonna work because Aaliyah music only works with her soul mate," he told REVOLT in 2013. "Which is *me*." He later apologized to Brown over Twitter for his comments, explaining Aaliyah is a sensitive subject for him.

It was 40 who was crushed the most by the disapproval, over not understanding the complicated dynamic of Aaliyah's estate, family, and fandom. "I was naïve to the politics surrounding Aaliyah's legacy and a bit ignorant to Timbaland's relationship and everybody else involved and how they'd feel," 40 explained to *Vibe* magazine in 2014. "Tim said to me, 'Don't stop. Make the album.' I think that was Tim taking the position of, 'I'm not going to stop you. If you're not going to do it, that's your decision.'" It was Aaliyah's mother who sealed the project's fate, by saying she didn't want the album out. By 2014, it was agreed upon that the project was canned. "The world reacting to Drake's involvement so negatively, I just wanted nothing to do with it," 40 told *Vibe*. "Ultimately, I wasn't comfortable and didn't like the stigma." This wasn't the only instance where artists were approached to utilize Aaliyah's vocals by one representative of Aaliyah's estate, only to be told by another that it's against the family's wishes. It's a confusing game at best, where any artist would give anything to work with Aaliyah, even posthumously. Maybe one day these unfinished tracks will all come to light in the form of a long-awaited new album. Then again, maybe not.

Aaliyah's songs have been sampled numerous times, as everyone from Gucci Mane to Ariana Grande has grabbed a sample or two and added it to their own tracks. Over the years, many artists from DJ Khaled to Kendrick Lamar have even name-checked Aaliyah in their songs, honoring her in little ways.

Over the years, some Aaliyah tracks have leaked. In 2016, one of Drake's songs using Aaliyah's vocals (called "Talk Is Cheap") surfaced. Years prior, "They Say (Quit Hatin')" and "Girl Friends" leaked, along with "Where Could He Be," which was initially supposed to appear on the *Aaliyah* album, and a cover of Donny Hathaway's "Giving Up." Sometimes songs will surface online and immediately disappear. Other times a batch of reference tracks and demos will surface, where Static Major sings and Aaliyah chimes in with ad-libs. Aaliyah's music has even been illegally uploaded to streaming platforms and circulated like wildfire, before promptly being pulled right back down. It's become a mind game, at best. Her videos have all been uploaded to an "official" YouTube channel, though in 2020 it was found that even that channel was managed by a fan and not Blackground. Fans had begun to publicly challenge anyone remotely associated with the distribution of Aaliyah's music over social media, including Reservoir. By the end of 2020, the estate publicly announced they were taking the reins on Aaliyah's YouTube channel.

On August 25, 2017, Reservoir released a statement explaining their place in Aaliyah's legacy, which was to "represent her catalog's songs, songwriters, and copyrights through careful administration and licensing, as it is our privilege to do." They then continued to advise that they do not own her masters, despite the original reported structure of their deal with Hankerson. "While Reservoir is honored to work with songs written for Aaliyah in this capacity, we do not represent any songs written by Aaliyah herself, nor can we act as a distributor of any of her recorded music as a record label would. We do not own her master recordings and thus, cannot make them available for streaming or sale."

Within a few years, Aaliyah was seemingly removed from their website, and in an anonymous email from a Reservoir employee they specify: "We previously published the Blackground catalog, and I'm not able to discuss Aaliyah as we are in a non-disclosure agreement with them."

So the onus, presumably, returns to Barry Hankerson.

As Barry Hankerson continues to hold his catalog hostage, where does that leave an artist like Aaliyah, who has no one but her fans fighting to hear her music?

For years, the only music of Aaliyah's that's been available on streaming platforms is in the form of some scattered collaborations and soundtrack appearances and the entire *Age Ain't Nothing but a Number* album, because it was released by Jive and at the time Hankerson didn't own her masters. That means that once again, R. Kelly becomes associated with Aaliyah's music and success. Not to mention, his publishing points attached to every stream. How is *that* fair? Well, it isn't, but the powers that be have made it this way for decades now.

What it has done, however, is increased the novelty value of Aaliyah's catalog in physical form. Vinyl, cassettes, and CDs all cost upwards of $50 or more on various bidding sites like eBay and other music marketplaces. Her *Aaliyah* and *One in a Million* vinyl records are often sold for hundreds of dollars. For most, it's no longer about opening it and listening to it, either. Aaliyah has become a collectible, which again has prevented her musical legacy from thriving.

The question remains, why is Barry Hankerson holding his niece's music so tightly? While he's hardly spoken publicly on it, many believe that it's because of the overwhelming guilt he's felt for her untimely death, and he is willfully not capitalizing on her catalog as a sign of respect to her mother and brother (since he's the owner of her masters). Conversely, others believe he is waiting for the right time to strike, as if every piece of music held valuable stock potential and he's anxiously awaiting their IPOs. There is no perfect time to strike. No anniversary that will somehow validate the release. The demand for Aaliyah's music has remained consistent, and with every passing birthday of hers or milestone year commemorating her passing, fans anxiously hope that *that* day is *the* day. In the spring of 2020, fans rallied together and formed the hashtag #FreeAaliyahMusic along with an entire Instagram page dedicated to promoting the music, as well as an online petition. The concept started during the COVID-19 pandemic, when Timbaland and Swizz Beatz formed the digital battle between artists called #Verzuz and fans wanted Aaliyah somehow in on it, especially when both Timbaland and Johntá Austin played her music during their respective battles.

There have been a series of undelivered promises on when

the music will finally be released, though some light has been flashed at the end of the tunnel.

On August 25, 2020, representatives for Aaliyah's estate made the following announcement about the status of her catalog on streaming platforms:

> *TO OUR LOYAL FANS*
> *We are excited to announce that communication has commenced between the estate and various record labels about the status of Aaliyah's music catalog, as well as its availability on streaming platforms in the near future. Thank you for your continued love and support. More updates to come.*

They returned again with an announcement on Aaliyah's birthday (January 16, 2021) to state that the music matters "are not within our control" and "unfortunately, take time." The estate collaborated with the company Bumpboxx, and that same day released a limited-run series of Aaliyah-stamped speakers, through which ironically her music can't even be streamed and played.

We may never have the opportunity to hear her unreleased material in full, but by the time these lines are read maybe Aaliyah's released music will be back out in the world. It may even have a new home at a brand-new record label. Maybe Aaliyah will no longer continue to be stigmatized by R. Kelly, since a search on streaming platforms will again only lead to work with his name on it. It's a connection that still haunts her, even when the counterargument is that their association should be wiped from our memory. But how? No one can open streaming sites and listen to her work in succession, marveling at her incomparable growth over seven years. No. They have one album to stream from an anxious fifteen-year-old, hedging her bets on stardom through a predator she thought she loved. Further, through every stream of *Age Ain't Nothing but a Number* there's only one person winning both musically and financially—and that's R. Kelly. Maybe her catalog will finally be released in full and new fans will finally begin to discover her magic, while old fans can relive the glory days of when Aaliyah once walked the planet.

It's a devastatingly open-ended answer to the long-asked question of when can we finally hear Aaliyah's music again?

CHAPTER THIRTEEN: CAME TO GIVE LOVE

I came to spread my love to the fans across the world.
Reach out to you, touch the hearts of boys and girls.

—Aaliyah, "Came to Give Love"

In a world where recognition from your favorite artist is just a retweet away, loving Aaliyah is a thankless job. Still, she has an army ready, willing, and able to fight—assembled and maintaining her legacy for no glory. It's not as if they will be able to show up side-stage at her concert waiting for a wave, or at a meet and greet where she would see her core fans and call them by their names. There's no acceptance speech at award shows, where they can hear her thank them on national television for their decades of loyalty. There's no T-shirt, CD, or press photo for her to sign, where they forever keep the pen. No, these are dedicated fans who exist for the love and the love alone. They excavate through the catacombs of the deep internet, in search of more bread crumbs—though not ones that lead to Aaliyah's whereabouts, since we all unfortunately know that answer. Rather, they lead to new information about her, new photos, new insight on their fallen star, and, if the fans are really lucky, new music.

Considering digital service providers (also called DSPs) like Spotify, Apple Music, and TIDAL are the new norm for how we receive our music—and CDs are practically a thing of the past—the lengthy absence of Aaliyah's music on all of the streaming platforms almost did more to amplify the magnitude of her legacy for new fans, especially. Kids born after her passing are not used to a world where they're told no, especially in an era where the solution to every problem is "there's an app for that." There's something dynamic about this Generation Z and their willingness to fight for something they want, whereas the generations before them (Generation X, Xennials, and even Millennials) sort of surrendered to the notion that they would just never hear Aaliyah in digital form. They hug her CDs tightly, probably have some ripped MP3s on their computers (since they're all a part of the Napster generation), and if they were proactive (or have $100 for eBay) they have Aaliyah's vinyl. Generation Z is different. They mobilize and form mini armies, complete with petitions and demands for the music they want to hear and projects they want to be seen. They also worked harder to be Aaliyah fans. They don't remember her heyday; most weren't even alive when she was. They've learned about Aaliyah from their parents now, or they catch on to the references made from artists out today. The point is, Aaliyah is now their Bob Marley. She's their Jimi Hendrix, their Kurt Cobain, Janis Joplin, John Lennon, Jim Morrison. She's their fallen idol, an iconoclast who is the reason their favorite living singers even have a shot at fame.

But with this fandom comes great responsibility. It's more than wearing a shirt with her face on it or putting a friend in their peer group on to her music. These fans—both new and old—are keeping her legacy alive. Through them, new fans are born, and so the movement continues. For some, it's a whole other job. They dedicate hours of their day to working toward this cause—by either creating graphics or digging through countless magazine articles and uploading them to the web, ripping old video interviews to social media—and they're not paid to do it. So why continue on this mission? The answer is quite simple.

Aaliyah loved her fans. So much so that she wrote a whole song about them. Right before she passed, her fans had a real surprise when she hopped on the message boards for her website, Aaliyah2001.com. It was the first real time she came on the boards to spend significant time, and as fate would have it, was her last. She came on July 27, 2001, to tell the fans that there were some technical issues they were working through. "When I can, I'll occasionally check in myself but I really hope you like what we're doing here," she wrote. "Peace & Blessings, A."

Aaliyah then came on again three weeks before her death, on August 2, 2001, to tell fans that she would soon be looking for message board moderators. "I'm still learning this stuff, but it's all very exciting," she said, before letting everyone know that she would be hanging around for a bit to answer some questions. When she was asked about her next single and video, she replied, " 'More than a Woman.' We're working out the details now." Before she left, she told her fans that she loved them. These screenshots from her now-defunct website have filtered through fan forums and Instagram pages for two decades as cherished relics of the last real time that Aaliyah spoke directly to her fans. "It was always a shock where someone would just have a general conversation starter and she would go on there and just respond to something," remembers Aaliyah2001.com board moderator Tonica Johnson, known online as Strawliyah. "She was just so cool and laid back, it was like she was one of us. It was always a real surprise whenever she did respond to something you were talking about, rather than a question directly to her or just in general to everyone reading it." Johnson heard that Aaliyah signed another fan's guest book on their fan page, which led her to build up her fan page Aaliyah Unleashed in the hopes of the same happening for her. To date, Aaliyah Unleashed is one of the longest-running Aaliyah fan sites created while she was still alive and continues on in her absence. "I felt like when she was there everybody was just trying to be as close as possible to her and connect to her, and it was like having a trophy or an award whenever she acknowledged a post you made," Johnson continues. "After she died, I would say things did change a little bit because everyone just got a little closer and got to know each other a little bit more, and we just more so went from strangers to family." For those who were on the boards back then, it was in real time, but even for those accessing these screenshots even years later, it's like she was still speaking to them, showing she cared about their experience and letting them know that she loved them. Eventually, Aaliyah2001.com ceased operation and Aaliyah. com was formed. "The fact that her family set up the website was a beautiful thing for fans to take part in, and we greatly appreciated the opportunity to have a home to go to," remembers Bashir Faddoul, whose online handle was 22Aaliyah2001. "There were so many kind, generous, and creative members who would design 'blends' or 'siggies' of different Aaliyah images, we had 'Blend Awards' where artistic fans created graphic images and were rewarded, fans shared poems about Aaliyah, rare pictures, and fond stories/memories of how they discovered Aaliyah. We worked together and were excited about sharing Aaliyah's music and her legacy, and many of us worked tirelessly to keep it alive and strong." Faddoul also ran the Aaliyah pages on both MySpace and Facebook following her passing. "Back then, we used to wish for an Aaliyah wax statue at Madame Tussauds, as well as a Hollywood Star on the Walk of Fame . . . and of course an Aaliyah movie for the big screen," Faddoul continues. "I am still in contact with, and even met many fans from the message boards over the years while visiting Aaliyah's resting place, participating in nine Revlon Run/Walks for Cancer as Aaliyah's Cancer Awareness Angels. They are all my friends for life and we are connected by our bond that is simply being Aaliyah fans. All I've ever tried to do is keep Aaliyah's legacy alive so that others can learn about her and how great of an entertainer she was."

Over the years, the fandom has only grown, and it varies in levels of both affection and intensity. Some outlier fans will simply pen fan fiction about her, while others take it to another level and state that they are the love children of Aaliyah's, suggesting she carried a baby to term in secrecy. Some fans act as mediums, holding seances on Instagram Live where they claim to be speaking to Aaliyah from the dead and request that viewers ask questions, which have included "Were you murdered?" and "Was Damon Dash the love of your life?" Others will play her music backwards, alleging that they hear messages of help or, even further, that she is addressing the Illuminati. Then of course there are the fans who will travel across social media, policing any mentions of Aaliyah's name and correcting any revisionists on historical facts, which even include knowing the exact person who gifted her every ring on her finger in photos. These fans vary in age, from as young as twelve and thirteen to as old as even fifty-plus, and they are from all corners of the world.

When they mobilize, amazing things have happened.

In July 2015, two fans named Regina Allen and Traesha Burke tweeted to Rashad Haughton about pushing to have an Aaliyah cosmetics line for MAC. What followed was a petition with twenty-six thousand signatures, requesting that MAC create the line. In June 2018, MAC announced the release of MAC x Aaliyah, featuring makeup that referenced her hit singles, with a replica of her autograph on the packaging. Eric Ferrell was the creative lead. Washington Football Team cheerleader Ashley Dickens was one of the fans who helped push the petition forward and was recognized for it. Dickens became popular with other fans, where every Halloween she would replicate various Aaliyah looks, starting with "Rock the Boat." When Dickens saw the petition for MAC, she felt it was a no-brainer to support it. "I was sending the petition to people, getting them to sign it when it came out," Dickens remembers. "I was in line at the store like seven AM. I was the first in line, then I immediately put out a review for the makeup line on YouTube and Rashad happened to see it, and he loved it." From that point on, Dickens served as one of the fans assisting with some promotional materials and providing feedback, including on the Aaliyah app. She was also invited to Las Vegas in 2019 for Aaliyah's wax figure unveiling at Madame Tussauds. Again, that figure happened after years of fans pushing for it.

The fans have also been instrumental in assisting the estate with their official releases, including the aforementioned Aaliyah app, and the Aaliyah fragrance developed with her family and Austin-based perfumery Xyrena back in 2015. It's also backfired, when fans expected music in 2020 and instead were met with an Aaliyah jigsaw puzzle, which led to a tsunami of backlash on social media.

Younger fans had enough and wanted to voice their frustration publicly. The fan-derived #FreeAaliyahMusic hashtag was also met with a petition to release her music, and an Instagram account that facilitated the petition. "I was frustrated that her first album is the only one available for streaming," says Nathan Hamlet, the fan who started @FreeAaliyahMusic. "I was so confused; where's the rest of her catalog? So we all came together and we set up this page to continue the legacy as she wants to be remembered: an entertainer. But we also want to let the world know that her music is missing for quite a few years now." Hamlet is eighteen, a younger fan who first learned about Aaliyah from his mother. Twenty-year-old Terrell Benson echoes a similar sentiment. "There are certain people that you just connect to and you're like, 'Wait a minute, now I have to protect this person, and I have to help this person's legacy,'" he says of Aaliyah. He first formed the Instagram page @AaliyahMemes but later formed @AaliyahsHistory, which included facts about the singer and new information as it surfaced. "It was about spreading positivity," he adds.

"The younger fans didn't get to have the same experience older fans had with her music," says Aali Cortes, a thirty-year-old graphic designer who services multimedia to fan pages. "We have CDs and I still even have an iPod with her music somewhere, so these younger fans are really just fighting for their own experience with her music like we had." Cortes is a longtime Aaliyah fan, who even had his name legally changed to Aali and has dedicated the greater part of his graphics career to assist in her visual legacy. "I learned how to draw when I was thirteen, because I wanted to draw her," he expresses of Aaliyah. "And that was my first inclination that there was something within me that I wanted to express when it came to her, whether it was for her or for her to other people. So I learned how to draw and quickly found Photoshop after that, and the rest as they say is history. I think I provide a different kind of artwork, very much entrenched in emotion and legacy and wanting people to think of Aaliyah in the bigger picture."

International accounts like @WeLoveAaliyahHaughton, @Aaliyah_Spain, and @AaliyahAlways have become global hubs, where fans from across the world connect. "The interesting part is, you can be friends with an eighteen-year-old, because you share this commonality, and there's nothing weird about it, because it's a shared community," says Frances Kondis, who manages the Australian-based account @AaliyahAlways. "You're all exchanging information and having conversations about this core subject, which is something that in modern society doesn't really exist." Kondis also had a limited-run Aaliyah merch line, which she coordinated with the estate. She is now a director of sorts for other fan sites to refer to for fact-checking and exclusive content. "She continues to inspire me daily, in the way she treated people and the way she lived her life," Kondis says of Aaliyah. "I try to always keep that in mind often. What would Aaliyah do? I try to hold myself to that same standard, even now at thirty-six years old. I still look to her like she was way older than me."

Erica Dove manages the widely popular @AaliyahHaughton Instagram account, and while the mononym @Aaliyah page exists, it's Dove's that has become a destination. "Aaliyah worked so hard, and just seeing other artists' legacies—like Michael Jackson's and even Selena's—I just feel like it's an obligation to help Aaliyah's," Dove explains. "Aaliyah was so much more than an entertainer for us, so I try to do my part." That includes not only sharing Aaliyah news and posting exclusive photos of Aaliyah but also sharing fan contributions and their own re-creations of Aaliyah's looks. It's as if she's taken the lead and continued celebrating fan participation in a way that the official account should have done. "It just breaks my heart that her music is just collecting dust," the twenty-five-year-old continues, though she's amassed an extensive collection of original vinyl, CDs, and cassettes through online digging and visiting various record stores with her father throughout Houston.

And then there is UK-based @AaliyahArchives. The page, run by graphic designer Sandhya Nandra, feeds into her site AaliyahArchives.com, which has become a music industry standard for all things Aaliyah. The site functions as a timeline of Aaliyah's history, where fans can find rare Aaliyah articles, photos, videos, information, and interviews. The site relaunched on January 16, 2021, complete with a message board that was a callback to Aaliyah's original site. As news about Aaliyah continues to circulate, Nandra keeps the Archives running. As a fan since childhood, thirty-two-year-old Nandra recognized that so much of Aaliyah's content was missing from the internet, leaving newer fans especially unaware of the singer's deep history. "Back in 2013, I wasn't seeing anything as a fan in terms of archiving Aaliyah's legacy and also keeping fans up to date on what's been going on," Nandra expresses. "I wanted to create a place where fans can come together and have a source of information—finding information that they normally wouldn't find elsewhere. I wanted to do justice by Baby Girl, which in my opinion is what her estate should be doing."

Over the years, Aaliyah's fan base has formed a sense of community unlike no other. While Beyoncé's Beyhive or Nicki Minaj's Barbz will often scour social media in an effort to challenge the latest bit of information that has trickled in from their favorite artist's news cycle, Aaliyah's fans are fighting for her survival, since she's no longer here to fight for it herself.

Call them what you want: Aaliyah Army, Team Aaliyah, Aaliyah's Angels, Young Nation, Down with the Clique, or even, as Diane Haughton affectionately calls them, Special Ones: these fan hives are responsible for keeping Aaliyah at the forefront of everyone's minds. They're the ones who have maintained her legacy—from YouTube to the MAC counter. They fight for her memory and their right to preserve it. They now refer to themselves as Aaliyah's Estate and in a way they're right, because they are the true gatekeepers to demystifying Aaliyah while simultaneously still protecting her. The only thing that's been missing is her music, which for them is really the only gift they want in return. Hopefully it won't last forever, this inconclusive, open-ended legacy. It's the words of young Nathan Hamlet that really sum it all up: "I don't feel like Aaliyah will be completely at rest until her music is back out in the world," he says. "Her music was her life, and she wanted us to hear it."

It's the next generation who feel it the most, especially when they discover her and then learn that she's gone. It's like they've just met her and now lost her; a different kind of grief.

In a strangely unique way, this is their answer to the question: *Where were you when you heard that Aaliyah died?*

CHAPTER FOURTEEN: 4-PAGE LETTERS

F ans from all around the world have written letters, either to Aaliyah or about Aaliyah, to show their appreciation for her.

In one of her last interviews, Aaliyah said something that resonates with me during hard times in my life. She had just released her self-titled album on July 7, 2001, and flew to Paris, France, for promotional work. Resting on the couch, visibly jet lagged but still her classy and good-natured self, Aaliyah said referring to her career as a singer: "Rejection is painful, but I felt deep in my heart and in my soul that I had it and that I would do it and that I could do it. And I honestly believed that, no matter what anybody said. And I continued and I said 'fine, you don't want me, somebody else will. And I will prove it; I will get out there and I will be a star.' And I really meant it. And you have to have that frame of mind, you have to have that kind of confidence to make it in this industry or you won't make it. So I did it and I'm very proud of the fact that I did."

Aaliyah's story is full of rejection—from her losing on *Star Search* as a ten-year-old to being turned down by countless record labels who did not believe in her. Then, during her 1994 debut, she faced unfair ridicule and sexism following the marriage scandal. Even today, years after her passing, naysayers continue to deny her talent and question her everlasting legacy. Despite these almost career-ending struggles, Aaliyah remained as resilient and radiant as a diamond under thousands of years of pressure. She never lost her grace, like a ballerina with painful blisters on her feet. No matter what happened, her faith never waned and she worked tirelessly for everything she wanted. By 2001, she achieved all her dreams—from releasing platinum hits to starring in blockbuster movies. Aaliyah became a model, actress, singer, entertainer, and role model for young people around the world.

I always aspire to be like Aaliyah—to weather the storms with no hair out of place, always poised and lovely, and with my confidence intact. As I go through the rejections of life—those painful job interviews, when no one believes in me or my dreams, and when others try to put me down—I remind myself that Aaliyah faced similar hurdles, picked herself up when she fell, tried again, and never gave up. Even as a young girl, her brother, Rashad, recalled her staying behind after losing on *Star Search*, drying her tears and watching the rest of the show. She pursued her dreams at full speed with no brakes, knowing that, with her hard work and the support of God and her loved ones, she would make it. And she did it.

Aaliyah taught me that you can achieve your goals and all your dreams can come true with hard work and strong faith. When you feel your hope fading and your dreams are billions of miles away, remember her beautiful advice: "Keep working hard and you can get anything that you want. If God gave you the talent, you should go for it. But don't think it's going to be easy. It's hard!"

Yordel Jackson

Age 24

Toronto, Ontario

Dear Aaliyah,

When I hear your name, there's always one memory that instantly comes to mind and fills me with happiness. I think of the night you performed "Journey To The Past" during the Oscars in 1998. I was so thrilled to see you share your magic on such a huge night, and I made my mother sit on the couch with me and watch your big moment. You looked beautiful as always, and I beamed at the sight of you in a beautiful gown. Your fans had only seen you in your cool baggy jeans aesthetic. It's just one of the lasting impressions you've left on my life.

You came into my musical existence when I was 11 years old, a time when I was so shy, quiet, and only confident about school. In you, I saw a role model to help me find my way, and you validated some of my traits. You modeled calm, quiet confidence for me at a time when I needed it most. And in my way, I adopted you as my big sister. Now that I'm an adult, I think of the memories you didn't get to make in your own life. Would you have done more movies? Or perhaps launch a MAC collection yourself, designed with your personal touch? What would have been? Decades later, your music sounds as current (and dare I say, even better) as music on the radio today. Babies are still named after

you, and teens wear T-shirts with your likeness all the time. I
picture you growing as timeless as one of your idols, Sade. In 22
years, you showed us a full, warm, kind, beautiful life well-lived.
And I carry your memory with me as long as I am on this earth.

With all the love in my heart to our little purple star,

Jada Gomez

Dear Aaliyah,

Words could never begin to describe the impact you've had on
my life. Not just as a girl growing up, but as a performer. What
I've taken away from you is the constant need to stay true to
myself and my heart's happiness. Your effortless and unapologetic
authenticity continues to light the way in the lives of artists of
all forms. *One in a Million* was the first album I ever owned as
a young and heartbroken girl. Still trying to make sense of my
parents' divorce and getting used to a new normal, your voice
and music was my constant escape. It essentially sparked my
desire to express myself as an artist on stage.

I choke back tears as I write this because it's still difficult to
accept that this ever-changing world of the arts moved forward
without such a guiding bright star. We never felt entirely worthy
of your genius, but we sure were ready for it, Baby Girl. So
up with the greats you are, where your untouched legacy
continues to live on in the hearts of us all . . . How fortunate
we all were to live in your radiating era of brilliance, style and
otherworldly energy. Aaliyah, I will forever be grateful to you . . .
For Everything.

Love you Li-Li,

Margarita N.

Dear Aaliyah,

Your music is timeless

Your beauty is ethereal

Your humility is warm and inviting

Your style unparalleled

"Street but sweet" as you would call it

Mixing the gritty and rawness from hip-hop with that beautiful soul sweetness from R&B

Truly making you *One in a Million*

Your talent remarkable

Recreating the face of hip hop and R&B

Your soft airy angelic voice with jazzy undertones layered over futuristic beats

I feel like I've known you for eternity

Having a spiritual and emotional connection to you

Like you're somewhat of a guardian angel

I look to you for reassurance and advice

You and your music are one thing I know I can count on to make me feel better no matter what

It pains me to know that you're not here

That I never got to see your face

Or witness your stunning beauty and charm

I'll never get to hear you laugh I'll never get to see you smile

I'll never be able to tell you how much I love your music and thank you for truly being yourself

It's hard to believe that you actually once graced this earth

Because you truly were an angelic individual

I know you're up there with God looking down at all of your fans and still appreciating us for supporting you

Although you're gone I still feel your presence through your music

I know that I can count on you

And that if I ever fail at something all I need to do is dust myself off and try again.

J. R., Age 16

Battle Creek, MI

Dear Aaliyah,

I was 11 years old when I discovered who you were. I remember seeing your music video, "Are You That Somebody?" and I instantly loved you. I was simply captivated by your talent from dancing and singing. The two things I have always dreamed of becoming and you embodied the very essence of who I wanted to be. I asked my mom to buy me the *Doctor Dolittle* soundtrack and she also bought me a boombox. I carried that boombox with me everywhere I went that Summer replaying your song over and over again. I studied your music video and copied your moves as best as I could. Fast forward, you got into acting and you played a role of a woman who fell in love with Jet Li. Jet Li is of Asian descent and someone who looked like me was on the big screen and played a role with someone I looked up to. I just felt so confident that one day I could also cross paths with you. It truly broke my heart when I found out that you died . . . how you died. You had so much more to give and so much more to do. I even made Aaliyah tribute mixtapes. You are definitely one of my inspirations, how I fell into music and turned it into a career. Thank you for that. I love you and miss you. If you are seeing this or hearing this, I hope you are proud of me.

-CYD

Aaliyah was truly "one in a million"—a huge talent, a constant innovator, a true beauty, an icon. But her biggest impact to me was being like a big sister to me. Although Aaliyah will never know, she held my hand during many struggles, big and small.

She made dressing like a tomboy acceptable, sexy even. She was effortlessly cool and stylish. Sure, she wore designers sometimes, but more often than not she wore brands the everyday girl could cop. The Aaliyah look was unique, but accessible.

Baby Girl, like me, was petite. I was incredibly insecure, but Aaliyah was the picture of confidence and she helped me to accept the body I was gifted. Our bond went deeper than that though. Aaliyah wasn't the biggest talker, but she was a calculated speaker who I could've sworn left messages just for me.

In early August 2001, Canada's music channel, MuchMusic, announced Aaliyah was going to host one of the final episodes of the iconic urban music show "Da Mix" in September. I was going to have the opportunity to finally meet my hero, my "big sister." I was prepared to cut school for the first time ever just to line up and be sure to get a good spot and hopefully have the chance to speak with her. I still mourn that lost opportunity. I mourn the loss of promise and opportunities she had laid out in front of her. It felt like my "secret find" was finally going to cross over. But more often I celebrate her accomplishments, her perseverance and persistence, her big heart and her eternal talent. She accomplished her dreams. And although she's an iconic public figure, I'll cherish the intimate memories she left me with.

Carol Santos
Baby Girl's "sister" in Toronto, Canada

When "Back & Forth" came out, I could tell that an infatuation with Aaliyah was imminent. I was immediately entranced with her dance moves, her flawless style, her angelic voice and of course, her often imitated never duplicated swagger. As crazy as it sounds, I felt like I knew her intimately, even though she just was a 2D image on a magazine page or on television. As a tom boy myself, she empowered me to always stay true to myself and she taught me that "Tommy Boy Fly" (thank you Rapsody!) meant I could have a little tom boy style, but I could remain feminine and sexy by adding a little Aaliyah flare. My sister and I spent weeks trying to learn the choreography to "Are you that Somebody?", realizing rather quickly that we were not up to par with her moves! She was the ultimate embodiment of cool, and stayed so humble throughout her success and her music always brought me joy and comfort. Her passing was devastating, especially so soon after the release of *Aaliyah*, an album which exhibited a growth in not only her maturity as a person, but her talent and breadth as an artist. It seemed so unreal, hearing that news on the radio while working my summer job—my heart sunk and I thought endearingly of her life as an artist, icon and someone who changed how I live every day. I will always remember her, will honor her goddess energy as often as I can, and will always be thankful and helpful for the imprint she has left on my life and her fan base around the world.

Forever in my heart, Baby Girl.

Maggie S, 38

Brooklyn NY

Dear Aaliyah,

Not a day goes by that I don't think of your kind spirit every day. Ever since I listened to your song "Try Again" on the radio, I was always curious asking myself, "Who is this woman with the most beautiful, timeless, angelic, calming voice my ears had ever heard?" Not knowing you were already gone at the time, your voice did stay in my mind for the longest. It wasn't until I heard you again from the song "Where Could He Be?" that caught my attention even more so to speak. Hearing your voice and hearing that mysterious vibe really not only gave me chills, but inspired me to do the same. I never thought I learned so much from you. Not just your singing, but your personality in general. From your fashion sense to your kindness and hard work and dedication all around. Your tomboy street style has really transcended the next generation. Looking at your style, evolution was even more fascinating, learning that you wore custom made or recycle version of regular t-shirts to beautiful fashion staple blouses around 2000—especially hearing the stories from your great friends like Kidada Jones and your stylist Derek Lee on how your style came to be. But one thing I love about you more is that how confident you are with everything coming in your way, good or bad. Even if you fall, you came back up. You absolutely competed with yourself to be the best. That's what inspired me the most about you. And I'm grateful to be influenced by you. Even though I never got a chance to meet you, but I will forever remember you as an artist, icon, and a kind-hearted person. And always, I will talk about you to the next generation like me.

We love you and miss you BabyGirl.

Love, Arce

Age 18

California, USA

Dearest Aaliyah,

Since the first time I saw you in "Back & Forth" music video, I got a connection right away with your energy, and your incredible voice. I identified with your style, and I loved the way you wear bandanas, as I used to wear. You inspired me, not just in your style, but also your own way, just for being who you are. You're so kind and wonderful with everybody. Not satisfied to see just one music video and hear one song, I searched for all your discography and see all the interviews, trying collect your CDs, read magazines about you. However, I know that never will be enough to really know you for real. You are definitely one in a million, that's why I made this letter. It isn't four pages, but is enough to express how much I love you. As fans, we will never let your legacy be forgotten. You was on earth. Everything that you strive for, and I'm extremely proud for who you were, our everlasting BabyGirl.

Maria Estela

Age 19

Brazil

Aaliyah is part of my life from a real long time. I remember discovering the "Age Ain't Nothing but a Number" single which was part of a compilation album that my father had bought. I was 7 and I never forgot this song. Few years later when I was a teen, I really discovered the whole talented artist Aaliyah was but it was a too short time before Aaliyah's sudden death. My passion for her made me improve my English, I wanted to understand everything she sings and I wanted to understand every interview I could find. So I started translating her songs and I shared my passion with her French fanbase. Thanks to Aaliyah I learnt English, I've never been abroad during my studies but my English became good enough to teach it. I can't really explain everything she represents to me, but anyone knows me knows that Aaliyah is a huge part of my life. My last tribute to her was to dance on her music for the opening of my wedding ball and I'm glad that thanks to that, people could still discover her music and share my passion for her. Aaliyah will never be forgotten, and I hope to have a daughter one day to name her after the incredible woman Aaliyah was.

Farah Benrehab

Age 32

Paris, France

Dear Aaliyah,

From the moment 5-year-old me saw you walking on walls with Jet Li, I knew you were the coolest girl in the world! In that moment, that was it—I wanted to be just like you when I grew up. Aaliyah, you have remained a constant in my life. There through it all: joy, grief, graduations and relationships. At 15, the Red album got me through a painful loss, it was one of the first things I found real joy and life in when everything around me felt grey.

Today, 25-year-old me still looks up to you. Your authenticity, sunny disposition, and the way you carried yourself still inspire me. From you, I have learned the importance of staying true to myself, to compete only with myself, and remain graceful through the ups and downs. These are the greatest gifts of all. Thank you for meaning so much to so many. Love and miss you, always.

Ikra, 25

London, UK

I started listening to Aaliyah not so long ago, so I'm not one "of the old" fans. But in my opinion, I could definitely be classified into the club of Aaliyah's real fans. Aaliyah was truly an angel on earth. She was incredibly pretty, funny and kind. Not to mention that she was extremely classy. She didn't need to show much to be looked at. Even when she was fully dressed, she could have all eyes on her 'cause she had that rare beauty. Aaliyah was the person that was loved by all of the people that were surrounded by her and nobody had to say something negative about her.

These are only some of the main features of her personality, that made me such a big fan, besides her amazing talent in music. Aaliyah's voice was so angelic. It was smooth and peaceful, but at the same time it was strong and was well controlled by her. Aaliyah had the kind of voice that you are able to listen to for hours and not get tired of, or get used to and that is something that you can rarely find in a singer. Not even one of her songs is tedious and all of them give you peace. These were only a little information for people that do not know much about her, but would love to get to know her a little bit more, just like I did. Aaliyah, if I could tell you one thing that would be that I truly love you. I love your character, your strength, your voice, your songs and your humor. I wish with all of my heart that you would still be here to bless us with your talent and to see how much we the fans and all of the people that were close to you, love you. I wish that you could be here to enjoy life and its beauty. I wish that you could be here to see what an impact you have to generations to this day, about two decades later. I want to be sure, as a fan, that I will keep your legacy alive and that you and your incredible talent, will never be forgotten. I miss you and I hope that you have found serenity.

With eternal love,

Angeliki Mavra, Age 20

Greece

Aaliyah, I wish I had the possibility to be alive around the same time you were rocking the whole world. I can't properly express how you affected and changed my life. I was born two years after your death, but eventually, in my childhood, I got familiar and I fell in love with your distinctive, angelical and precious voice, alongside with your brilliant work. And this passion just grew stronger, you helped me throughout my teenage years, high school, and now as I'm reaching adulthood, my love for you couldn't be more powerful. Your legacy won't ever be forgotten, and your art will forever transcend generations. Thank you for everything. Keep resting in paradise, Baby Girl.

Reydnée Souza

17 years old

Brazil

Dear Aaliyah,

I still have trouble accepting the fact that you're gone at 31, so I just won't. I struggled on whether to submit this or not because my feelings about you I hold dear to my heart and anyone who knows me knows this. But as I sit and reflect on the last 19 years without you, I think it's only right that the world knows how I feel. I know God doesn't make any mistakes, so even questioning why seems wrong, so I won't. . . I just know that you should be here. . . Your style your street but sweet smooth angelic voice your mysterious persona such a rare soul that is much needed in today's time . . .

I remember getting pregnant at 15 and a classmate asking how's Aaliyah and I'm like huh and they're like your baby and I'm like oh I might name her that and them being completely flabbergasted that I didn't . . . And I couldn't, Aaliyah, no one could ever live up to your name, the soul, the woman behind that . . . I remember the group home staff taking me to Ferncliff to see you at 14 twice, risking her job because she knew how much you meant to me . . . You were my heart . . . I remember the fire department telling the staff at Little Flower Children's Services it was a fire hazard having your pics wallpapered on my wall and them allowing me to keep them on until I left . . . Aaliyah, I still have your name etched on my leg that I did at 11. My house embodies, you my daughter sends me news clippings and people all over (even your friends) now follow me because they know they feel the genuine love I've always have, but I know no one loves you more than Mama Diane, so I'm content with being called the special one (the nickname Mama D gave a few of us, including rednyc).

Whenever I have a bad day, your song comes on so I know that's your own little way of assuring me everything will be ok . . . Until we meet again sweet LiLi . . . Some people come into our lives some people go . . . Some stay for a while and leave footprints on our hearts and we are never the same.

Love Always, Your Special One,

Lesley Lyons

Age 31

Brooklyn, NY

Dear Aaliyah,

Almost two years ago I discovered you by way of a Chris Brown song "Don't Think They Know." When I heard your voice, I was mesmerized. At the time, I didn't know you had passed, so I found your other music on YouTube and I was blown away. Soon after, I found out you had passed almost 17 years ago. This made me want to do some research into what you were like, what was your character, who did you work with, and why you died. Doing some digging, I've listened and watched your interviews and noticing what a sweet humble spirit you were.

On August 25th, 2001 at 6:50 pm the world lost a star, who was gonna shine even brighter than you already were. I noticed over the 2 years I've known about you we have some things in common. Like our love for Egypt, music and art. We were so robbed Aaliyah, I wish I could just go back in time and tell you not to get on that plane. You like so many others have inspired my love and appreciation for music and art. And all I want to say is Thank You, AALIYAH.

Peace and Love,

Z., Age 15

Indiana

Dear Aaliyah,

Ever since I can remember, you have always came across my TV screen and your songs played on the radio frequently when I was younger. You stood out to me so much that one day I just screamed to the top of my lungs "MOM WHO IS THIS, WHAT'S HER NAME!?" when she replied "Aaliyah." I was totally mesmerized. I wasn't even in kindergarten yet. You definitely had me at a young age. My eyes were glued to the TV when your videos came on and I tuned out any other noise in the car when your songs played on the radio. As I grew older, I noticed I always seen the same videos, never seen you at any award shows that I would watch and heard the same songs from you. I took it upon myself to find more from you and that's when I discovered you were no longer with us.

I was born in 2003. I was 9 years old at the time I realized you were gone. I was beyond hurt because I would think in my head all the time, "I would love to go to an Aaliyah concert" or "I wanna meet her," and to know I didn't get to experience you while you were here on this earth made me sad, but at least I have your music, movies and fashion that has inspired me and millions of others around the world to remember you by. I didn't realize how much you were an inspiration to me (other than listening to your music) until I became a teenager. I would watch all of your old interviews and you taught me that there is nothing wrong with being you and being original. You taught me that if I work hard for what I want in life, I will get it. When I strive for something that I want and I get tired and want to quit, I think of why I'm doing it and why I can't quit, but I have also thought, "What would Aaliyah do??"

I learned from you that I don't have to ever put myself against anyone to come out the greatest. That is why my favorite quote from you will forever be, "I'm competing with myself to be the best." There isn't a day that goes by where I don't think of you and what you could be doing if you were still here. I just want you to know that you're an inspiration to me and your impact is still felt by many, including people like myself who didn't experience you while you were here. Thank you for the unmatched beauty, talent and timeless music that you have shared with us in your lifetime. Thank you for always being so humble, and so kind. Thanks for being a role model to me, and thanks for always being AALIYAH. I love you, Aaliyah, keep resting in perfect peace.

> With appreciation,
>
> Nisa
>
> Saint Louis, MO

Aaliyah, you have helped me through so much in life because of the lyrics in your music. You have inspired me to never give up on a dream and to always stay true to myself. I just want to say thank you for just being you! I started listening to your music when I was 6 years old and I remember hearing "One in a Million" playing inside a Beauty Supply Store and your voice sounded soothing to me. It calmed me just for a moment. The song "One in a Million" became my favorite song ever since. Whenever I'm feeling nervous or just want comfort, I listen to this song just to take me into a different place. You have songs for every mood or emotion, and I really like that because I can relate to all of them whenever I'm feeling a certain way. I love your style and how you were a trendsetter. You inspired me to wear baggy clothes. I really hated wearing dresses and skirts because it wasn't for me. You inspired a lot of your fans that were tomboys who hated wearing girly stuff. You helped me find myself through rough times. The way you never got mad about anything helped me change for the better. So thank you for that. I believe the most exciting thing to have in my life is having the same birthday as your favorite singer. You don't see a fan with the same birthday as another famous person. Now that's rare to me. Thank you Aaliyah for the love you shown, you will always have a special place in my heart. I really miss you BabyGirl. Lots of Love from your biggest fan.

Da'Mya Buford

Age 17

Holly Springs, MS

Aaliyah has changed my life from a very young age. My mom had her CDs. *Age Ain't Nothing but a Number, One in a Million, Aaliyah.* My mom had a whole collection of CDs of artists from the 90s to current day at that time. I would go through all the CDs, I was maybe 6 or 7, and look at the album covers. I didn't know any of the artists. I would look at the cover art and something drew me to Aaliyah's *Aaliyah* CD, so I asked my mom "who is that?" and she replied "Aaliyah" and I said "Can I listen to it?" and ever since then I've been a fan. I would sing "At Your Best" to the top of my lungs and my mom would say "Why are you yelling? Is she yelling?" Then I'd laugh. Aaliyah definitely defines who the person I am today in terms of music wise and fashion wise. I always admired her fashion and loved her humbleness. My favorite music video when I was younger was "Are You That Somebody." I am now 15 and I am on my way to beginning my music career. As a fan I hope I can collect all three of Aaliyah's vinyl records. I never want to forget about her she's always in my heart.

Love, A.

Age 15

Queens, NY

Aaliyah has changed my life by making me more confident and happy with how I look. She showed me that I can be beautiful just the way I am and inspired me to be successful. I always think of the lyrics, "If at first you don't succeed, dust yourself off and try again," from the song "Try Again" to keep me motivated. The first song of hers I remember listening to was "One In A Million" and I instantly fell in love with her voice. Knowing she released *One In A Million* in 1996 when she was 17 made me believe that people can accomplish a lot at a young age. She also inspired a bit of my style. I started wearing baggy pants with small tops and big jackets because I would see how stunning she looked with that style. Watching her music videos, live performances, interviews, behind the scenes, home videos, and funny moments makes me wish I had met her; she was such a nice humble person that cared so much for everyone. I recently wanted to get into dance after seeing her dance moves in her music videos and live performances. I am currently collecting her posters, records, and CDs. I can't wait to show my collection to other people.

Her music will always inspire me to never give up and to keep growing and moving forward.

Savannah Mercedes Casillas

Age 20

Dallas, Texas

Aaliyah was my first introduction to being a softer version of myself. I always had a tough exterior, but when I heard "One in a Million" for the first time, it woke something up. Even now as I write this letter, I'm listening to it in the headphones, and a part of me always arrives to a place as an adult I often shut down. It's as beautiful as she is: vibrant, full of colors that to this day we cannot describe. Her music is timeless, and if you were to toss it on the airwaves now it would be just as relevant as the day it was first played; that's classic.

When Aaliyah died, I cried for days. I remember the day clearly. I had come home from volleyball practice and my mom told me, "One of your singers died in a plane crash." My heart sank when I saw the news. Unaware of how important she was to me, my mom was shocked at how much I cried as I sat on the couch in shock. I had never been so emotional over someone I never met. This hit me deep.

It was truly a loss to the world, and to me, a young woman who didn't have too much guidance on how to be a *woman* in the sense. Sensual, strong, fearless, mysterious, commanding, kind, all at once without forcing to be the center of attention. That in itself was magic; that was Aaliyah to me. Come to think of it, as a grown woman, this is how I move in my daily life and I owe a lot of it to Aaliyah and her music. Having been in the music industry, I learned of course it takes more than just the artist to make the music legendary, but what is a journey without a ship to take it there? She was, and continues to be the vessel, for all of us that were witness to her greatness.

Thank you, Baby Girl.

Sincerely, Yaya Martinez

Age 36

Phoenix, AZ

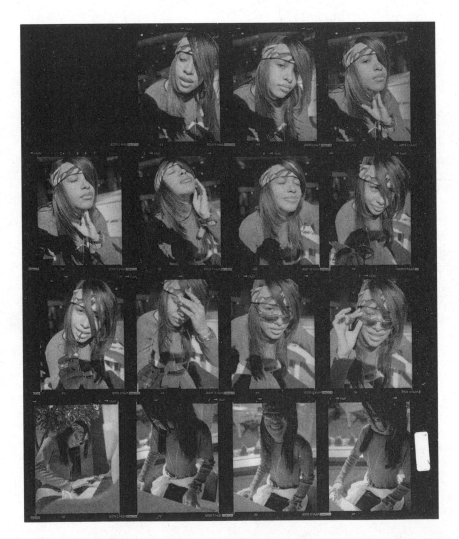

PHOTO OUTRO ONE: SHOOTING YOUR SHOT

In 1994, Aaliyah traveled overseas, doing international press for *Age Ain't Nothing but a Number*. It was then that photographer Eddie OTCHERE met Aaliyah. He was around nineteen and shooting the photos for his friend Andrew Green's interview with Aaliyah for his fanzine. Someone was missing from the equation during this press run: R. Kelly. At that point, it was a rarity, since he was with her for the most part wherever she went. Across the pond, she didn't have him beside her, which presented an interesting opportunity for the interviewer to maybe lay into Aaliyah about the details of her and R. Kelly's working relationship.

That didn't go at all as planned.

Aaliyah was fifteen yet poised. She sat at the table ready to be questioned by the interviewer, and you can see from the contact sheet that her doe eyes were already piercing into the interviewer's and OTCHERE's souls before the interview even began. When she opened her mouth to speak, it was almost like she sang her answers, even the "ummms" and "ahhhs." "And it was fucking in key!" OTCHERE exclaims. "Then she would speak and go up an octave! It's like what? Wow, like how do you do that? Like, can you just say my name, just so I know the natural keys of my name? The music was just pouring out of her." Any line of questioning completely escaped the interviewer, so he couldn't even get his bearings. "He's like talking to her and he's melting into the table," OTCHERE continues, "and before you know it, his face is on the table, he's looking like a child. I'm thinking, 'Andrew, pull your fucking self together, bro! What's going on? Don't lose yourself!'"

But it was too late. Aaliyah charmed him.

"Andrew was gone. He was like . . . he was melting. He was gonna ask all these questions about R. Kelly and shit and then he met her and it's like, 'Nah, I can't even go there.' Like, 'You're amazing; what's going on in your world? Tell me more.'"

It was safe to say that Aaliyah was on the verge. Stardom was within her reach, and this was one of the few moments that captured her being on the brink of something special. For the photo shoot, Aaliyah was dressed in a large white Nike polo, with the infamous Tasmanian Devil chain around her neck. She had a ring on her left ring finger, which fans have speculated was a gift from her grandmother, though the choice of finger placement raised some eyebrows given her relationship status. Her hair was pin straight and she wore dark glasses, that is, until OTCHERE asked her to take them off. "I did ask her to take her glasses off, and she didn't feel totally comfortable with that," OTCHERE says, but she did take them off for a few shots.

Cut to just a few short years later, when Aaliyah returned to London for early promo around *One in a Million*. The glasses were still on, yet the artist had changed some, and she was even more accepting of taking those glasses off. Aaliyah was a star, and she was also entering womanhood. OTCHERE was again assigned to shoot her for a magazine spread. This time her clothes were more fitted—she was in a long-sleeved top with more fitted jeans and a shirt tied around her waist. She wore a camouflage bandana. The Tasmanian Devil chain was gone. "She's not wearing baggy clothes and she had hips now," OTCHERE says. She also wasn't resigned to the requisite hip-hop-style, beginner's photo-shoot poses she had done at fifteen. Now she knew how to work the camera and pose effectively. She even walked up to a piano in the room and just started playing it. The music was still pouring out of her. She still spoke in key. Again, the whole room was completely taken by her, "but we all felt we were punching above our weight just to even try it," he adds with a laugh. "It's like you just, you met her and you fell in love with her and that was the end." He later named his first daughter Aaliyah in her honor.

His photos were later featured in the 2018 book *Contact High: A Visual History of Hip-Hop*. "I thought Eddie's photos captured her being her," says Vikki Tobak, author of *Contact High*, "which was kind of like cool, vulnerable, effortless. Plus she was super-young, just starting out."

Few photographers got to witness that flip of a switch in Aaliyah. OTCHERE caught her right before stardom and again right before those glasses came off for good and Aaliyah fully embraced her womanhood. "To watch her grow was a beautiful thing," he says. The impact she left on him will last forever.

"She was like an angel, way above anything mere mortals were destined to be, and for me it came across in her voice," he explains. "Just the way she spoke was like wow, she was just literally talking and singing at the same time. That's a gift. For me, it's now become the mark of a great artist . . . if you speak in key."

PHOTO OUTRO TWO: THE PERFECT SHOT

Photographer Jonathan Mannion is known for capturing moments in his art that otherwise would have never been captured had he not been the man behind the lens. He has a well-documented history of being a camera titan, as his work has become the visual accompaniment to many, many classic hip-hop albums. He's become a staple for Jay-Z's album covers, ranging from *Reasonable Doubt*; *In My Lifetime, Vol. 1*; *Vol. 2 . . . Hard Knock Life*; *Streets Is Watching*; and *Vol. 3 . . . Life and Times of S. Carter* to even *The Blueprint*, *The Black Album*, and the list goes on and on. While Mannion has photographed many legends, most artists would return the accolades and declare that they too were in the presence of a legend. While known for particularly masculine subjects, Mannion has a history of shining when he's able to show what he's capable of with female artists, as he was also the photographer who shot Lauryn Hill's iconic photo of her in all black against a yellow background for the cover of *Honey* magazine while she was pregnant for the first time. Mannion had the honor of shooting Aaliyah's domestic and international promotional materials for her *Aaliyah* album in 2001, as well as taking the photographs that would later be used for her 2002 posthumous EP *I Care 4 U*.

The collection of photos were taken in one shoot, over the course of around five hours, with locations changing around during that time frame, scattered throughout Lower Manhattan. Mannion was supposed to have four hours in the morning to shoot with Aaliyah, before she headed to a separate magazine photo shoot. "The night before, they decided they wanted to swap the day," Mannion remembers. "It was better for the other photographer to shoot in the morning and then [Aaliyah] comes to me and finishes out the day." The entire shoot was already planned and mapped out, so they had to "unproduce it all and reproduce it," as Mannion explains. Permits had already been secured, cars were rented, props were ordered, yet everything had to be flipped around in the wee hours of the morning leading up to the shoot, now later in the day.

"I was required to do ten shots for international press and publicity," Mannion adds, still in disbelief that the large quantity was the photo requirement within such a short time frame. The shots all had to be with unique setups, as well. Meaning, no two shots could look alike, with the same background, outfit, et cetera. "I'm like, 'How am I gonna make this happen? In four hours, ten shots?'" Mannion continues. But it was for Aaliyah, an emerging icon, so the hassle was worth it. He had a team huddle and was ready to make it happen. "'All right, guys, we're gonna rise to this occasion,'" he remembers telling his team. "'Let's show up, because she's magic.'"

Mannion and Aaliyah had only met in passing prior to the

shoot, at a nightclub while she was with Damon Dash, where they exchanged some hellos and pleasantries. Like most of Mannion's work, he has the gift of connecting with his subject through the lens, and despite only being acquaintances beforehand, they ended that photo session as friends. "Working with her was a reward for me for working with the different artists on Blackground Records," Mannion says. "Having shot Tank and Bradshaw and Timbaland and Magoo—all of the people that they were pushing forward—that was in my understood wheelhouse of what I did and who I was as a photographer. It was like shooting primarily men: the Jay-Z album covers, Ja Rule, DMX. 'Let's give him men, because that's what he really does.' But my roots are really in fashion, so for me to be able to spend time in a different capacity, you know, with this incredibly talented, beautiful sweet soul . . . it made me rise to another level."

It was a special day all around; Aaliyah didn't mind hitting up the projects to shoot, nor did she take any umbrage at glamming it up for some looks in studio. She was flexible and kind, and despite being one of the most important artists in R&B at that very moment, she was unshakably humble. So the goal for Mannion was to capture all of that in as many moments as possible. A legend in his own right, he rose to the occasion. It wasn't that hard given the subject.

"My thought process was to give them the widest range of her personality in order to give that to the world," Mannion adds. He curated shots that would take Aaliyah outside of the comfort zone of her public persona, even ordering a bed for the final set scene to give, as he puts it, a "Cuban bedroom" theme. At first the label was concerned that the shot might be too "racy" and "outside of her character," but Mannion urged them to let Aaliyah explore the opportunity, and if they didn't want the shot they could scrap it. "There wasn't any real demands, but I was like, 'Look, we're here; let's finish strong,'" Mannion expresses. "She looked amazing; let's give it to the world. If you don't want to use it, you guys are in control." Over the years, it's become one of the more widely circulated shots among her fan base.

The photos taken that day run the gamut of Aaliyah's personality, just as Mannion intended. Each frame depicts Aaliyah in a whole different space and time. The locations included everywhere from the Jacob Javits Center to the housing projects that touch the far end of New York's Chelsea neighborhood, and a giant block-long photography studio space just a few blocks away from there. The selections that were chosen are some of the most famous photos of Aaliyah, especially since they were taken within the last year of her life. A Post-it on one of the contact sheets shows a delivery date of June 6, 2001, less than three months before her passing.

Each photo screams "Aaliyah" in different ways. There's the photo showing a more rock 'n' roll aesthetic that she was later leaning toward, as Aaliyah is decked in black leather and leaned up against a hot rod with flames chasing along the side of the car. Another look includes Aaliyah wearing a crop top with her real hometown of "Brooklyn" sprawled across her chest. The background varies from a deep blue to one where she's posted up with the projects in the distance, in a New York City public playground, leaned against a geometric jungle-gym dome.

There's the shot of her in the Roberto Cavalli dress that's so long it kisses the floor, as Aaliyah looks almost like an angelic mermaid posing gracefully for the camera. Another shot shows Aaliyah in a denim bikini top lying against a patchwork tapestry made of various sewn-together denim fabric pieces (some even have jeans pockets). Another studio shot shows Aaliyah dressed in a formfitting fur coat with snow leopard-print pants, leaned casually on a weathered brown leather chair. The aforementioned Cuban bedroom décor shot was taken in an ocean-blue scenery with a white bed, as Aaliyah is clad in a dress that matches the blue walls, gazing seductively into the camera.

Then, of course, there's the fluffy cheetah-print faux fur coat and white pants ensemble, as Aaliyah dons rose-tinted shield sunglasses. These shots were later used as the artwork for the *I Care 4 U* project. "Some of them had to be pretty simple," Mannion explains, "because it was press; it wasn't about a super-elaborate setup. We got through it, and we gave it all a different vibe through the styling, coupled with the simple sets we brought in."

Mannion portrayed Aaliyah as multidimensional, which was accurate, considering she was then twenty-two years old, full of experiences in both her personal and professional life. She had fully come into her own, as an R&B princess who had taken form and was on the brink of stardom. Looking back, the shoot runs almost like a timeline of the span of her career—from her youthful *Age Ain't Nothing but a Number* days, to her *One in a Million* era, with flames and leather, to entering a more seductive phase as she entered adulthood with *Aaliyah*. This shoot had it all, serving as the most comprehensive visual journey of Baby Girl.

"How can I say it more eloquently? It's like, she's our version of Marilyn Monroe," Mannion says. "She dealt with a lot, survived a lot, like really battled through, still made really pure, amazing music from her soul—working with incredibly talented artists like Tank and Static Major. And you know, it's just like, those are the people that you really want to win and deserve to win."

In just a few short hours, Mannion managed to capture the essence of Aaliyah. The photo shoot became iconic. So much so that years later Jonathan Mannion gifted Drake a giant original print from the shoot to hang on his wall. Mannion knew that Drake had a tattoo of Aaliyah on his back, and when he visited Drake's home he saw that there were empty walls with no art. Aaliyah's portrait ultimately began Drake's art collection, as prior to that Drake was photocopying images and hanging them on his walls, not investing in high art. Now he had Baby Girl as the first of his art pieces.

Given the switch in Aaliyah's schedule that day, this photo shoot would be regarded as Aaliyah's last, and had the magazine photographer not changed the timing of the second shoot of the day, Mannion's photo shoot wouldn't have been the one to visually close out her legacy.

"I used it in one of my TED Talks actually," Mannion reflects on that shoot. "It's like you never know what moment is going to be a really critical moment, years from the moment that you're experiencing. I think that this was one of those things. Like, had I not given the energy that I did, maybe I would have gotten five shots. Maybe it would have been like, 'Oh, man, it was just too hard to get these other ones.' But to say now that I just gave it my all—and then to know that I did that and achieved the pictures that I did—now means something more to the world because they're the final images that were taken on a professional level. So you look back at these things, and it holds more weight."

If on an abstract level a photograph is intended to take a still of the spirit of its subject, then Jonathan Mannion succeeded tenfold in his shoot with Aaliyah. It marked a strong finish to her history, while also leaving an impression on Mannion that he still thinks about to this day.

"Quite frankly, when people are like, 'What's the most important photo shoots that you did? What's your sort of *favorite*?' this is always in the top three," Mannion admits. "There's something about her, where everybody wanted to embrace her and protect her and really cherish the sweetness of her spirit."

PHOTO OUTRO THREE: THE FINAL SHOT

In November 2001, *Vibe* magazine released what many regard as Aaliyah's final cover story. The whirlwind of events that happened in the United States from Aaliyah's death in August until the magazine's release made her passing a delayed reaction for the world. It somehow was solidified as *real* with this cover. On the cover is Aaliyah in black and white, wearing a spaghetti-strapped white slip dress. In block letters at the bottom it reads: "AALIYAH DANA HAUGHTON, 1979–2001." There it was: set in stone. She was gone. The photo remains a vivid part of her memory, perceived as the final image captured of Aaliyah. It wasn't the last photo physically taken, yet it was the last photo seen by the world.

New York City photographer Eric Johnson met with Aaliyah for their photo shoot in 2001, right before her world started moving quickly. Johnson was and still is the quintessential representation of the gritty New York City photographers who so brilliantly capture the spirit of their subjects. He is a self-defined outcast of popular culture, yet his work has become cultural moments for everyone. Johnson is known for iconic photos, like The Notorious B.I.G. cuddled up next to Faith Evans in the car; a pic from that shoot also became the cover art for his eponymous single, "The Notorious B.I.G." Johnson also shot the infamous visuals for Lauryn Hill's masterpiece *The Miseducation of Lauryn Hill* and his photos for Maxwell, Bruno Mars, and Lady Gaga all equally achieve Johnson's gift for freezing a soul in time from behind the lens. His loft in midtown Manhattan became the stuff of legend, where he would throw epic parties and also photograph his subjects. It's affectionately called Upstairs at Eric's. To this day, Johnson shoots some of the most groundbreaking artists, using a combination of his own flare for edginess and the artist's true essence. The day he shot Aaliyah, all bets were off on his traditional formula.

Aaliyah met Eric in passing prior to the shoot, exchanging hellos at one point or another at a restaurant in the city. He was assigned a photo feature in *Entertainment Weekly* with Aaliyah as she was in the chaotic promotional cycle for her final album. "Honestly, I would have definitely shot Aaliyah for any publication," Johnson explains, "but once *VIBE* used the photos, it kind of took away from the fact that they started at *EW*." He knew that her star was rising and that she was becoming a big deal in multiple industries. "They were preparing to make her the doll in films, which was rare," he says, noting that musicians rarely make a successful transition to the movie world, but per industry rumblings, he heard that Aaliyah was going to be really groomed for Hollywood. That wasn't why he agreed to shoot her; he genuinely enjoyed who she was and the music she was making. The fact that she was gorgeous and a "doll" (as he reiterates) made her the perfect muse for his camera lens.

It wasn't his thing, really, to take very conventional photos of stars. On the contrary, he loved pushing his subjects to their creative limits. There was something different about Aaliyah from the moment he walked into the studio. The shoot took place in New York's Pier59 Studios, just off the West Side Highway. Johnson arrived hungover after a night of raging, and Aaliyah was already there getting ready. "Her being bad the bitch that led, she got there early to set everything up," he remembers. "She was someone on a mission, who knew what she was doing."

Aaliyah arrived with a very specific vision for the shoot. She wanted it clean and stripped down. Her hair wasn't in its usual poker-straight style, but full and wavy. She was made up, but not dramatic—just a simple pink lip and a little eye shadow. Her shimmery slip dress was a stark contrast to the black and leather rock star chic phase she was just entering into with her final album. "A lot of those photos of Aaliyah, they could be in like a beauty campaign or something," Johnson adds, "but you will never find another photo shoot of mine that 'clean' in a way. I feel like I really followed her lead—and I've worked with everybody—but there was something about her that I really respected, like *she's the boss*. Whatever she wants. This is Aaliyah's world and I just wanted everything to be nice."

That "clean" look went against the grain of who Aaliyah was becoming, and instead of utilizing the creative eye of a photographer known for exploring that darker side, she posed a challenge for him to keep it light. It was a first for both of them. "I didn't feel inspired to make her look like she was try-ing to be cool or edgy or any of those kinds of things," Johnson continues. "These photos felt like just for her in particular."

In the midst of the photo shoot, Eric recognized something in Aaliyah, where the two connected. "She knew who to click with, not based on us having a history," he expresses. They saw each other. He was Eric Johnson, legendary photographer who preferred to exist on the outskirts of the mainstream. He was known to get "live" as he put it, parlaying the NYC party life. She was Aaliyah Haughton, musician who chose to work with fellow outcasts Missy Elliott and Timbaland to create something beautiful and substantial. She lived on pop music's periphery; she wasn't saccharine yet still came with the sweet-ness. He felt it; she felt it. During her prep of hair and makeup, a friend of Eric's called him in the middle of the shoot. It was Michael Boadi, famed British hairstylist who Eric described as "cheeky, Black, and eccentric." When Eric told him that he was shooting Aaliyah that day, his friend responded, "Let me speak to her." Boadi and Aaliyah had actually known each other. Eric wasn't handing the phone over that easily. "You would never have an artist on set and say, 'Oh, my friend wants to speak to you,'" Eric adds, but given this unspoken connection, he acquiesced and asked Aaliyah if she would speak to his friend. "She was like 'Gimme that phone!'" he continues, relaying how he watched Aaliyah gleefully chat with his friend. "They were like schoolgirls on the phone while she was getting made up. It was just another testament to how down she was." To grab a phone and chat with an eccentric hairstylist was not out of the ordinary for someone as down as Baby Girl.

The photo shoot was immaculate and gorgeous. Aaliyah

changes looks, from the *Vibe* cover's white outfit to a black tank top, and then a black and gray marbled top, made of two pieces of fabric that meet in a cross at the front. Her poses are delicate, but without the fashion and makeup bells and whistles you see something greater: Aaliyah as an adult. This was not the same girl in her baggy pants, hiding behind dark sunglasses. She didn't need a bandana or a beanie cap or even a flatiron to perfect her hairstyle. It was tousled and natural. She was a woman, and her spirit was captured in those photos before it was time for her to go.

After the shoot, Aaliyah reached out about the photos, which in and of itself was unique, judging from Johnson's past experiences. "She wanted to see them. I feel like that's rarely the case. Those people get shot all the time," he explains. Aaliyah took the time to even survey the whole contact sheet and return it back to him. "She marked *X*s on them and *O*s for the ones she appreciated, and the ones that she didn't," he says. It felt like everything moved far too quickly after that. "She asked for the photos, she signed which ones she liked, and then she passed away."

He did get to see her one last time, however, which is how he knows his was not the last official photo shoot. "The last time I saw Aaliyah, I was walking the streets of New York and I walked past my one friend and he was with Aaliyah and they were doing a shoot for *i-D* magazine," he explains. "My shoot was definitely one of the last, but it wasn't *the* last." The night she died, he was at a house party in Greenwich Village with Boadi. The radio was blaring Aaliyah back to back until they all paused to finally listen to the DJ's interjections as to why this playlist was happening. That's when he learned that she died. He and his friend were devastated but remembered that moment they both shared not too long ago. "It was cool we were together, because we had a connection together," he remarks. "She was connected to us, somehow; we were like all real outcasts."

The one image in white that has now circulated was defined as her last one. "The photos took on a life of their own," he adds. Since *Vibe* used it for their cover, that became the story: Aaliyah's last photo shoot was for *Vibe* magazine. "The kids online like to say that," Johnson says. "People think they were for *Vibe*; they asked to see [the shoot] for their tribute cover and then they became iconic."

His shoot was also featured in Vikki Tobak's *Contact High*. "I mean, the thing I love about Eric's photos is the story of how he showed her the images and she marked up which images she liked, which made it kind of collaborative," Tobak says. "I was sort of taken aback at how many images she didn't like; they're all so beautiful, you know? They're all perfect, but it just reminded me even a little bit about how women are when they look at photos of themselves, or when they try to, like, capture themselves in photos and they're so critical. I was like, 'Oh, right, Aaliyah is still that girl'; she was very much like every girl, you know, every girl in hip-hop, making her way in the world. I felt the photographs captured that expression."

Over the years, Johnson has given fans the gift of the *X* and the *O* shots from that fateful photo shoot. While Aaliyah in the moment didn't approve of certain shots—which he expresses were all categorically perfect thanks to the subject—in the absence of other relics from her stardom, he wanted to contribute to her legacy still in some way for the fans. There's a lack of enough content from such a short life as it is, but even bigger than that, these were images that he held near and dear to his heart. It's an act of kindness, while also making a statement. "When I look around and I see her image on all of this cheap bootleg stuff and see how people can rarely find her music, I kind of feel as if it is a bit of my responsibility to tell the story in a way," he explains.

That day at Pier59 Studios was more special than either even imagined on the day it happened, yet there's a reason why Aaliyah came with her own goal for the shoot in mind and blueprint for how the photos would and should look. It was like she chose the photographer for it, without even realizing it. "We landed in front of each other with a specific purpose that neither of us knew at the time," Johnson remarks. The purpose was to create a final image of Aaliyah, where she looked so angelic that the image looks as though it were taken in the afterlife. And like so many, he says that she embodied that angelic aura, here on earth. "I just want kids to know that this was not because she passed away," Johnson adds. "There was something about her when she was here. There was something deep inside of her that we all caught wind of but couldn't explain it."

ACKNOWLEDGMENTS

First and foremost, thank you, God, for always keeping me and my pen up high (even when I'm low).

Thank you, Aaliyah. I hope you view this book from the heavens as a love letter to you. You were strong, you were brave, you were bold. You are my hero. I hope I made you proud.

To my mother, Anna Acquaviva Iandoli. Mommy, you are the angel on my shoulder and the light of my life, always. I know you and Grandma (and Pop-Pop and Great-Great) will continue to watch over me. I love you and miss you so much. #AnniesDaughter forever.

Prodigy, I hope you're hanging out with my mom up there. Miss you.

To the Haughton and Hankerson family, thank you for birthing an icon. Rest In Peace to Michael Haughton, Mintis Hankerson, Eric Ferrell, Static Major, and DMX.

To Robert Guinsler and Sterling Lord Literistic. Thank you for always believing in me and my literary vision. And also for being my friend. Love you.

To Will Watkins and ICM, thank you for your support.

To Amar Deol and Atria Books/Simon & Schuster. I appreciate all of your help with this and talking me through this process. Thank you to Rakesh Satyal for bringing me into Atria, too!

Thank you Daddy and Rosie for checking in to see how my writing was going (in a pandemic). My sister Gina, my brother-in-law Travis, my brother Jimmy and my sister-in-law Ev. Love you all. To my nephew Tommy, get used to seeing your name in books. Zia loves you.

To Aunt Camille, for being my sounding board and fairy godmother, always. Love you, and Aunt Gae, Uncle Mike, Kevin, Kelsey, Danielle, and our angel Vince.

Thank you to Uncle Joe, Aunt Nancy, Kim, and Joe. Love you all.

To all of my Iandoli, Acquaviva, and Saccomano family. Much love and appreciation. Love you and thank you to my godmother, Roe, as well as Robin, Gloria, Felicia, Anita, and Mary Lou.

To my best friend, Maryum, for being right there with me when I went to Aaliyah's gravesite. You literally are always beside me. I love you mostestest.

To my cousin Jenn and the Barber Family, for having a permanent scar, just so we could jump into the AstroTurf at Giants Stadium in '98 to be closer to Aaliyah. Love you for always being down to ride. Hi Luvenci (and Nesta!).

To Christina, who cut off all of her hair when Baby Girl died. We mourned together that day. I'm still so sorry she passed on your birthday.

To Paulie, for being there through most of my Aaliyah fandom. Love you, Boo Boo!

To Chica (Albania): the day you were Aaliyah for Halloween was the day I knew you would be my friend forever. L.A.V.

To Steph, who read this book before the world did and hears all of my thoughts on anything and everything. I couldn't have asked for a better accountability partner and friend. Keith loves Stove forever.

To Tamika, I seriously don't know what I would do without you. You have kept me from spiraling so many days of every week. I love you so much and can never repay you. Glad you, me, and Maggie have this #BrewHa crew, ha. Love you Mags! And of course, hi Kennedy!

To Jonathan, who sees my potential even when I don't. You are the greatest. Love you.

To KC, for always being my light in transit. You bring out the #writer in me. Love you.

To Janice, for being my musical partner in crime and in cry hahaha. Love you!!

To Munny, for being so supportive through this process and always. Love you so much.

To Tra and Bree, I love you my sisters (Kel too haha!). I can't thank you both enough for being the best support system since we were kids. You mean the world to me.

To Porscha, for always listening and being my partner in water sign crime. I love you, P. Your pep talks are epic. Can't wait to keep our teamwork going in this space.

To Georgette, for the Aaliyah candle that I've burned at every milestone. Love you Gza!

To Laura Stylez, for being the first to know about this book. Thank you for being the best. Love you! Love to Ricardo and Kenza too!

To Marvis, for being my favorite sparring partner hahaha. You're the greatest.

To Lil' Kim, for coming through with stories about Baby Girl. Every time you talk, you know I'm listening, in awe of you. Appreciate you always, my friend.

To Phoebe Robinson, for commiserating with me during this entire ride!

To Chanel Pettaway, for being an amazing friend (and publicist).

To Dart Adams, for helping me with these thank you's.

To Simone Amelia Jordan, Roderick Scott, Marsha Gosho Oakes (Hawk), and Michael Gonzales, for digging up treasured Aaliyah relics for my research. I appreciate you, friends.

To dream hampton, for taking part in this book and for also being a wonderful mentor and friend. Also, thank you for always laughing at my jokes. Someone has to.

To Rapsody, Lolo Zouaï, Kash Doll, Jim Jones, Ja Rule, Vikki Tobak, Tameka Foster, Jimmy Douglass, April Walker, Kimya Warfield-Rainge, and Cola Walker (the queens of Walker Wear), Jim DeRogatis, Tim Barnett, Donnie Scantz, Bashir, Eddie OTCHERE, Eric Johnson, and of course Jonathan Mannion. Your input was so valued for this book. I can't thank you all enough.

To Kingsley Russell, your bravery in telling your story is so appreciated.

To #TeamAaliyah, who became my friends: Aali, Sandy, Erica, Frances, Ashley, Terrell, Nathan, and Tonica. As an Aaliyah fan, I never had a place to really talk about just how much she impacted my life. You all provided that (and so much more). Sandy, you and Erica are my favorite five-hour convos. Aali, Indie says hi.

Thank you also to Shonda Rhimes, Alison Eakle and the team at Shondaland, my dear friends Kim Osorio and Vanessa Satten, my lil' sis Se'era Ricks, my forever girl Marisa Mendez, Questlove, Robert Glasper, Vic Mensa, Nina Sky, India Shawn, Jada Gomez, Daniel Sozomenu, Amaiya Davis, B. Dot, Rebstar, JFK, Leah McSweeney, JoJo, Kid Sister, Leandra Williams, Ebro, Peter Rosenberg, Carl Lamarre, Jake Paine, Alvin "Aqua" Blanco, Chuck Creekmur, Jermaine Hall, Jerry Barrow, Big Ced, Jahi Sundance, Dove, Cherry Martinez, Queen D. Scott, Marisa Mendez, Se'era Spragley Ricks, Dan Charnas, Elliott Wilson, Clover Hope, Kierna Mayo, Marisa Bianco, Joe Carozza, Ashley Kalmanowitz, Jason Davis, Jamie Sward, Low Key, Kaz, Soren Baker, J57, Erin and MadeMe, Mary Pryor, FWMJ, D, Sarah Mary Cunningham, Krista Schlueter, Toni and Haus of Swag, Jaime and WKiD Creations, Victoria Hernandez, MC Debbie D, Neil Martinez-Belkin, Marcus J. Moore, Thembisa Mshaka, Adelle Platon, Gary Suarez, Sean Kantrowitz, Eric Diep, Sara Marcus, Andres Tardio, Tai Saint Louis, William Ketchum III, Theola Borden, Skoob, Paul Cantor, Ayanna Wilks, Nicole Hajjar, Dana Meyerson, Tracy G, Nadia Ali, Keyaira Boone, Jemeni, Rashaun Hall, Cassandra Spangler, Karissa Kindy, Jamal Jimoh, Gabby Rosenthal, Mecca, Roberta Magrini, Trent Clark, Tommy Cherian, Michelle McDevitt, Lydia Kanuga, Kierra Felton, Kristin Somin, Amanda Zimmerman, Chantz Brewer, Vanderslice, Laura (my bae-bor and London), Kiara, Nuri, Ginetta, Alissa, Caca (Lorena), Dita, Russ, Pri, Dunny (Lauren), Jasmine (My Jazzy), Jay, Sally, Huron, and all of my other friends and colleagues. Sorry if I've missed anyone.

To Indie, my dogter, who can now bark all the words to every Aaliyah song. You still sound better than me.

To everyone who reads this book, it's like Aaliyah said: "You have to love what you do to want to do it every day." Thank you for making that possible by reading.

ABOUT THE AUTHOR

Kathy Iandoli is a critically acclaimed journalist and author. Her work has appeared in *Billboard*, *The Guardian*, *Pitchfork*, *Rolling Stone*, *Playboy*, *PAPER*, *Teen Vogue*, VICE, *The Village Voice*, *Cosmopolitan*, and many other outlets. She has held editorial positions at top hip-hop/urban websites, including AllHipHop .com, HipHopDX.com, and BET.com. In 2019, she released the book *God Save the Queens: The Essential History of Women in Hip-Hop* through Dey Street Books / HarperCollins. Iandoli is an alumna-in-residence of Music Business at New York University and has appeared across the media, in television and on radio and panels discussing hip-hop and gender. She lives in the New York metropolitan area.

BIBLIOGRAPHY

VIDEO

"Aaliyah & Jet Li—Romeo Must Die Interviews & BTS." YouTube video, 4:31. "AaliyahPL." https://www.youtube.com/watch?v=AowVx4SikuA

"Aaliyah and R. Kelly: Jewelry Connection (1994–1996)." YouTube video, 1:56.
   "AaliyahAndRKelly," December 16, 2015. https://www.youtube.com/watch?v=
   -nc_A-ImG4E

"Aaliyah and R. Kelly on Video Soul Gold [1994]." YouTube video, 5:59. "GMON-
   EYHAWK." https://www.youtube.com/watch?v=TGCHvpMco3A&t=262s

"Aaliyah @ 'Romeo Must Die' Premiere 3-20-00." YouTube video, 1:47. "Hollywood
   Archive." April 2020. https://www.youtube.com/watch?v=ELAlU3NBg2E

"Aaliyah at the Premiere of Romeo Must Die." YouTube video, 1:57. "Aaliyah
   Haughton." https://www.youtube.com/watch?v=965ZXGeRyjM

"Aaliyah CBS Interview." YouTube video, 10:28. "CrystalVisions21," June 11, 2016.
   https://www.youtube.com/watch?v=XynzyQPiLnE

"Aaliyah | Teen People's 21 Hottest Stars under 21 (May 21, 1999)." YouTube video,
   2:30. "Aaliyah's Gems," July 2, 2020. https://www.youtube.com/watch?v=fZEE
   bq9cBNw

"Aaliyah Interview on BET Show In Your Ear February 1995." YouTube video, 7:49.
   "BeatleMay," October 1, 2017. https://www.youtube.com/watch?v=Cb6k4rl91to

"Aaliyah—Making of 'Journey to the Past' 1997. [Aaliyah.pl]." YouTube video, 3:37.
   "AaliyahPL," January 23, 2016. https://www.youtube.com/watch?v=gKA3JzE
   Fbns&feature=youtu.be

"Aaliyah—Making the Video: 'We Need a Resolution.'" YouTube video, 4:47. "Aaliyah," September 14, 2008. https://www.youtube.com/watch?v=qSlyL6m384Y

"Aaliyah MTV Stripped Interview." YouTube video, 17:57. "James Bishop," August 25,
   2019. https://www.youtube.com/watch?feature=youtu.be&v=HeoF3a5GPzY

"Aaliyah MTV Tribute (feat. Timbaland and Puffy)." YouTube video, 9:17. "Kenneth Antonsen." https://www.youtube.com/watch?v=1fJruAcR8Jo

"Aaliyah on the Set of Queen of the Damned." YouTube video, 8:56. "TeamAali-
   yah79." https://www.youtube.com/watch?v=Vt08QzYDwK4

"Aaliyah: One in a Million (BET Special) Pt. 1." YouTube video, 4:18. "Anthony22," August 17, 2016. https://www.youtube.com/watch?v=yR6PWlb6_VE

"Aaliyah: One in a Million (BET Special). Pt. 3." YouTube video, 7:33. "Anthony22," August 17, 2016. https://www.youtube.com/watch?v=yR6PWIbS_VE

"Aaliyah: One in a Million (BET Special) Pt. 4." YouTube video, 8:34. "Anthony22," August 17, 2016. https://www.youtube.com/watch?v=3Z617qryo2E

"Aaliyah, One in a Million (BET Special) Pt. 5." YouTube video, 1:02. "Anthony22," August 17, 2016. https://www.youtube.com/watch?vdafaseQ229

"Aaliyah One in a Million Part 2." YouTube video, 3:01. "AaliyahFans4ever," August 26, 2011. https://www.youtube.com/watch?v=Ghe5SzSMShY

"Aaliyah—'Rock the Boat' BET Access Granted." YouTube video, 21:50. "Aaliyah-PL." https://www.youtube.com/watch?v=nhEH2WBX-bI

"Aaliyah—CBS Interview." YouTube video, 4:58. "CrystalVisions21." https://www.youtube.com/watch?feature=youtu.be&v=XynzyQPiLnE

"Aaliyah—Romeo Must Die Junket Interview." YouTube video, 3:53. "Marilyn King," November 1, 2017. https://www.youtube.com/watch?v=OQp3FzAHB-U

"Aaliyah Teen People 21 Interview." YouTube video, 2:14. "MusicLatte," June 21, 2016. https://www.youtube.com/watch?v=Vpy9zGyqEpM&feature=youtu.be

"Aaliyah Tribute." YouTube video, 5:24. "HottDame36," September 26, 2008. https://www.youtube.com/watch?v=1jDgXogoQc0

"Aaliyah—Video Music Box Interview 1995." YouTube video, 11:44. "AaliyahPL," January 26, 2019. https://www.youtube.com/watch?v=2kdcHWOQuS4

"Aaliyah's Interview after the 2000 VMAs." YouTube video, 1:19. "OnTheTLCTip," August 22, 2020. https://www.youtube.com/watch?feature=youtu.be&v=Bc4FdPOng5g

"Aaliyah's Last Ever Radio Interview in August 2001." YouTube video, 20:00. "The Hip-Hop Historian," September 2, 2016. https://www.youtube.com/watch?v=sMyOiw3cPuQ

"Aaliyah's Mother Finally Reveals the Truth about Aaliyah's Relationship with R. Kelly." YouTube video, 3:14. January 3, 2019. https://www.youtube.com/watch?v=2Q7Ak2dI0S4

"'Cannon's Class'" ft. Dame Dash." YouTube video, 1:11:14. "Nick Cannon," January 10, 2019. https://www.youtube.com/watch?v=B8iV4ZaSFjE&t=3200s

"Damon Dash on Aaliyah's Untimely Death." YouTube video, 1:32. "The Real Daytime," April 19, 2016. https://www.youtube.com/watch?v=auJCO_wQYgc

"Dame Dash Opens Up about Losing Aaliyah | Family Therapy with Dr. Jenn." YouTube video, 2:04. "VH1," April 13, 2016. https://www.youtube.com/watch?v=WVT5biOy_d4

"Damon Dash: When Jay Worked with R. Kelly . . . (Aaliyah's Experience)." YouTube video, 34:59. "Hip Hop Motivation," January 5, 2019. https://www.youtube.com/watch?v=0E34YAJnrME

"Drake Reflects: 'Aaliyah Had the Biggest Influence on My Music.'" YouTube video, 3:44. "SoulCulture," January 16, 2011. https://www.youtube.com/watch?v=wuZYQ5lg5Ck&feature=youtu.be

"Farrakhan Warned R. Kelly about His Former Manager Barry Hankerson." YouTube video, 18:13. "Prima Donna," October 23, 2019. https://www.youtube.com/watch?v=kRznW1jr1mQ

"Full Aaliyah Interview! - *Rare* (1997)." YouTube video, 3:34. "AaliyahCentral,"
    August 31, 2014. https://www.youtube.com/watch?v=xSE4bmzEZ1o
"Ginuwine Opens about Aaliyah's Passing, Making of 'Pony,' TGT + More." You-
    Tube video, 1:06:37. "Premier Live TV," June 30, 2020. https://www.youtube
    .com/watch?v=2q2Ysaz4Qtg
"Gladys Knight Interview (2004)." YouTube video, 3:50. "Largo3point0." https://
    www.youtube.com/watch?v=msmBoK87yUk
"How Hip-Hop Celebrates Aaliyah with Beats, Rhymes & References | Genius
    News." YouTube video, 4:51. "Genius," August 23, 2018. https://www.youtube
    .com/watch?feature=youtu.be&v=3TB9wZ38QZA
"Inside of Aaliyah's Manhattan Condo." YouTube video, 3:20. "Tony Turner," June 2,
    2020. https://www.youtube.com/watch?v=90-kEGInJHo
"Jazze Pha Speaks on Producing for Aaliyah & Ciara." YouTube video, 9:05. "My-
    NameIsMyName." https://www.youtube.com/watch?v=2_EpOXpaImw
"Jet Li Talks Mulan & Remembers Aaliyah Romeo Must Die Co-star." You-
    Tube video, 5:20. "Sade Spence." https://www.youtube.com/watch?v=2m
    -6TSiQzj4
"Lisa Van Allen on R. Kelly, Aaliyah, Aaliyah's Mother, Arrests, Trial (Full Inter-
    view)." YouTube video, 1:09:27. "DJ Vlad," March 20, 2019. https://www.you
    tube.com/watch?v=COanAq2iUF4
"Losing Aaliyah Part 1. Avi." YouTube video, 9:45. "Via_Purifco," June 12, 2010.
    https://www.youtube.com/watch?v=_092AXPIQY8
"Losing Aaliyah Part 2. Avi." YouTube video, 8:04. "Via_Purifco," June 12, 2010.
    https://www.youtube.com/watch?v=SSipfcEYxYs&t=301s
"Missy Elliot and Timbaland on Drake & Aaliyah Album." YouTube video, 9:07.
    "Hot 97," September 18, 2012. https://www.youtube.com/watch?v=XgW8B
    mg1Buw&t=3s
"MTV Europe Select—Aaliyah Interview, 2000, Romeo Must Die." YouTube video,
    8:27. "Olevish." https://www.youtube.com/watch?v=fVYUOD0JpFE
"'Queen of the Damned' Crew Interviews (NY Times)." YouTube video, 10:39. "Aa-
    liyahPL." https://www.youtube.com/watch?v=CCpADdC-u_M
"R. Kelly 'Do You Like Teenage Girls?' Interview." YouTube video, 4:19. "US Now,"
    January 4, 2019. https://www.youtube.com/watch?v=MX1qybUYFjg
"RARE: Aaliyah in Annie Rehearsals (1988)." YouTube video, 2:49. "Baby Girl."
    https://www.youtube.com/watch?v=M7yHKc02hj0
"RCMS with Wanda Smith Interview Cousin of Aaliyah, The." YouTube video,
    12:26. June 24, 2014. https://www.youtube.com/watch?v=379aa7q7MyY
"Star Search—Katrina vs. Aaliyah." YouTube video, 5:54. "Katrina Woolverton,"
    October 14, 2011. https://www.youtube.com/watch?v=1Dx_5SLhIvM
"Surprising Things We Learned about Aaliyah after Her Death." YouTube video,
    5:13. "Nicki Swift," January 29, 2018. https://www.youtube.com/watch?v=W
    za0rmJQNNU
"Throwback News: Aaliyah Marries R. Kelly (1994)." YouTube video, 0:32. "Klas-
    sicThrowbackTV," July 17, 2013. https://www.youtube.com/watch?v=H7mZv
    2vHx58
"Timbaland Making Beats in the Studio!" YouTube video, 4:33. "Mc Cabe," De-
    cember 14, 2017. https://www.youtube.com/watch?v=7ufpCF3OKsU&t=130s

"What the End of Aaliyah's Life Was Really Like." YouTube video, 11:01. "Grunge," August 15, 2020. https://www.youtube.com/watch?feature=youtu.be&v=2FzugVWR288

RECORDING

Aaliyah: Open-Ended Interview. Jive Records, 1994. Compact disc.

FILM

Bellis, Nigel, and Astral Finnie. *Surviving R. Kelly.* Aired on Lifetime. Kreativ Inc. Bunim/Murray Productions, 2019.

Bellis, Nigel, and Astral Finnie. *Surviving R. Kelly Part II: The Reckoning.* Aired on Lifetime. Kreativ Inc. Bunim/Murray Productions, 2020.

BOOKS

Brackett, Nathan, and Christian Hoard (eds.). *The New Rolling Stone Album Guide.* New York: Fireside Books, 2004.

DeRogatis, Jim. *Soulless: The Case Against R. Kelly.* New York: Harry N. Abrams, 2019.

Farley, Christopher John. *Aaliyah: More than a Woman.* New York: MTV Books, 2002.

Footman, Tim. *Aaliyah.* Medford, NJ: Plexus, 2003.

Iandoli, Kathy. *God Save the Queens: The Essential History of Women in Hip-Hop.* New York: Dey Street Books, 2019.

Smith, Demetrius. *The Man Behind the Man: Looking from the Inside Out.* Bloomington, IN: Xlibris, 2011.

Timbaland and Veronica Chambers. *The Emperor of Sound: A Memoir.* New York: Amistad, 2016.

VIBE Magazine. *Hip-Hop Divas.* New York: Three Rivers Press, 2001.

Warner, Jennifer. *Aaliyah: A Biography.* BookCaps Study Guides, 2014.

DIGITAL AND PRINT ARTICLES

"Aaliyah: Angel So Fly." TheFADER.com, August 25, 2011: https://www.thefader.com/2011/08/25/aaliyah-angel-so-fly-2

"Aaliyah Concert Setlists & Tour Dates." Setlist.fm, n.d.: https://www.setlist.fm/setlists/aaliyah-2bd69c16.html

"Aaliyah Dana Haughton—Facts." Its_All_About_Howie.Tripod.com, n.d.: http://its_all_bout_howie.tripod.com/aaliyah/id1.html

"Aaliyah Hits Find Home with Apple Music—Illegally." JetMag.com, January 12, 2017: https://www.jetmag.com/entertainment/aaliyah-compilation-apple-music

"Aaliyah Likes the Way Virgin Puts Out." HitsDailyDouble.com, May 5, 2000: https://hitsdailydouble.com/news&id=273432&title+AALIYAH-LIKES-THE-WAY-VIRGIN-PUTS-OUT

"Aaliyah Often Had Her Left Eye Covered, under the Advice of Her Mother." CapitalXtra.com, n.d.: https://www.capitalxtra.com/features/lists/aaliyah-facts/no-family-on-rock-the-boat-video-shoot

"Aaliyah Plane Was Overloaded by Hundreds of Pounds." CNN.com, August 31, 2001: https://edition.cnn.com/2001/WORLD/americas/08/30/aaliyah.crash

"Aaliyah, R. Kelly Named in Copyright Lawsuit." MTV.com, May 7, 1997: http://www.mtv.com/news/1424665/aaliyah-r-kelly-named-in-copyright-lawsuit

"Aaliyah, Usher & Others for Tommy Hilfiger." LipstickAlley.com, April 20, 2014: https://www.lipstickalley.com/threads/aaliyah-usher-others-for-tommy-hilfiger.690691

"Aaliyah's Mom Is Not Here for 'Surviving R. Kelly' Docuseries by @robinrazzi." Whur.com, January 3, 2019: https://whur.com/entertainment/whats-the-tea-wrazzi/aaliyahs-mom-speaks-out-against-surviving-r-kelly-docuseries

ABC News. "Aaliyah Stars in 'Queen of the Damned.'" ABCNews.com, February 22, 2002: https://abcnews.go.com/Entertainment/story?id=101275&page=1

Alexander, Brenda. "Aaliyah's Brother Shares Behind-the-Scenes Video of Her Tommy Hilfiger Campaign." Cheatsheet.com, June 30, 2020: https://www.cheatsheet.com/entertainment/aaliyahs-brother-shares-behind-the-scenes-video-of-her-tommy-hilfiger-campaign.html

Alexander, Brenda. "Damon Dash Reveals How R. Kelly Is Part of the Reason His Business Relationship with Jay-Z Ended on 'Surviving R. Kelly.'" Cheatsheet.com, January 4, 2020: https://wwww.cheatsheet.com/entertainment/damon-dash-reveals-how-r-kelly-is-part-of-the-reason-his-business-relationship-with-jay-z-ended-on-surviving-r-kelly.html

Alexander, Brenda. "One of Rapper Eve's Biggest Songs Was Originally Meant for Aaliyah." Cheatsheet.com, May 13, 2020: https://www.cheatsheet.com/entertainment/one-of-rapper-eves-biggest-songs-was-originally-meant-for-aaliyah.html

Alexander, Brenda. "The Unconventional Outfit Aaliyah Almost Wore to Her Senior Prom." Cheatsheet.com, May 13, 2020: https://www.cheatsheet.com/entertainment/the-unconventional-outfit-aaliyah-almost-wore-to-her-senior-prom.html

Ali, Rasha. "Aaliyah's 'Queen of the Damned' 15th Anniversary: 10 Things You Didn't Know about Vampire Thriller." TheWrap.com, February 22, 2017: https://www.thewrap.com/aaliyahs-queen-of-the-damned-15th-anniversary-10-things-you-didnt-know/#

"Always Remember." TheFADER.com, May 21, 2008: https://www.thefader.com/2008/05/21/always-remember

Anderson, Trevor. "Rewinding the Charts: In 1994, Aaliyah Went 'Forth' & Conquered." Billboard.com, May 21, 2016: https://www.billboard.com/articles/columns/chart-beat/7378340/rewinding-the-charts-in-1994-aaliyah-went-forth-conquered

"Are You That Somebody?" Songfacts.com, n.d.: https://www.songfacts.com/facts/aaliyah/are-you-that-somebody

Augustin, Camille. "Aaliyah Week: 'Age Ain't Nothing but a Number' & the Isley Brothers Cover That Placed Aaliyah on the Map." Vibe.com, August 26, 2016: https://www.vibe.com/2016/08/age-aint-nothing-but-a-number-aaliyah-week

Augustin, Camille. "Aaliyah Week: How 'One in a Million' Pushed the Envelope of R&B." Vibe.com., August 26, 2016: https://www.vibe.com/2016/08/one-in-a-million-album-aaliyah-week

Augustin, Camille. "Aaliyah Week: An Ode to Static Major, the Pen behind Aaliyah's Self-Titled Album." Vibe.com, August 24, 2016: https://www.vibe.com/2016/08/static-major-aaliyah-week

Augustin, Camille. "Aaliyah Week: Remembering Aaliyah's Final Musical Journey." Vibe.com, August 26, 2016: https://www.vibe.com/2016/08/aaliyah-album-aaliyah-week

Augustin, Camille "From Baby Girl to More than a Woman: A Look at Aaliyah's Growth from Fashion to Dance." Vibe.com, August 22, 2016: https://www.vibe.com/2016/08/derek-lee-fatima-robinson-eric-ferrell-interivew-aaliyah-week

Avins, Mimi. "Take a Spin Inside Tommy Hilfiger's Fashion Cuisinart." LATimes.com, August 25, 1996: https://www.latimes.com/archives/la-xpm-1996-08-25-tm-37378-story.html

Baltin, Steve. "Artists Mourn Aaliyah." RollingStone.com. August 29, 2001: https://www.rollingstone.com/music/music-news/artists-mourn-aaliyah-235480

BARRY SONS INC v. INSTINCT PRODUCTIONS LLC: https://caselaw.findlaw.com/ny-supreme-court/1483266.html

Bautz, Mark. "Aaliyah Dies in a Plane Crash." EW.com, August 28, 2001: https://ew.com/article/2001/08/28/aaliyah-dies-plane-crash

"Been Around the World: Before Kool & Dre or the Neptunes, There Were the Hitmen. On One Legendary Trip, They Earned Their Name." Vibe, November 2006, accessed at: https://books.google.com/books?id=9SYEAAAAMBAJ&pg=PA136&lpg=PA136&dq=did+puffy+want+to+sign+aaliyah&source=bl&ots=7mFJ25BjUk&sig=ACfU3U3MPnoPVvBmc1ZjqTCGjTR8k sao_A&hl=en&sa=X&ved=2ahUKEwjx34Tzw8rqAhXog31EHW-6D3oQ6A EwGHoECAoQAQ#v=onepage&q=did%20puffy%20want%20to%20sign%20 aaliyah&f=false

Berkowitz, Joe. "We Were Warned: A Timeline of R. Kelly's Many Sexual Abuse Allegations." FastCompany.com. January 4, 2019: https://www.fastcompany.com/90288224/we-were-warned-a-timeline-of-r-kellys-many-sexual-abuse-allegations

Billboard Staff. "Aaliyah's Parents Settle Plane Crash Suit." Billboard.com, September 9, 2003: https://www.billboard.com/articles/news/69189/aaliyahs-parents-settle-plane-crash-suit

Billboard Staff. "Coroner's Inquest Opens in Aaliyah Crash." Billboard.com, November 18, 2003: https://www.billboard.com/articles/news/68116/coroners-inquest-opens-in-aaliyah-crash

Billboard Staff. "Update: Aaliyah Killed in Bahamas Plane Crash." Billboard.com, August 26, 2001: https://www.billboard.com/articles/news/78580/update-aaliyah-killed-in-bahamas-plane-crash

"Blackground Deal Finally Closes." HitsDailyDouble.com, August 11, 2000: https://hitsdailydouble.com/news&id=272862&title+BLACKGROUND-DEAL-FIN ALLY-CLOSES

Bobila, Maria. "Aaliyah's Stylist Derek Lee on Her Most Fashionable Music Video Moments." Nylon.com, August 21, 2020: https://www.nylon.com/fashion/der ek-lee-on-styling-aaliyah-her-most-fashionable-music-videos

Boucher, Geoff. "Aaliyah's Fans Keep Her Music Alive." LATimes.com, Decem-

ber 19, 2002: https://www.latimes.com/archives/la-xpm-2002-dec-19-wk
-albums19-story.html

Broughton, Philip Delves. "Why Music Is Still Mourning the Loss of Aaliyah."
Telegraph.co.uk, August 26, 2015: https://www.telegraph.co.uk/music/artists
/why-music-still-mourns-aaliyah-anniversary/

"Career of Aaliyah from Former Blackground Associate's Perspective (Exclusive Interview), The." YouKnowIGotSoul.com, October 18, 12012: https://youknow
igotsoul.com/interview-the-career-of-aaliyah-from-former-blackground
-associates-perspective

Carra, Mallory. "Aaliyah's Parents' Negligence Suit Had Sad Details." Bustle.com, November 15, 2014: https://www.bustle.com/articles/49168-aaliyahs-parents-lawsuit-
over-her-death-revealed-upsetting-details-about-the-plane-crash-that-took-her

Celebretainment. "Aaliyah's Music Could Come to Streaming Services in 'Near Future.'" https://www.celebretainment.com/music/aaliyahs-music-could-come
-to-streaming-services-in-near-future/article_c3c068fc-267c-5078-af2c
-182424565929.html

Chavez, Danette. "*Romeo Must Die* Was Another Bad Movie with a Great Aaliyah
Song." AVClub.com, October 2, 2015: https://music.avclub.com/romeo-must
-die-was-another-bad-movie-with-a-great-aaliy-1798285015

Chernikoff, Leah. "Tommy Hilfiger Addresses Those Racist Rumors from 1996
One More Time." Fashionista.com, January 14, 2015: https://fashionista
.com/2012/03/tommy-hilfiger-addresses-those-racist-rumors-from-1996
-one-more-time

Cinquemani, Sal. "Review: Aaliyah, *Aaliyah*." SlantMagazine.com, July 17, 2001:
https://www.slantmagazine.com/music/aaliyah-aaliyah

Cochrane, Naima. "The Superfriends." Medium.com, July 22, 2018: https://medi
um.com/musicsermon/the-superfriends-548351645d2e

Colon, Yves, Elaine De Valle, and Martin Merzer. "R&B Star, 8 Others Killed in
Plane Crash." MTStandard.com, August 26, 2001: https://mtstandard.com
/news/national/r-b-star-8-others-killed-in-plane-crash/article_ba15e121
-2d7e-5154-bd57-91626faac3b2.html

"Congress Passes Mann Act, Aimed at Curbing Sex Trafficking." History.com,
November 13, 2009: https://www.history.com/this-day-in-history/congress
-passes-mann-act

"Court Dismisses Suit over Aaliyah's Death." APNews.com, January 6, 2005: https://
apnews.com/article/4393d1b6d26cd92203aa072100d4099d

"Court Records Show Aaliyah's Pilot Had Drug Record." Chron.com, August 29, 2001:
https://www.chron.com/entertainment/music/article/Court-records-show
-aaliyahs-pilot-had-drug-record-2052452.php

Craig, Brenda. "Some Good 'Lawyering' Returns $3.3 Million In Harassment Case."
LawyersandSettlements.com, April 21, 2011: https://www.lawyersandsettle
ments.com/legal-news/harassment/interview-sexual-harassment-in-work
place-hostile-16502.html

Cross, Latoya. "Aaliyah Biopic Inspires the Most Hilarious Memes." JetMag.com,
November 17, 2014: https://www.jetmag.com/entertainment/aaliyah-biopic
-inspires-hilarious-memes

Cross, Latoya. "Listen: Ana Lou Covers Aaliyah's 'At Your Best.'" JetMag.com, November 14, 2014: https://www.jetmag.com/entertainment/listen-ana-lou-covers-aaliyahs-best

Cross, Latoya "Listen: BJ the Chicago Kid Covers Aaliyah." JetMag.com, November 20, 2014: https://www.jetmag.com/entertainment/listen-bj-the-chicago-kid-covers-aaliyah/

Cross, Latoya. "Watch: 'Aaliyah: The Princess of R&B' Trailer." JetMag.com, October 24, 2014: https://www.jetmag.com/entertainment/aaliyah-princess-rb-full-trailer

"Dame Dash Gets 'Real' about Aaliyah." JetMag.com, April 19, 2016: https://www.jetmag.com/entertainment/dame-dash-aaliyah-the-real

Davey D. "Star, Aaliyah, and Hot 97." DaveyD.com, http://www.daveyd.com/staraaliyah.html

DeRogatis, Jim. "How the Story of R. Kelly's 'Sex Cult' Finally Went Public—and Quickly Exploded." Buzzfeed.com, June 5, 2019: https://www.buzzfeednews.com/article/jimderogatis/i-thought-the-world-would-never-know-about-r-kelly

DeRogatis, Jim. "Personal History: R. Kelly and the Damage Done." NewYorker.com, June 3, 2019: https://www.newyorker.com/culture/personal-history/r-kelly-and-the-damage-done

DeRogatis, Jim, and Abdon Pallasch. "R. Kelly Accused of Sex with Teenage Girls." Chicago.SunTimes.com, December 21, 2000: https://chicago.suntimes.com/2000/12/21/18423229/r-kelly-accused-of-sex-with-teenage-girls

"Details of Aaliyah's Fatal Plane Crash Slowly Surfacing." Top40-Charts.com, August 28, 2001: https://top40-charts.com/news.php?nid=728&cat=

DIANE HAUGTON ET AL VS VIRGIN RECORDS AMERICA ET AL: https://unicourt.com/case/ca-la22-diane-haugton-et-al-vs-virgin-records-america-et-al-463303

Dorsey, Avon. "One in a Million! Aaliyah Loved Street Style but She Slayed High-Fashion Dresses." Essence.com, August 25, 2018: https://www.essence.com/fashion/aaliyah-best-red-carpet-looks

Easlea, Daryl. "Aaliyah, Aaliyah Review." BBC.co.uk, 2009: https://www.bbc.co.uk/music/reviews/2wjw

Eb the Celeb. "25 Days of Aaliyah: Millicent Shelton Remembers . . ." BET.com, August 9, 2015: https://www.bet.com/shows/bet-music-special/news/aaliyah-millicent-shelton.html

Ebert, Roger. "Romeo Must Die." RogerEbert.com, March 22, 2000: https://www.rogerebert.com/reviews/romeo-must-die-2000

"Economy in the 1980s, The." CountryStudies.us, n.d.: http://countrystudies.us/united-states/history-137.html

Edgers, Geoff. "How the Music Industry Overlooked R. Kelly's Alleged Abuse of Young Women." WashingtonPost.com. May 4, 2018: https://www.washingtonpost.com/news/style/wp/2018/05/04/feature/how-the-music-industry-overlooked-r-kellys-alleged-abuse-of-young-women

Ehrlich, Dimitri. "Age Ain't Nothing but a Number." EW.com, June 17, 1994: https://ew.com/article/1994/06/17/age-aint-nothing-number

Eichenwald, Kurt, with Robin Pogrebin. "Haste, Errors and a Fallen Star." NY Times.com, September 8, 2001: https://www.nytimes.com/2001/09/08/arts/haste-errors-and-a-fallen-star.html

Elliott, Missy. "Aaliyah: 1.16.1979–8.25.2001." EW.com, January 4, 2002: https://ew.com/article/2002/01/04/aaliyah-1161979-8252001

Ex, Kris. "Got to Give It Up." *Vibe*, December 1996. Accessed at: https://www.aaliyah archives.com/2014/02/aaliyah-vibe-magazine-dec-1996-jan-1997.html?m=1

"Exclusive: The Producers of 'Aaliyah' Take Us behind the Scenes into Making of This Classic." YouKnowIGotSoul.com, July 17, 2011: http://youknowigotsoul .com/aaliyah

Farley, Christopher John. "Siren of Subtlety." Time.com, August 26, 2001: http://content.time.com/time/arts/article/0,8599,172511,00.html

Feitelberg, Rosemary. "Getting to the Heart of Tommy Hilfiger." WWD.com, March 12, 2012: https://wwd.com/fashion-news/designer-luxury/getting-to-the-heart-of-hilfiger-5789723

Filip, Iulia. "Producer Claims Blackground Records Cheated." CourtHouse News.com, February 27, 2013: https://www.courthousenews.com/producer-claims-blackground-records-cheated

Flick, Larry (ed.). "1998 May 30. Singles." *Billboard* 110, no. 22 (May 30, 1998): 28.

Fuertes-Knight, Jo. "The Noisey Guide to Aaliyah." Vice.com, May 30, 2013: https://www.vice.com/en/article/r3vkv6/the-noisey-guide-to-aaliyah-us

Gaudette, Emily. "Why Can't I Stream Aaliyah? Late R&B Singer's Discography Still Locked Down by Her Uncle." Newsweek.com, January 16, 2018: https://www.newsweek.com/aaliyah-streaming-online-apple-music-spotify-782787

"George and Regina Daniels' Daughter Speaks Out about R. Kelly Fling." STL American.com, February 19, 2008: http://www.stlamerican.com/entertainment/living_it/george-and-regina-daniels-daughter-speaks-out-about-r-kelly-fling/article_c3ba0c95-1cdd-588e-b17c-d0aa6700bf16.html

"Gladys Knight Mourns Niece Aaliyah." News.BBC.co.uk, August 28, 2001: http://news.bbc.co.uk/2/hi/entertainment/1513515.stm#:Ã¥Ã¥:text=Soul%20legend%20Gladys%20Knight%20has,a%20plane%20crash%20on%20Saturday.&text=Knight%2C%20who%20was%20married%20to,her%20special%20and%20unique%20talents

Glanton, Dahleen. "Column: An Alleged Sexual Assault Victim May Have Lied to Help Acquit R. Kelly in 2008. Her Cooperation This Time Is an Act of Bravery." ChicagoTribune.com, July 18, 2019: https://www.chicagotribune.com/columns/dahleen-glanton/ct-dahleen-glanton-r-kelly-child-victims-20190718-bqdmog5pcrfj5b22ka5uvlx2cq-story.html

Gonzales, Michael. "Look Back: 20 Years On the Short but Influential Career of Aaliyah." April 2020. WaxPoetics.com, https://www.waxpoetics.com/blog/features/articles/look-back-20-years-on-the-short-but-influential-career-of-aaliyah

Good, Dan. "Reflections on the Real Aaliyah." ABCNews.go.com, November 17, 2014: https://abcnews.go.com/amp/Entertainment/reflections-real-aaliyah/story?id=26963755

Greene, Michael W. "Black Caucus Vows Fight for Funds." *Indianapolis Recorder*, March 10, 1979. Accessed at: https://newspapers.library.in.gov/cgi-bin/indiana?a=d&d=INR19790310-01.1.1&e=-------en-20--1--txt-txIN-------

Greenwald, Judy. "Firm Barred from Seeking Damages in Singer's Death." BusinessInsurance.com, January 16, 2005: https://www.businessinsurance.com/article/20050116/STORY/100016044?template=printart

Greenwood, Douglas. "H.E.R.: 'When I See Tommy Hilfiger, I Think of Aaliyah.'" I-D.Vice.com, February 18, 2020: https://i-d.vice.com/en_uk/article/5dm59q/her-tommy-hilfiger-capsule-collection-interview

Grossberg, Josh. "Aaliyah Wrongful-Death Suit Tossed." EOnline.com, January 7, 2005: https://www.eonline.com/news/48975/aaliyah-wrongful-death-suit-tossed

Guzman, Jayden. "The History of Hip Hop Fashion: How Street Culture Became Fashion's Biggest Influence." AfterGlowATX.com, March 26, 2019: https://www.afterglowatx.com/blog/2019/3/26/the-history-of-hip-hop-fashion-how-street-culture-became-fashions-biggest-influence

hampton, dream. "Aaliyah 'One in a Million.'" Vibe, October 1996: accessed at https://books.google.com/books?id=4SsEAAAAMBAJ&printsec=frontcover&source=gbs_ge_summary_r&cad=0#v=snippet&q=aaliyah&f=false

hampton, dream. "Man in the Mirror." Vibe, November 2000: accessed at https://books.google.com/books?id=-CcEAAAAMBAJ&pg=PA165&dq=vibe+november+2000&hl=en&sa=X&ved=2ahUKEwjd2t-snLLtAhXWLc0KHc4UCQ0Q6AEwCXoECAIQAg#v=onepage&q=mirror&f=false

Haughton, Rashad. "Eulogy Given by Aaliyah's Brother at Her Funeral." Angelfire.com: https://www.angelfire.com/celeb2/aaliyahalways

Haynes, Clarence. "Inside the Plane Crash That Took Aaliyah's Life." Biography.com, November 12, 2020: https://www.biography.com/news/aaliyah-plane-crash-died

Heath, Chris. "The Confessions of R. Kelly." GQ.com, January 20, 2016: https://www.gq.com/story/r-kelly-confessions

Hilburn, Robert. "'Aaliyah' Tops the Charts after Singer's Death." LATimes.com, September 6, 2001: https://www.latimes.com/archives/la-xpm-2001-sep-06-ca-42571-story.html

Hobbs, Linda. "One in a Million." Vibe, December 2008: accessed at https://books.google.com/books?id=qiYEAAAAMBAJ&printsec=frontcover&source=gbs_ge_summary_r&cad=0#v=onepage&q&f=false

Hong, Nicole. "R. Kelly Used Bribe to Marry Aaliyah When She Was 15, Charges Say." NYTimes, December 5, 2019: https://www.nytimes.com/2019/12/05/nyregion/rkelly-aaliyah.html

Hopsicker, Daniel. "Charter Company Ran Second Jet off Runway." MadCowProd.com, February 24, 2009: https://www.madcowprod.com/2009/02/24/charter-company-ran-second-jet-off-runway/

Huhn, Mary. "Aaaah, Aaliyah! This 22-Year-Old R&B Singer Has Her Eyes on the Prize." NyPost.com, July 15, 2001:https://nypost.com/2001/07/15/aaaah-aaliyah-this-22-year-old-rb-singer-has-her-eyes-on-the-prize/

Humblestone, Stephanie. "Inquest Begins in Aaliyah Crash." The Abaconian, 11, no. 22 (December 1, 2003).

Iandoli, Kathy. "Aaliyah: Still Stylin' on 'Em." LifeAndTimes.com, January 16, 2014: https://lifeandtimes.com/aaliyah-still-stylin-on-em

Iandoli, Kathy. "I Finally Met Aaliyah." AllHipHop.com, August 28, 2003: https://allhiphop.com/opinion/i-finally-met-aaliyah

Iandoli, Kathy. "6 Fashion and Music Experts Speak on Aaliyah's Trendsetting Style." TheBoomBox.com, November 3, 2014: https://theboombox.com/6-fashion-music-experts-speak-on-aaliyahs-style

Iandoli, Kathy. "What I Learned about Style from Aaliyah's 'We Need a Resolu-
    tion.'" Vice.com, January 16, 2014: https://www.vice.com/en/article/rgmamr
    /what-i-learned-about-style-from-aaliyahs-we-need-a-resolution

Jasper, Kenji. "Aaliyah at 40: Reminiscing on Baby Girl after a Random New York
    Run-In." Essence.com, January 17, 2019: https://www.essence.com/entertain
    ment/only-essence/aaliyah-at-40-reminiscing-on-baby-girl-after-a-random
    -new-york-run-in

Johnson, Connie. "Aaliyah's Spirit Sounds like a 'Million.'" LATimes.com, Sep-
    tember 28, 1996: https://www.latimes.com/archives/la-xpm-1996-09-28-ca
    -48232-story.html

Jones, Nate. "Skeleton Crew: Meet the Band Who Beat a Young Beyoncé on *Star
    Search*." People.com, December 22, 2013: https://people.com/celebrity/skele
    ton-crew-meet-the-band-that-beat-beyonce-on-star-search

Jones, Tashara. "Damon Dash Claims Jay-Z Had a Crush on Aaliyah." PageSix.com,
    November 28, 2019: https://pagesix.com/2019/11/28/damon-dash-claims-jay
    -z-had-a-crush-on-aaliyah

Kane, Ashleigh. "Six Times Aaliyah's Style Slayed in Romeo Must Die." Dazed
    Digital.com, March 20, 2015: https://www.dazeddigital.com/artsandculture
    /article/24155/1/six-times-aaliyah-s-style-slayed-in-romeo-must-die

Kaye, Ken. "Aaliyah Plane Crash Spurs Another Lawsuit." Sun-Sentinel.com,
    March 2, 2002: https://www.sun-sentinel.com/news/fl-xpm-2002-03-02
    -0203020219-story.html

Kennedy, Gerrick. "The Arrival (and Disappearance) of Aaliyah's Greatest Hits
    Collection Is the Latest in Saga of Late Singer's Catalog." LATimes.com, Janu-
    ary 13, 2017: https://www.latimes.com/entertainment/music/la-et-ms-aaliyah
    -posthumous-collection-20170112-story.html

Kennedy, Gerrick. "Drake Releases Posthumous Aaliyah Single 'Enough Said.'"
    LATimes.com, August 6, 2012: https://www.latimes.com/entertainment
    /music/la-xpm-2012-aug-06-la-et-ms-drake-releases-posthumous-aaliyah
    -single-enough-said-20120806-story.html

Kennedy, Gerrick. "Posthumous Aaliyah Album to Come from Drake?" LATimes
    .com, August 4, 2012: https://www.latimes.com/entertainment/music/la-xpm
    -2012-aug-04-la-et-ms-posthumous-aaliyah-to-come-from-drake-story
    .html

Kennedy, Gerrick. "Timbaland: Aaliyah Collaborations Only Work 'with Its Soul-
    mate.'" LATimes.com, July 24, 2013: https://www.latimes.com/entertainment
    /music/la-xpm-2013-jul-24-la-et-ms-timbaland-not-a-fan-of-posthumous
    -aaliyah-collaborations-20130723-story.html

Kim, Hyun. "Revisit Aaliyah's August 2001 Cover Story: 'What Lies Beneath?'"
    Vibe.com, July 7, 2020: https://www.vibe.com/featured/aaliyah-august-2001
    -cover-story-what-lies-beneath

Kimble, Julian. "Why We Are in Danger of Losing Aaliyah's Voice." Vox.com, Sep-
    tember 4, 2019: https://www.vox.com/the-highlight/2019/8/28/20825657/aa
    liyah-r-kelly-wax-museum-death

"Kindness Meets Eric Johnson, Esteemed Photographer of Musical Icons." Daily
    .RedBullMusicAcademy.com, August 25, 2016: https://daily.redbullmusic
    academy.com/2016/08/kindness-meets-eric-johnson

Krol, Charlotte. "Resurfaced R. Kelly Video Proves Singer Knew Aaliyah's Age at 14." NME.com, January 14, 2019: https://www.nme.com/news/music/r-kelly -footage-proves-he-knew-aaliyah-14-married-2430924

Larson, Jeremy D. "Who Was the Baby on Aaliyah's 'Are You That Somebody?'" Daily .RedBullMusicAcademy.com, July 15, 2016: https://daily.redbullmusicacade my.com/2016/07/who-was-the-baby-on-aaliyah-s-are-you-that-somebody

Lavin, Will. "Puff Daddy's Label Powerhouse Celebrates 20 Years in the Game." GigWise.com, August 9, 2016: https://www.gigwise.com/features/107841 /cant-stop-wont-stop-20-of-bad-boys-best-albums

Leischow, Dagmar. "Aaliyah Ich hebe ab, ich fühle mich frei." Zeit.De, August 30, 2001: https://www.zeit.de/2001/36/AALIYAH¬≠_ich_hebe_ab_ich_fuhle_frei. Translated via Google Translate.

Lockett, Dee. "Stream Aaliyah's Greatest Hits for the First Time While You Still Can." Vulture.com, January 12, 2017: https://www.vulture.com/2017/01/aali yahs-greatest-hits-are-finally-streaming.html

Lueck, Thomas J. "New York Fans Grieve over Death of Aaliyah." NYTimes.com, August 29, 2001: https://www.nytimes.com/2001/08/29/us/new-york-fans -grieve-over-death-of-aaliyah.html

"MAC to Honour Aaliyah with Make-up Line After Fan Petition Goes Viral." Hel loMagazine.com: https://www.hellomagazine.com/healthandbeauty/make up/2017082541892/aaliyah-fan-s-petition-prompts-mac-to-launch-make -up-line/

Madden, Sidney. "19 Hip-Hop Songs That Pay Homage to Aaliyah." XXLMag.com, August 25, 2015: https://www.xxlmag.com/hip-hop-songs-that-pay-homage -to-aaliyah

Mahadevan, Tara C. "Aaliyah's Estate Shares Message on Future Availability of Her Music Catalog on Streaming Platforms." Complex.com, August 25, 2020: https://www.complex.com/music/2020/08/aaliyah-estate-shares-message -future-availability-music-catalog-streaming-platforms

Marthe, Emalie. "Journey to the Past: The Making of the Forgotten Aaliyah Song from 'Anastasia.'" Vice.com, February 23, 2017: https://www.vice.com/en/arti cle/8x4njb/journey-to-the-past-making-of-forgotten-aaliyah-song-anastasia

Martin, Andrew, and Kiana Fitzgerald. "A History of Drake's Obsession with Aaliyah." Complex.com, July 3, 2018: https://www.complex.com/music /2018/07/a-history-of-drakes-obsession-with-aaliyah/

McNamara, Audrey. "Aaliyah's Ex Damon Dash Says She Couldn't Talk about R. Kelly." TheDailyBeast.com, January 10, 2019: https://www.thedailybeast .com/aaliyahs-ex-damon-dash-says-she-couldnt-talk-about-r-kelly

Minsker, Evan. "Aaliyah's Hits Removed from Apple Music after Brief Appearance." Pitchfork.com, January 12, 2017: https://pitchfork.com/news/70847-aaliyahs -hits-long-unavailable-online-appear-on-apple-music

"Missy Elliott on Writing for Aaliyah, Beyonce and Herself." Billboard.com, Novem- ber 29, 2018: https:// www.billboard.com/articles/columns/hip-hop/8487105 /missy-elliott-writing-for-aaliyah-beyonce-herself

Mitchell, Elvis. "'Romeo Must Die': Hip-Hop Joins Martial Arts but Lets Plot Mus- cle In." NYTimes.com, March 22, 2000: https://archive.nytimes.com/www .nytimes.com/library/film/032200romeo-film-review.html

Moss, Corey. "Cocaine, Alcohol Found in Pilot of Aaliyah's Plane." MTV.com, July 16, 2002: http://www.mtv.com/news/1456119/cocaine-alcohol-found-in-pilot-of-aaliyahs-plane

"Motown: The Sound That Changed America." MotownMuseum.org, n.d.: https://www.motownmuseum.org/story/motown

Munoz, Lorenza. "After A Star's Death, a Delicate Marketing Task." LATimes.com, February 22, 2002: https://www.latimes.com/archives/la-xpm-2002-feb-22-et-munoz22-story.html

Nessif, Bruna. "Timbaland Spills Secrets about Aaliyah: 'I Was Once in Love with Her.'" EOnline.com, December 16, 2011: https://www.eonline.com/news/281124/timbaland-spills-secret-about-aaliyah-i-was-in-love-with-her

"Nostalgic Scoop: Aaliyah and Kidada Jones Were in the Process of Starting a Clothing Line." NostalgicExpress.com, November 7, 2019: https://www.nostalgicexpress.com/post/nostalgic-scoop-aaliyah-and-kidada-jones-were-in-the-process-of-starting-a-clothing-line

NS [@Nygelsartorial]. (2019, August 25). Paul Hunter's written treatment for Aaliyah's 'We Need a Resolution' Music Video (3/27/2001) *"This story unfolds like we're an editorial spread of Italian Vogue and on every page is @Aaliyah. She leads us from one surreal scene to the next . . . all within her own world."* [Tweet: link to article]. Twitter: https://twitter.com/nygelsartorial/status/1165682971023724546

Nunez, Amalia Isabel. "Late R&B Singer Aaliyah Inspires Makeup Collection." CBSNews.com, June 22, 2018: https://www.cbsnews.com/news/aaliyah-mac-makeup-collection

"Officials Seek Clues in Aaliyah Plane Crash." Billboard.com, August 29, 2001: https://www.billboard.com/articles/news/78552/officials-seek-clues-in-aaliyah-plane-crash

Okoth-Obbo, Vanessa. "One in 35 Million: How Unlicensed Music by Aaliyah Ended Up on Spotify." Factmag.com: https://www.factmag.com/2018/03/11/aaliyah-bootleg-spotify-report

O'Neill, Ann W. "Suits Filed in Singer's Crash." LATimes.com, February 28, 2002: https://www.latimes.com/archives/la-xpm-2002-feb-28-fi-virgin28-story.html

Oppelaar, Justin. "Aaliyah Label, U Ink Pact." Variety.com, November 29, 2001: https://variety.com/2001/music/news/aaliyah-label-u-ink-pact-1117856519

Ottaway, Amanda. "R. Kelly Pleads Not Guilty on Charges Linked to Aaliyah Marriage." Courthousenews.com, December 18, 2019: https://www.courthousenews.com/r-kelly-pleads-not-guilty-on-charged-linked-to-aaliyah-marriage

Pareles, Jon. "Aaliyah, 22, Singer Who First Hit the Charts at 14." NYTimes.com, August 27, 2001: https://www.nytimes.com/2001/08/27/arts/aaliyah-22-singer-who-first-hit-the-charts-at-14.html

Parker, Najja. "Could a Second Aaliyah Biopic Be in the Making?" JetMag.com, July 13, 2014: https://www.jetmag.com/entertainment/second-aaliyah-biopic-making

Parker, Najja. "Petition for Aaliyah MAC Line Circulates." JetMag.com, August 3, 2015: https://www.jetmag.com/entertainment/petition-aaliyah-mac-line-circulates

Parker, Najja. "Timbaland Teases New Aaliyah Music." JetMag.com, August 10,
    2015: https://www.Jetmag.com/entertainment/timbaland-teases-new-aaliyah
    -music

Partridge, Kenneth. "Aaliyah's 'One in a Million' Turns 20: How Her Second Album
    Predicted R&B's Future." Billboard.com, August 27, 2016: https://www.billboard
    .com/articles/news/7487855/aaliyah-one-in-a-million-album-anniversary

Pattenden, Siân. "Classic Cover Story: When Aaliyah Reigned Supreme." Mixmag
    .net, January 16, 2019: https://mixmag.net/feature/aaliyah-mixmag-cover-fea
    ture-august-2001

"Production Set to Begin in May on Romeo Must Die Starring Jet Li." Warner-
    Media, April 23, 1999: https://warnermediagroup.com/newsroom/press
    -releases/1999/04/23/production-set-to-begin-in-may-on-romeo-must-die
    -starring-jet-li

"R. Kelly 'Arrested on Federal Sex Trafficking Charges.'" BBC.com, July 12, 2019:
    https://www.bbc.com/news/newsbeat-48960545

"R. Kelly 'Underage Sex Videotape' Surfaces." NME.com, February 27, 2002:
    https://www.nme.com/news/music/r-kelly-110-1373243

"R. Kelly's Old Video with Aaliyah Proves He Lied about Not Knowing Her Age."
    BET.com, January 14, 2019: https://www.bet.com/music/2019/01/14r-kelly
    -aaliyah-age-old-video-.html

Rabin, Nathan. "Aaliyah: Aaliyah." AVClub.com, July 17, 2001: https://music.av
    club.com/aaliyah-aaliyah-1798192710

Ramirez, Erika. "Brandy Speaks on Her Friendship with Aaliyah." Billboard.com. Au-
    gust 25: 2011: https://www.billboard.com/articles/columns/the-juice/467746/
    brandy-speaks-on-her-friendship-with-aaliyah

Ramirez, Erika. "DMX Talks 'Priceless' Moments with Aaliyah." Billboard.com, Au-
    gust 24, 2011: https://www.billboard.com/articles/columns/the-juice/467772
    /dmx-talks-priceless-moments-with-aaliyah

Real, Evan. "Former Intern Claims R. Kelly Sexually Abused Her as a Teen."
    HollywoodReporter.com, January 18, 2019: https://www.hollywoodreport
    er.com/news/intern-tracy-sampson-claims-r-kelly-sexually-abused-her-as
    -teen-1177217

Respers, Lisa. "Remembering Aaliyah: Late Icon's Stylist Derek Lee Remembers the
    R&B Superstar." PhilaSun.com, August 26, 2017: https://www.philasun.com
    /entertainment/remembering-aliyah-late-icons-stylist-derek-lee-remembers
    -icon-fateful-day

Reynolds, J. R. "Aaliyah Set Courts Broader Fan Base." Billboard 108, no. 29 (July 20,
    1996): 15.

Reynolds, Matt. "Woman Sues Record Producer Ex for Millions." Courthouse
    News.com, January 12, 2015: https://www.courthousenews.com/woman
    -sues-record-producer-ex-for-millions

Reynolds, Simon. "Aaliyah, Aaliyah." ReynoldsRetro.Blogspot.com, April 13, 2013:
    http://reynoldsretro.blogspot.com/2013/04/aaliyah-aaliyah-unpublished
    -review.html

Rogo, Paula. "Aaliyah's Wax Figure Unveiled at Madame Tussauds in Las Vegas."
    Essence.com, August 22, 2019: https://www.essence.com/celebrity/aaliyahs
    -wax-figure-unveiled-at-madame-tussauds-in-las-vegas

Rogo, Paula. "Dame Dash Calls Out Jay-Z for Collaborating with R. Kelly: 'I Knew, Morally, We Weren't the Same.'" Essence.com, January 6. 2019: https://www .essence.com/celebrity/dame-dash-jay-z-r-kellys-collaboration-i-never-want ed-no-part-of-that

Rosen, Miss. "The Story behind These Photographs of a 15-Year-Old Aaliyah." DazedDigital.com, November 20, 2018: https://www.dazeddigital.com /art-photography/article/42272/1/eddie-otchere-story-photography-15-year -old-aaliyah-london-contact-high-book

Rubenstein, Janine. "R. Kelly Had Sex with Underaged Aaliyah and Members of His Entourage Witnessed It, Claims Former Backup Singer." People.com, De- cember 31, 2018: https://people.com/music/r-kelly-sex-underaged-aaliyah -on-tour-bus-surviving-r-kelly-lifetime

Runtagh, Jordan. "Aaliyah's *Age Ain't Nothing but a Number* at 25: Revisiting Its Complex Legacy amid R. Kelly Reckoning." People.com, May 24, 2019: https:// people.com/music/aaliyah-age-aint-nothing-but-a-number-25-anniversary -r-kelly-relationship

Rush, George, Joanna Molloy, Lola Ogunnaike, and Kasia Anderson. "Star Falls Faster after Aaliyah 'Joke.'" NYDailyNews.com, August 31, 2001: https:// www.nydailynews.com/archives/gossip/star-falls-faster-aaliyah-joke-article -1.929910

Sanchez, Karizza. "Top Gear: The Oral History of Hip-Hop's Love Affair with Tommy Hilfiger." Compex.com, August 22, 2016: https://www.complex.com /style/2016/08/tommy-hilfiger-hiphop-oral-history

Sanneh, Kelefa. "A Pioneer, Briefly, of a New Sound." NYTimes.com, September 2, 2001: https://www.nytimes.com/2001/09/02/arts/a-pioneer-briefly-of-a-new -sound.html

Sarah. "Romeo Must Die Turns 20." LaineyGossip.com, March 19, 2020: https:// www.laineygossip.com/look-back-on-romeo-must-die-starring-jet-li-and -aaliyah-on-20th-anniversary/65818

Saulny, Susan. "Record Company Can Sue over Popular Singer's Death." NYTimes .com, May 29, 2004: https://www.nytimes.com/2004/05/29/nyregion/record -company-can-sue-over-popular-singer-s-death.html

Savage, Mark. "R. Kelly: The History of Allegations against Him." BBC.com, Au- gust 28, 2020: https://www.bbc.com/news/entertainment-arts-40635526

Scheerer, Mark. "'Romeo Must Die': On a Hip-Hop Kick." CNN.com, March 28, 2000: https://www.cnn.com/2000/SHOWBIZ/Movies/03/28/romeo.must.die

Schumacher-Rasmussen, Eric. "Jermaine Dupri, Hype Williams, Others Recall Aa- liyah as 'Risk Taker,' 'Groundbreaker': Rodney Jerkins, Treach, Directors Cite Late Singer's Hands-on Approach to Music, Film." MTV.com, August 28, 2001: http://www.mtv.com/news/1448464/jermaine-dupri-hype-williams-others -recall-aaliyah-as-risk-taker-groundbreaker

Schumacher-Rasmussen, Eric. "Timbaland, P. Diddy, Other Artists, React to Aali- yah's Death." MTV.com, August 27, 2001: http://www.mtv.com/news/1448422 /timbaland-p-diddy-other-artists-react-to-aaliyahs-death

Silverman, Stephen M. "Aaliyah's Parents Settle Crash Lawsuit." People.com, September 9, 2003: https://people.com/celebrity/aaliyahs-parents-settle-crash -lawsuit

Silverman, Stephen M. "Aunt Gladys Knight Remembers Aaliyah." People.com, January 16, 2002: https://people.com/celebrity/aunt-gladys-knight-remembers-aaliyah

Sinha, Shreeya. "Aaliyah, Whose Soaring Career Was Cut Short by a Tragedy." *NYTimes*, August 25, 2016: https://www.nytimes.com/interactive/projects/cp/obituaries/archives/aaliyah

Smith, Danyel. "Revisit R. Kelly's Dec 1994/Jan 1995 Cover Story: Superfreak." Vibe.com, January 4, 2019: https://www.vibe.com/featured/r-kellys-dec-1994-jan-1995-cover-story-superfreak

Spargo, Chris. "Lawyer for R Kelly Confirms That the Singer Married Aaliyah When She Was Just 15, but Says His Client Had 'No Idea' She Was a Minor Because 'She Lied about Her Age.'" Dailymail.co.uk, January 11, 2019: https://www.dailymail.co.uk/news/article-6582323/R-Kelly-confirms-married-Aaliyah-just-15-says-late-singer-lied-age.html

Staff. "Marketing of a Star after Death." LATimes.com, September 24, 2001: https://www.latimes.com/archives/la-xpm-2001-sep-24-ca-49180-story.html

Staff. "Queen of the Damned Reviews Pouring In!! It Sucked!!" AintItCool.com, October 10, 2001: http://legacy.aintitcool.com/node/10454

Stegemoeller, Kristen. "Aaliyah Is Getting Her Own MAC Collection, Thanks to a Group of Her Superfans." PAPERmag.com, August 25, 2017: https://www.papermag.com/aaliyah-is-getting-her-own-mac-collection-thanks-to-a-group-of-her-superfans-2477010824.html

Stewart, Chelsea. "Inside the Plane Crash That Claimed the Life of Aaliyah." Cheatsheet.com. November 10, 2020: https://www.cheatsheet.com/entertainment/was-aaliyahs-body-found.html

Stewart, Chelsea. "The Real Reason You Can't Stream Aaliyah's Music." Cheatsheet.com, April 7, 2020: https://www.cheatsheet.com/entertainment/the-real-reason-you-cant-stream-aaliyahs-music.html/

Stewart, Chelsea. "What Happened to Aaliyah's Posthumous Album?" Cheatsheet.com, August 25, 2020: https://www.cheatsheet.com/entertainment/what-happened-to-aaliyahs-posthumous-album.html

"Sultry Singer Aaliyah on Why It's Cool to Be So Hot." *Jet*, July 23, 2001: accessed at https://www.aaliyaharchives.com/2013/12-aaliyah-jet-magazine-july-23rd-2001.html?m=1

Susman, Gary. "Aaliyah Mortician Says Label Reneged on $68K Bill." EW.com, August 13, 2002: https://ew.com/article/2002/08/13/aaliyah-mortician-says-label-reneged-68k-bill

Swan, Betsy. "Avenatti: New Tape Shows R. Kelly Urinating on 14-Year-Old Girl's Face." TheDailyBeast.com, February 27, 2019: https://www.thedailybeast.com/avenatti-new-tape-shows-r-kelly-urinating-on-14-year-old-girls-face

Tai, Cordelia. "Aaliyah for MAC Is Finally Happening, Thanks to Thousands of Seriously Devoted Fans." TheFashionSpot.com, August 24, 2017: https://www.thefashionspot.com/beauty/762391-aaliyah-for-mac-cosmetics

Tardio, Andres. "Just Blaze Mourns Aaliyah's Passing, Says They Were Scheduled to Collaborate." HipHopDX.com, October 25, 2012: https://hiphopdx.com/news/id.21643/title.just-blaze-mourns-aaliyahs-passing-says-they-were-scheduled-to-collaborate.

"10 Facts about Aaliyah You Might Not Know." Complex.com, August 24, 2011: https://www.complex.com/music/2011/08/10-facts-about-aaliyah-you -might-not-know

"39 Things You Didn't Know about Aaliyah." CapitalXtra.com, n.d.: https://www .capitalxtra.com/features/lists/aaliyah-fact/wages-paid-in-films

Thompson, Desire. "Fans Rally for Aaliyah's Discography to Be Released on Streaming Platforms." Vibe.com. April 2, 2020: https://www.vibe.com/2020/04/fans -rally-for-aaliyahs-discography-to-be-released-on-streaming-platforms

Tietjen, Alexa. "How Instagram Willed a MAC X Aaliyah Collaboration to Fruition." LATimes.com, June 19, 2018: https://www.latimes.com/fashion /la-ig-wwd-mac-aaliyah-collaboration-20180619-story.html

Timbaland. "Song Origins: 'Are You That Somebody?'" MasterClass.com, n.d.: https://www.masterclass.com/classes/timbaland-teaches-producing-and -beatmaking/chapters/song-origins-are-you-that-somebody#transcript

"Timbaland Caught Up in Fresh Aaliyah Scandal following R. Kelly Documentary." Amp.CapitalXtra.com, January 7, 2019: https://amp.capitalxtra.com/artists /timbaland/aaliyah-relationship-wife

"Timbaland Tells SXSW Crowd That Aaliyah Spoke to Him in a Dream and Said Tink Was 'the One.'" Factmag.com, n.d.: https://www.factmag .com/2015/03/22/timbaland-tells-sxsw-crowd-that-aaliyah-spoke-to-him-in -a-dream-and-said-tink-was-the-one

Tinsley, Justin. "The Notorious Night Biggie Was Murdered in Los Angeles." TheUndefeated.com, March 8, 2017: https://theundefeated.com/features/the -notorious-night-biggie-was-murdered-in-los-angeles

"To Release a 'Aaliyah for MAC' Limited Edition Collection #AaliyahFor MAC." Change.org: https://www.change.org/p/mac-cosmetics-estee-lauder -to-release-a-aaliyah-for-mac-limited-edition-collection-aaliyahformac

Touré. "Aaliyah: 1979–2001." RollingStone.com, October 11, 2001: https://www .rollingstone.com/music/music-news/aaliyah-1979-2001-192667

Touré. "R. Kelly Backlash Is Not a 'Lynching' but a Reckoning." RollingStone.com, May 3, 2018: https://www.rollingstone.com/culture/culture-news/toure-r-kelly -backlash-is-not-a-lynching-but-a-reckoning-628995

Tsioulcas, Anastasia. "New York Federal Prosecutors File New Charges against R. Kelly." NPR.org, March 13, 2020: https://www.npr.org/2020/03/13/815500741 /new-york-federal-prosecutors-file-new-charges-against-r-kelly

Tsioulcas, Anastasia, and Colin Dwyer. "The Allegations against R. Kelly: An Abridged History." NPR. Capradio.org, January 11, 2019: https://www.capra dio.org/news/npr/story?storyid=683936629

"Twitter Remembers Aaliyah." JetMag.com, August 25, 2016: https://www.jetmag .com/entertainment/aaliyah-twitter-remembers

"U.S. Investigators to Probe Aaliyah Crash." CNN.com, August 27, 2001: https:// www.cnn.com/2001/SHOWBIZ/Music/08/26/death.aaliyah

Van Der Merwe, Lea-Ann. "Remember Rapper Static Major? His Wife Is Sure He Died Due to Hospital's Mistake." AmoMama.com, July 16, 2018: https://news .amomama.com/94260-remember-rapper-static-major-his-wife-di.html

Venezia, Todd. "R. Kelly in Sex Arrest." NewYorkPost.com, June 6, 2002: https:// nypost.com/2002/06/06/r-kelly-in-sex-arrest

Verna, Paul, Marilyn A. Gillen, and Peter Cronin (eds.). "Album Reviews." *Billboard*, June 11, 1994. Accessed at: https://books.google.com/books?id=UAgEAAAAM BAJ&lpg=PA64&dq=aaliyah%20age%20ain%27t%20nothing%20but%20 a%20number&pg=PA64#v=onepage&q=aaliyah%20age%20ain't%20noth ing%20but%20a%20number&f=false

Wang, Amy X. "R. Kelly Hasn't Really Been 'Dropped' by Anyone in Music." Rolling Stone.com, January 22, 2019:https://www.rollingstone.com/pro/news/r-kelly -sony-universal-music-spotify-782119

Warikoo, Niraj. "New Book on History of Gesu Catholic Church and School in Detroit." Freep.com, October 12, 2017: https://www.freep.com/story/enter tainment/2017/10/11/book-history-gesu-catholic-church-school-detroit/ 752007001

Weber, Peter. "The Rise and Fall of Detroit: A Timeline." TheWeek.com, July 19, 2013: https://theweek.com/articles/461968/rise-fall-detroit-timeline

"Wendy Williams 'Proud' of 'Aaliyah' TV Movie." JetMag.com, November 17, 2014: https://www.jetmag.com/entertainment/wendy-williams-proud-aaliyah -tv-movie

White, Constance C. R. "If It Sings, Wear It; Tommy Hilfiger Dresses the Stars in Hopes That They Will Sell His Stuff." NYTimes.com, October 26, 1997: https:// www.nytimes.com/1997/10/26/style/if-it-sings-wear-it-tommy-hilfiger -dresses-stars-hopes-that-they-will-strut-his.html?searchResultPosition=4

Williams, Keishel. "Aaliyah's Secret Moments." CRFashionBook.com, January 16, 2019: https://www.crfashionbook.com/celebrity/g25859451/aaliyahs-secret -moments/?slide=8

Winfrey, Oprah. "Oprah Talks to Mary J. Blige." Oprah.com, May 2006: http:// www.oprah.com/omagazine/oprah-interviews-mary-j-blige/1?print=1

Witt, Stephen. "The Inexplicable Online Absence of Aaliyah's Best Music." Com plex.com, December 16, 2016: https://www.complex.com/music/2016/12/aa liyahs-music-isnt-online-and-her-uncle-barry-hankerson-is-the-reason-why

Witter, Brad. "The True Story of Aaliyah and R. Kelly's Relationship." Biogra phy.com, November 12, 2020: https://www.biography.com/.amp/news/aali yah-r-kelly-relationship-true-story

Wolton, Rebbekka. "17 Years Later, What We Really Know about Aaliyah's Death." MonaGiza.com, September 5, 2018: https://monagiza.com/stories /17-years-later-really-know-aaliyahs-death

Wong, Thom. "No Touching." Medium.com, March 24, 2016: https://medium .com/@thom/no-touching-e4d32d890be#:~:text=Still%2C%20Hollywood %20prevails%20uber%20alles,lead%20in%20the%20grand%20finale.&text =Respectfully%2C%20that%20is%20not%20why%20they%20don't%20kiss.

YKIGS. "Unsolving the Mystery: Sugar & Spice (Produced by Timbaland, Written by Missy Elliott)." YouKnowIGotSoul.com, August 25, 2011: https://youknow igotsoul.com/rare-gem-sugah-sugar-spice-tweets-former-group

Zafar, Aylin. "What It's Like When a Label Won't Release Your Album." Buzzfeed .com, May 12, 2013: https://www.buzzfeed.com/azafar/what-happens-when -your-favorite-artist-is-legally-unable-to

INTERVIEWS

Ed OTCHERE, WhatsApp interview 7/22/20
Donnie Scantz, phone interview 8/27/20
Rapsody, phone interview 10/28/20
Tameka Foster, phone interview 7/3/20
April Walker, Zoom interview 7/4/20
Kimya Warfield-Rainge, Zoom interview 7/4/20
Nicole "Cola" Walker, Zoom interview 7/4/20
Tonica Johnson, phone interview 12/22/20
Jim Jones, phone interview 2/18/20
Tim Barnett, phone interview 3/11/20
Jimmy Douglass, phone interview 3/11/20
Lolo Zouaï, phone interview 3/17/20
Eric Johnson, phone interview 7/2/20
dream hampton, phone interview 7/4/20
Jonathan Mannion, phone interview 7/9/20
Nathan Hamlet, FaceTime interview 8/23/20
Terrell Benson, FaceTime interview 8/23/20
Ja Rule, phone interview 8/24/20
Ashley Dickens, phone interview 8/24/20
Aali Cortes, FaceTime interview 8/25/20
Frances Kondis, Zoom interview 8/26/20
Sandhya Nandra, Zoom interview 8/28/20
Erica Dove, phone interview 8/30/20
Kash Doll, phone interview 9/1/20
Kingsley Russell, phone interview 9/17/20
Vikki Tobak, phone interview 10/27/20
Bashir Faddoul, email interview 12/23/20
Lil' Kim, phone interview 1/9/21

All original quotes by interview.
All lyrics provided by Genius.com.
All social media announcements by Twitter and Instagram.
All additional references provided by AaliyahArchives.com.

INDEX